ABOUT TH_ ____

Volume 1

ABOUT THE BIBLE

Volume 1

Genesis to Joshua

by

Nicholas Dunning

Dedication

This collection has taken several years to produce, and I took the opportunity during the Coronavirus lockdown in 2020-22 to sort the text into a final order.

The time I have spent producing this collection has taken my time away from others. Therefore this dedication can only be to my family and friends who can now see this finished product.

My special thanks must go to my wife and her constant inquiry about whether I have finished it yet.

Only when writing such a book, can you understand the enormity of the task and how it continues to expand in front of your eyes before finally taking its final form.

Table of Contents

LIST OF TABLES

PREFACE

How many people now actually read The Bible? Small sections are read at Christmas and Easter, perhaps, or Weddings and Funerals, but to many, the books are a mass of names, begats, and Letters. Some find it is not easy to pick up and actually read despite being commonly available. Many never investigate its contents and just find something else to do.

This collection of volumes provides a start-to-finish guide to the Bible and explains where it has come from and how it has ended up in our hands today.

Each volume includes the history of the adjoining regions that come into the Bible narrative at various stages—for example, the Egyptians, Assyrians, Romans, etc. It also covers the later influence of the Visigoths and Vandals, etc., continuing to the Reformation (AD 1521) and later.

Now reflect on the following, a situation from the past.

> You are looking after your family on your family land. All you own is around you, including your extended family, friends, goats, sheep and donkeys. You are content and happy. Your life is what you have made of it and is as perfect as it can be.

> Then, out of nowhere, an army appears and takes everything from you. Your way of life is devastated. Everybody and everything you have known is destroyed. You are in total despair.

> To rebuild requires considerable strength and guidance. It is this that the Bible has provided over centuries and will continue to. Indeed, destruction can appear at any time, totally out of the blue, to us all.

The story of Job is perhaps the oldest book in the Bible. It reflects on God and Satan destroying everything a man has bit by bit, including his family and health, to test his belief. He passed the test, and almost everything was restored to him. Unfortunately, his wife is not mentioned in the restoration, which is probably just a simple error.

But how would any of us pass a similar test today? We know our mental ability and strength only when faced with such an extreme situation.

The Bible text can be used to show:

- *The development of 'God',*
- *The reason for and introduction of his son, Jesus,*
- *The use of 'Jesus' to link the Old Testament and New Testament,*
- *Paul's development of the Christian Church,*
- *How the various philosophical arguments were resolved.*

The Christian Bible today provides a text which is the basis of the religion known as 'Christianity'. This work covers, in twelves volumes and an Appendix, the history of Christianity as follows:

No.	Subject	Approx. date range
1.	Creation - Joshua	- 1200BC
2.	Judges - Solomon	1200BC – 930BC
3.	The Kings - Exile	930BC – 582BC
4.	Babylon - The Return	582BC – 516BC
5.	Persians & Greeks	529BC – 175BC
6.	Jews v Romans	175BC – 70 AD
7.	Jesus	4BC – 34 AD
8.	Paul	34AD – 63 AD
9.	Acts & Letters	34AD – 70 AD
10.	The Early Church	70 – 325 AD
11.	The Church Divides	325 – 1073 AD
12.	Western Church	1073 -1517 AD +
	Appendix	

The Appendix volumes cover a range of subjects, expanding items covered and background subjects.

I am pleased to receive comments and feedback on this work. I intend to update the text via Amazon / Kindle every year. Please forward any feedback to the following:

aboutthebible@gmail.com

ACKNOWLEDGEMENTS

The reader will appreciate the various translations of the Bible are copyrighted. For my use, I have obtained permission to use the NET Bible, details are below. Please view their websites.

Their excellent websites will guide you to several useful Bible Study tools.

Scripture quoted by permission. Basic Bible text is taken from the NET Bible® copyright ©1996-2006 by Biblical Studies Press, L.L.C. www.bible.org. All rights reserved.

Another helpful website is www.e-sword.net, copyright © 2000-2021 by Rick Meyers. This site provides a means of quickly searching for phrases and words in many Bible versions. It is an outstanding reference source and well worth supporting.

The final reference work required is a Bible Atlas to show the relationships of towns, cities and kingdoms to each other. See, for example:

www.ruthenpaul.com/wp-content/uploads/OTS1/Oxford_Bible_Atlas _Fourth_Edition_2007.pdf

PROLOGUE

While the rest of the world was in relatively dark ages, the Hebrews were busy writing away, recording their religious history. This was later taken up by a new group, the Christians, and used as the basis of their holy text. Over time, the language changed from Hebrew to Aramaic to Greek and then Latin.

The development of the apocalyptic visions provides the narrative for the victory of Good over Evil, the End of the World, and Judgement Day.

The Hebrew writings of the Old Testament are based around God and his desire for the Children of Israel to be faithful to him. Unfortunately, they were not, and they began to worship other gods. Due to this, we are told, God brought armies from elsewhere to destroy the Hebrew's homeland, especially his temple in Jerusalem. Like many other temples of the period, the temple was seen as where God and the people communicated. The key activity was the provision of offerings to God, which the priests mostly received on his behalf.

With the destruction of the Temple, captured Hebrews were taken away to populate the Assyrian and Babylonian Empires. Many other Hebrews voluntarily left Judah and found sanctuary in Egypt.

When the Hebrews were allowed to return, they rebuilt the temple in Jerusalem. The temple was again destroyed following the Jewish civil war and revolt against the Roman Empire in AD 66-70. The indigenous population was again taken away. The Hebrew prophecy that God would protect them finally proved to be wrong.

In the meantime, Jesus provided an alternative interpretation of the Hebrew writings. Paul primarily developed this in his sect called 'The Way'. The sect developed in cities and ports around the Mediterranean under the name of 'Christianity'. It was not based on a temple location and was open to anybody, not just circumcised Jews.

Christianity spread widely once it was adopted by the Roman Empire under the Edict of Milan AD 313.

Today, Christianity is seen as monotheistic religion based on the life and teachings of Jesus of Nazareth. Jesus is seen as the Son of God, whose coming as the Messiah was prophesied in the Hebrew Bible (the Old Testament) and chronicled in the New Testament.

Nothing has been added for nearly two thousand years, but their stories are still relevant today.

Their writing has produced the culture at the very centre of our society. It forms the basis of our laws, cities, ceremonies, and so much more.

It is now the world's largest religion, with some 2.4 billion followers in 157 countries.

Set out in this series of books is the history of Christianity. From then till now.

The main books of the Old Testament provide the main storyline, but the twelve books named after the minor prophets are also crucial for later giving background for the New Testament.

1. Hosea (ca. 750–715)
2. Joel (ca. 500?)
3. Amos (ca. 760–750)
4. Obadiah (Ca. 587-515?)
5. Jonah (ca. 785–775)
6. Micah (ca. 735–690)
7. Nahum (ca. 630-612)
8. Habakkuk (after 605)
9. Zephaniah (ca. 630–620?)
10. Haggai (520)
11. Zechariah (520–518)
12. Malachi (ca. 450–430?)

INTRODUCTION

The land of Israel has been at the crossroads of history for thousands of years. Its people have come and gone, over the years, for one reason or another.

But its real fame comes from being the prime location of the book called today *'The Bible'* by Christians. This book is made up of two sections, referred today as the *'Old Testament'* and the *'New Testament'*.

The Old Testament draws on the Hebrew religious text and history. The New Testament is the story of Jesus and the founding of the Christian church in the eastern Mediterranean.

This work, *'About the Bible'* in a series of volumes, attempts to put the Bible into a historical context and to make the text readable in a clear story format. It follows the development of Christianity from its origin into its final form as one of the primary religions in the world today.

It is an easy reference for those interested, but it is not intended to replace anyone's much-loved version of *'The Bible'*.

Evolution of thought

The evolution of human thought has been by:

- *Word of mouth passing on concepts from generation to generation.*
- *Drawn and Written texts recording concepts to be read later by others.*

In each case, the chain could be broken by outside forces of nature or human intervention. What is surprising is what has come down to us directly. More is being rediscovery by archaeologists. In the past, the mixing of concepts from different locations spurred on their evolution. For example, Farming, Metallurgy, Geometry, Writing and Hieroglyphics.

Population growth required the concepts of control and order. Famine, disease, attrition, and war lead to the survivors seeking ways to preserve their futures: the result and the development of Laws, Enforcement, Discipline, Education and a Social structure.

Similarly, religion evolved. Different generations review the religion as handed down, and sharp direction changes occurred. For example:

- *Early form of Monotheism used by the Patriarchs (2000-1500 BC)*

- *'The Law' introduced by Moses (1500-1400 BC)*
- *Canaanite Religion used in parallel by the Israelites (1000=900BC)*
- *Jewish religion changed due to the discovery of old scrolls found in the Temple during repairs work under Josiah, King of Judah (640-609 BC)*
- *Development of Jewish Synagogue from the time of the Babylon Exile (c.587- 520 BC)*
- *Start and development of Christianity (30-70 AD)*
- *Council of Nicaea (325 AD)*
- *Establishment of the Roman Catholic Church (400-500 AD)*
- *The Reformation and Protestants, Puritans etc. (1500-1600 AD)*

In each case, the change occurred due to the acceptance of alternative or additional text. This changed the practice of religion. Also, changes have occurred over wider areas, from local, national, regional, and worldwide.

Hebrews

The term 'Hebrew' describes descendants from the biblical patriarch Abraham. They are identified as a nomadic group of the pre-monarchic period prior to the Bronze Age collapse (1200-1150 BC). They occupied Canaan and counted themselves as being separate from the Canaanites. They are traditionally identified by the use of the Semitic language *'Hebrew'*. The term is used throughout history despite the introduction of the *'Aramaic'* spoken language during the second temple period (516BC-70 AD).

Israelites

The term *'Israelite'* is a biblical term used to describe the descendants of Jacob, son of Isaac, grandson of Abraham.

The terms *'Hebrews'* and *'Israelites'* usually describe the same people but at different times in their history. For example:

- *Hebrews: before the conquest of the Land of Canaan.*
- *Israelites: after the conquest.*

The conquest dates from the time of the 'Sea People' and the result of the Bronze Age collapse.

As described in the Bible, the Israelites were organised into clans under a tribal chieftain. They occupied land on both sides of the Jordan.

The Jews

The term '*Jew*' has one or more of three possible definitions:

1. *A member of the tribe of 'Judah' only. It would exclude members of the other tribes of Israel.*
2. *A resident of the land of 'Judea'. Not from Galilee or Samaria.*
3. *A follower of the then-new 'Jewish' religion.*

The Israelis

The term refers to the citizens of modern Israel, a multi-ethnic society.

Generally

All these terms are often intermixed and used randomly in written work, documents, articles and books. However, the reason we know so much about the Hebrews, Israelites, and Jews is they wrote down their history and stories. Other people came and went without a written record; therefore, we know nothing of their names and events. We know of their existence simply by indestructible remains and records left by other people.

The Israelites say they were not skilful in homebuilding. Indeed when they arrived in their *'Promised Land',* they focused on finding readymade properties. They then drove away the current occupiers and took over their property. They took the Canaan highland while on the lowland bordering the Mediterranean Sea. They were sandwiched between the Philistines to the south and the Phoenicians to the north. The Bible describes how the Israelites were constantly at war with the Philistines, but the Phoenicians became their important cultural associates.

The Philistines

These were the remnants of the *'Sea People'* and processed advanced technology such as ironworking and sharping of blades which the Israelites took advantage of at times. They lived in five cities occupying a land strip on the Mediterranean coast. The southern half today forms – *'The Gaza Strip'*.

The Phoenicians

The Phoenicians provided the Israelites with advanced technology, materials, and labour to build palaces and their temple. When the Israelites discovered they did not have the skill to build, the Phoenicians were employed as contractors to project-manage, design, supply specialist skills, and build various projects.

The account of the building of Solomon's Temple and Palace explains how Hiram, King of Tyre, provided all the expertise and materials required. He sourced the timber (Cedars of Lebanon) used extensively in the new buildings. He also provided all the metalwork and luxuries the Israelites demanded. This all came from Hiram's extensive trading contacts around the Mediterranean.

Peace-keeping

The Phoenicians had no deity of war and did not glorify in it in any way. They developed initially as peaceful people, interested in practising their trade and not arguing or being hostile. They perfected merchant trade, shipbuilding and navigation. Later, Carthage, one of their colonises, took on Rome and lost.

Farming

The Israelites were primarily shepherds and Arable farmers. They had flocks of goats and sheep, which gave them wool, fleece, milk, and meat. Their grain was barley and wheat. They used oxen for ploughing power. They also kept Bees and made wine. Their food production is reflected in the gifts they give to their Temples. As a *'Thanks Giving'*, they would offer an amount of goods according to the requirements set out in the bible.

Religion

The centre of their culture was their religion. It was based around one god known as 'YWHW' (Yahweh), and his contract with the Hebrew people. This required them to worship and be faithful to him in exchange for their *'Promised Land'*. It was their failure to do this that led to their later downfall. They later reasoned that YWHW brought enemies to their door to punish them.

On the other hand, the strength of their beliefs led them to not work on the Sabbath, our Saturday. This was finally responsible for their downfall. They would not fight on the Sabbath. As a result, their enemies took advantage and attacked them on the Sabbath.

Metal and Timber

The supply of metal to regions lacking local sources laid the basis for an enduring trade network in various commodities. This, in turn, led to a new dependency between different regions and had profound social implications. Individuals and groups emerged to control production and distribution. In this way, metal and timber contributed in no small measure to the rise of social hierarchies across the Bronze Age Near East.

Timber was of limited use until copper tools were developed to cut and joint it. Demand for timber dramatically increased with the introduction of the saw, plane, mortise and tenon joints fixed with treenails.

One date we can use as a milestone is 2566 BC. This was when the timber boat of Pharaoh Khufu was built. In 1954 AD, it was found disassembled with 1,224 numbered pieces in a pit next to the Great Pyramid at Giza. The boat, some forty-three-metre long, is made of Cedar from Lebanon.

The only types of trees native to Egypt were the Palm and Acacia*. Neither produced any timber useful for construction. The timber Egypt required came from Lebanon, Cyprus, and later the Aegean.

Timber could be used for:

- *Boats and carts used for trade*
- *Levers for lifting for construction projects*
- *Columns, beams, ties,*
- *Siege tower and ladders*
- *Catapults and siege engines*

You can see the importance of timber and metal in the Bible. Indeed demonstrating your wealth in metal only attracted armies to take it, as the events of King Hezekiah's lifetime (715-686BC).

The Hebrews used acacia to make the Tabernacle's frames. They had nothing else until they reached the 'Promised land'.

Metal

Metal, in the form of gold, silver, copper, tin and iron, was used to provide military strength. In addition, it was used to hire mercenaries and equip soldiers. Metal is the result of an industrial-type process. Generally, it was mined and smelted into ingots by others, then transported and traded for other goods. Then, the new owners proceeded to manufacture the items they required. The alternative to using ingots was to take metal items from others and melt them down to make new items. The key to these processes was high heat.

Slaves

Mining processes were often difficult and dangerous, with slave labour extensively used. Slaves were traded the same as any commodity. Initially, the slaves came from overrun communities nearby, but as military strength increased, whole towns, cities, and even nations were captured. Defeated nations were stripped of their physically fit and were taken off for manual labour – mining, building defences, new cities, etc. Others were identified as craftsmen and taken for production and manufacturing. Women and young children were used as servants. Those identified as lacking value might be left, used for cruel sport, or killed to save food and water.

Passing armies

The Israelites occupied a relatively small piece of land, but throughout their history, the armies of many other nations passed nearby. It was often a matter of life or death. If a city did not surrender, a siege would be set with the aim of destroying all within. This served as an example to other cities nearby. An army just wanted to take the valuable resources and pass on to its final goal.

The passing armies in Israel included the following:

Table 1: Passing Armies

Egyptians	1550 – 550BC	Battle of Megiddo 1479BC, Battle of Kadesh 1274BC, On-going control of Israel.
Hittites	1750 - 1180BC	Battle of Kadesh 1274BC against Egypt.
Philistines	1175 -1100BC	On-going War with Israelites.
Neo-Assyrians	911 - 608BC	740-721BC: Kingdom of Israel was taken into exile and slavery.
Babylonians / Chalden	597 – 539BC	Kingdom of Judah taken into Exile.
Persians	550 - 336BC	Those in Exile were allowed to return from 539BC. Persia ruled Egypt. Invasions of Greece 492-490BC, 480-479BC.
Greeks / Seleucid	332 – 30BC	Alexander the Great destroys Tyre and takes Egypt in 332BC. Hellenization begins. Alexander ends the Persian Empire.
Romans	63BC – 639AD	Pompey made Syria a Roman Province, Resolved the civil war in Judea. Egypt became a Roman Province. Jewish civil war ended in the Fall of Jerusalem in 70AD.

The Israelites mostly watched these armies as they passed nearby their land, but occasionally they suffered considerable apocalyptic destruction. For example, the Assyrians took their northern kingdom population away in 721 BC, and no more was heard of them. The Southern kingdom was primarily split by evacuation to Babylon (597 and 583 BC) and desertion to Egypt. However, in both locations, the Jews prospered and became skilled traders, merchants and artisans.

Technological

Technological improvements to weapons, such as the change of design of bows, chariots, armour, swords, spears, etc., can all have a dramatic effect on battles. Domestication of animals, including the camel, provided further options. An army could be assembled from distant places and take food it found on the way as it marched through the countryside. This would devastate the land it passed through and deliver a deadly blow to an unprepared kingdom if it arrived out of the blue. Periods during which city walls were built and wells excavated demonstrate an initial problem. The later rebuilding of higher and thicker city walls, watchtowers and more wells show how attack and defence methods developed based on self-preservation.

Horses

The introduction into the region of the horse led to a dramatic change in how wars were conducted. The chariot produced a fighting platform, which proved to be an advantage in conflicts on the planes. Elsewhere the Donkey* continued as the main beast of burden.

The merit of using chariots first appears in Genesis with Joseph in Egypt. They were followed by the disadvantage at the crossing of the Red Sea.

Solomon demonstrated his wealth by the number of horses, chariots, and horsemen he owned.

'Donkey' is a 17th-century term for an 'Ass'. The name is not used in the KJV but is now common in later translations.

Roads

Initially, there were no roads, just easily navigable paths over the land, taking gentle routes between water sources or crossings. However, when an army used these paths, they became wider and worn to form roads. Messengers passed to and fro, and communications developed along the route. Certainly, these routes formed more or less permanent roads and were used continually—for example, The King's Highway and the Via Maris, which both linked Egypt to Mesopotamia.

The roads that took the Persians to Greece later took the Greeks in the reverse direction to Persia. It was also part of the route later used by the Romans to get its army to Egypt.

Materials for war, weapons, mercenaries, metals, 'money', and a strong army – could be collected along the away, as long as there was a belief in gaining wealth and winning. But often, a strong army melted away once the leader had been killed or simply died, and therefore, delivery of future benefits seemed unlikely. So it was essential to always be on the winning side.

Boats

Movement was quicker by boat, but this could provide limited access due to the tides and time of year. Ports were required to quickly land men and materials. They were also important for the building of ships and Galleys.

The main focus for the use of boats was around the Mediterranean and Black Seas. Rivers and other seas were of interest and provided access to other areas. But they required a different design of boat.

We learn of travel by boat from Jonah, who was thrown overboard by the crew to calm a storm. Later, Luke describes the terror of being shipwrecked.

Many cities were linked primarily by shipping, and passengers were taken on board for the journey.

The juggernauts of the shipping industry were the grain barges which travelled from Alexandra to Rome and were forty metres or more in length. Two of the most famous are 'Syracusia' (240 BC) and 'Isis' (150 AD).

Pirates and sea raiders were present at times. They would land and attack villages, taking away valuables and people as slaves. Those taken had little hope of return.

Cities also used boats to establish colonies elsewhere. Their selected citizens were sent to establish new cities elsewhere in the Mediterranean. This form of population control enabled the food supply to match those that remained. In addition, the locations of new colonies could be trading posts, where it was essential for the mother cities to retain access to important metals. Perhaps one of the most famous colonies was Carthage, founded by Tyre.

Boat Building

The building of a sea-going boat was a technical masterpiece. Made of wood, it would float naturally. The skill came with cutting and jointing the timber and fixing together with timber pegs or metal nails.

Large boats needed sails or oars for propulsion. Ships of war required arms and weapons. Phocaean penteconters of 535 BC were provided with a bronze bow to ram enemy ships. The later Greek Triemes dominated the Mediterranean. Roman war galleys became fighting platforms and transport ships for its armies.

But the fundamental problems were achieving and maintaining a water-tight hull and its speed in the water.

Navigation

The key to successful travel was knowing where you were going and how to get back home. Navigating an extensive area would have been difficult without charts and aids.

To repeatedly travel the same extended routes would have been straight forward. But if known routes were linked using skilled 'Pilots', then trade routes could be extended and navigation skills enhanced.

Night travel provided more guides employing the stars and planets. In clear water, sailing at night shortened the travel time. But night travel was too dangerous in whitewater areas with rocks.

The seasons also affect sea travel. For example, it was possible to sail from May to October as the sea was calm and warm. But during Autumn and winter, the sea was often too rough.

It was the Phoenicians who discovered the key to distance navigation. This was the magnetic needle, simply a thin suspended metal rod which always pointed north. It was made simply by hammering metal until it took on magnetic qualities. Such a guide permitted considerable advantage over others who had nothing.

Kingdoms

The ability of a man or family to control others gave them status but not security. They could easily be overthrown and replaced unless the system they had created could maintain their position. Loyalty was also required, and in return, the masses could be provided with protection in times of need. This included times of war or famine.

Social groups operate with a collective interest, generally assisting each other with knowledge and trade. However, a different group could be disruptive and act hostilely to the extent of murder and pillage. When living in an area where food was seasonal and in short supply, fighting for your existence was a necessity.

Records

Writing developed from Court records used for taxation. The oral tradition could be replaced by written text once it proved reliable and durable. But this was not accessible to everyone, only those educated in its use.

Records, be they written or drawn, only portray the events in the lives of the rich and powerful. The poor shepherd in his field does not record his life, so documents do not represent the complete spectrum of life. The history we see from the past involves only the top echelons of life.

After Death

The rich were buried with their grave goods. This was preferred to the body being burned or left out in the open, where wild animals would take it. It also removed considerable wealth from the successor.

Where the ground was hard, perhaps of rock, caves were used with access prevented by a pile of large stones.

The Soul

The change in a body before and after death was seen to be the result of the departure of the Soul, which maintained the physical body while it was used. The Soul required support during its onward journey to the afterlife. This was believed to be either above or below the earth -which was considered 'flat' at the time.

The Gods

The environment, climate, fertility, disasters, and warfare all led to the belief in gods, influencing the population's day-to-day lives. Different nations had different gods and beliefs.

Offerings to the gods were provided by the population and used to support the priests.

The Bible

The Bible (Old Testament) comprise many separate books with different reference and subject matter.

Originally passed down in a verbal tradition, like Homer's *Odyssey*, it was finally written down. It was then copied and edited, re-edited and re-copied etc. The Hand of the *'Deuteronomist'* (An Editor) appeared and set out the *'history books'* to demonstrate the failure of the Israelite covenant with YHWH, God.

Further books were added, including apocalyptic stories describing the end of the world, reflecting the feeling of the Jewish nation.

The Early Christians scoured the Old Testament for references and possible prophecies which could be used to justify the story of Jesus.

These were then woven into the New Testament narrative and the new Christian Religion tradition. These combined writings now form our Christian Bible.

Apocalyptic Stories

The old apocalyptic stories drive the narrative of the story of Jesus. The Christian Bible demonstrates how a prophecy from the Old Testament is used within the gospels. They provide authority as to the background and reason for the work of Jesus.

Not all Apocalyptic stories turn out as intended. Zechariah 14.2-4 introduced the belief that God would stand on the Mount of Olives and defeat all nations attacking Jerusalem. In August 70 AD, the two Jewish leaders at the Temple siege, John and Simon, Believed God would arrive and destroy the Romans who were about to take the Temple complex. But nothing happened, and the two were captured. John was sentenced to life imprisonment. But Simon, the enemy's general, was thrown off the Tarpeian Rock after the triumph parade in Rome.

The traditional means of execution for Roman traitors parallels the Hebrew Scapegoat of Azazel (Lev 16. Day of Atonement).

Dates

The Old Testament contains information on the following:

- *Time since the occurrence of major events*
- *Time since birth and death*
- *Names and events within other nations*

For example:

- *I Kings 6:I. In the four hundred and eightieth year after the Israelites left Egypt. . . .*
- *2Ch 36:22. In the first reign of King Cyrus of Persia.....*

But it was the Greek translation of the Old Testament, called 'LXX Septuagint', which was used for quotations within the New Testament. This was in preference to the older Hebrew text.

The date of Creation

Bishop James Ussher (1581-1656) established from The Hebrew Bible that the day of creation was Sunday, 23rd October 4004 BC. We now know the Hebrew Bible, Masoretic text, is a later interpretation of the Hebrew Text, and at variations with Christian Greek Text.

However, Bishop Ussher used it as if it were the original text and worked out the time from Creation to Solomon. He then added the time from Solomon to the destruction of the Jerusalem temple. Where the Bible was silent, he took other sources to establish the periods, e.g. Chaldeans, Persians, Romans etc. and came up with the round number of 4000BC.

When he found out that Herod the Great died in 4BC, he had to adjust the error in the Anno Domini numbering method originally calculated by Dionysius Exiguus (d.554 AD). He, therefore, moved the date of the birth of Jesus back four years and the Creation back to 4004BC.

From the Hebrew Bible, Ussher saw the world was created on the Sunday nearest the Autumnal equinox. From the Julian calendar, he worked out the date of 23rd October.

Ussher established the key event in Biblical history. Here they are set out against those deduced from the LXX Septuagint:

Table 2: Key events in Biblical History

Event	Ussher (BC)	Septuagint (BC)
Creation	4004	5501
Noah's Flood	2349-2348	3239
Abraham called by God	1921	2092
The Exodus from Egypt	1491	1448
Founding of the Jerusalem Temple	1012	968
Destruction of the Temple and the start of Babylonian captivity	588	586
Birth of Jesus	4	4

Dates established from the Bible after the Fall of the Temple in Jerusalem in 586 BC are generally reliable. But Dates before the Fall cannot be relied on, and outside sources need to be used.

Alpha and Omega

The Bible starts and finishes in the Garden of Eden, which was part of the Israelite religion and is represented using the Jerusalem Temple.

The Bible is an interesting source. Its text has been translated from ancient languages and passed down through the ages. As a result, many disputes continue regarding some sections' exact phrases and meanings. In addition, there is no single text version; all are slightly different.

There is considerable wordplay, and names, for example, may have some hidden meaning in the original tongue. The use of the Greek language has also added further word-play, e.g. ADAM related to the four-point of the compass. Indeed the names used in the Old and New Testaments are not the original names of the various characters.

The Old Testament presents a historical background story for general understanding.

Jewish Religious Text

The Old Testament, as a Jewish religious document, has been extensively studied by Rabies since the diaspora. In the various Jewish settlements, religious texts such as the Talmud, Midrash and Kabbalah, etc., were developed to explain the meaning through Jewish eyes.

This Volume 1

This volume covers the period from the Book of Genesis to the end of the Book of Joshua. Including:

- *Creation*
- *Adam and Eve*
- *Noah and the Flood*
- *Abraham*
- *Isaac*
- *Jacob*
- *Joseph, including entering Egypt*
- *Moses, including leaving Egypt*
- *Joshua, including entering the Promised Land*

Volume 2

More details of the following are contained in the Appendix of Volume 2

- **The Laws**
- **Feasts and Festivals**
- **Offerings**
- **The Priests**
- **Health**

GENESIS

The Original Creation Story

God made the heavens and the earth. The earth was bare, watered only by springs from below. God provided no rain as the land was uncultivated, as there were no men.

God then made man from the dust and breathed the breath of life into his nostril. Man then became a living being.

Creation story (Priest's version)

(This is a later Creation Story from the priests of the first temple. The temple layout and features were based on the Garden of Eden story, with Adam being the first High Priest.)

At the beginning of time, God formed the earth in the universe and developed it with life throughout six successive eras.

These Eras are now marked as 'Days'. "The evening and then the morning formed the first day." This is why the Jewish day starts at sunset.

Table 3: Eras of Creation Story

Era	Created
1	The Heavens and water covered the Earth. Light and Darkness separated into Day and Night,
2	Sky separated the waters of heaven and earth
3	The water covering the earth separated, which allowed the land to appear between seas and oceans. As a result, vegetation, plants and trees grew, spreading their seeds and fruits on the ground.
4	The Sun and Moon divided the day and night, and the stars marked the seasons and the years
5	The oceans became filled with large and small creatures. The sky filled with birds.
6	Livestock, wild animals and creatures that moved along the ground appeared on the land. Man, both male and female, ruled over the earth. All those that breathed were vegetarians and only ate green plants, seeds and fruit.
7	God rested and sanctified the seventh day

Note: Humans - Males and Females were created on the sixth day.

The Garden in Eden

The land was called Eden, and to the east, God planted a garden and put Man there to take care of it. All kinds of trees grew there, including those that were attractive and colourful and those that provided food.

At the centre of the garden were two trees:

- The Tree of life
- The Tree of Good and Evil Knowledge

A river flowed from Eden into the garden to provide the plants with water. From there, the river split into four main rivers as follows:

Table 4: Main rivers from the Garden of Eden

1	*Pishon (Karun)*	This river winds through the entire land of Havilah, which has gold, lapis lazuli and pearls.
2	*Gihon (Nile)*	This river winds through the entire land of Cush
3	*Tigris*	This river runs along the east side of Assyria
4	*Euphrates*	-

(Euphrates River location is not described, perhaps due to the author expecting the reader to know already).

God told the man he could eat from all the trees except the 'Tree of Good and Evil Knowledge', which was deadly. (*Was God telling the truth here?*).

Birds and Animals

He then provided Man with companions and formed birds and animals out of the soil. He brought each one to **Adam** (the *first time his name was used*) to be named. But Adam did not find any companion among them.

Woman

God made Adam fall into a deep sleep and then took out one of his ribs* and formed a Woman.

(*The rib – In John's account, when Jesus was crucified and pierced with a spear….blood and water flowed out …this is the sign of birth. Men and women have the same number of pairs of ribs.)

When the man saw her, he said:

> "This one, at last, is bone of my bone and flesh of my flesh. This one will be called 'woman', for she was taken out of man."

(That is why a man leaves his father and mother and unites with his wife, and they become a new family. Gen 2:24)

The man and his wife were both naked and were not embarrassed.

The Temptation and the Fall

The serpent is the shrewdest of all the wild animals which God made. So it spoke to the woman and said, "Did God tell you not to eat from any tree in the garden?"

The woman replied, "We can eat from any tree except the one in the middle, which God said would kill us."

The serpent said, "You will not die. God knows when you eat from this tree, your eyes will be opened, and you will be like gods, knowing good and evil."

The woman saw the tree had produced fruits that were:

- Good for Food
- Attractive to the eye
- Desirable for making one wise

The woman took some fruits and ate them. She then gave some to her husband, who was nearby. They both gained knowledge and realised they were naked. To cover themselves, they sewed together fig leaves to form aprons.

The Judgment Oracles of God at the Fall

(The term 'The Fall' is developed by St Augustine of Hippo (354-430AD)

In the cool of the day, Adam and his wife heard God walking in the garden and decided to hide from him. God called out to Adam and asked why he could not see him.

Adam replied, "I heard you walking in the garden and hid as I was naked".

God asked, "Who said you were naked? Have you eaten from one of the two trees?"

Adam replied, "The woman gave me some fruit to eat?"

The woman said, "The serpent tricked me into eating some fruit."

God then gave each of them, in turn, a punishment:

Table 5: Punishment of the Serpent, Woman and Adam

Serpent	You will have no legs and simply crawl on your stomach and eat dust all your life. Everyone will try to kill you. They will try to crush your head while you will try to bite their heels.
Woman	You will have terrible pain when you give birth to children. Your husband will rule you, and you will desire him.
Adam	You will now eat the food you grow through your efforts. You are the dust of the ground, and when you die, you will return to the dust.

The man called himself 'Adam' and his wife 'Eve', meaning 'life'.

(The Greek word 'Adam', when split into four letters, A, D, A, and M, stand for the initial letters of the earth's four quarters. Anatolh / East, Dusis / West, Arktos / North, Meshmbria / South).

God made clothes for them from animal skin and dressed them. Then, he said, "Now that man has become like one of us, knowing good and evil, he must not be allowed to stretch out his hand and take from the tree of life and live forever."

God drove them out from the Garden in Eden and told them to cultivate the soil from which they were made. Then, on the east side of the garden, God placed Cherubim with flaming swords to guard the way back to the tree of life.

(This later symbolically appeared in the design of the Temple curtain. This curtain hung in front of the partition, which divided off the Holy-of-Holies within the tabernacle / temple.)

The Story of Cain and Abel

Adam made love to his wife, Eve, and she became pregnant. She gave birth to a son they called Cain. Eve said, "I have created a man just as God did." *(Biblically - Cain would have been the first to have a tummy button!)*

She then gave birth to another baby boy, who they called Abel.

- Abel took care of the flock
- Cain cultivated the soil

At the time of the Harvest, Abel gave God an offering of the best fattest firstborn lambs. God was very pleased. Cain presented God with an offering of the best fruits. As God did not seem very pleased, Cain became angry and upset.

God told Cain, "It was fine to be happy when what you do is right, but the minute something goes wrong, Sin is there to take you, and you must subdue it."

Cain invited Abel to go out in the field together, and he killed Abel there.

God came and asked Cain, "Where is your brother Abel?"

Cain replied, "I do not know – Am I my brother's keeper?"

God then said, "What have you done? The voice of your brother's blood is crying out to me from the ground!"

He added, "You are now banished from the ground, which has opened its mouth to receive your brother's blood from your hand. When you try to cultivate the ground, it will no longer yield its best for you. You will be a homeless wanderer on the earth."

Cain complained that this punishment was too great to endure. He would be homeless on the earth, and anyone who found him would kill him.

God agreed and told Cain that if anyone killed him, he would be avenged seven times as much. God then put a distinctive mark on Cain so no one could strike him down. (This distinctive mark is unknown)

Cain left the presence of God and went and lived in the land of Nod, east of Eden.

(Cain and Abel showed a comparison between Animal and Fruit sacrifices, and animal sacrifices prevailed)

Farming

The story of the Garden of Eden reflects the actual change from hunter-gathering to farming. This occurred in the Middle East, probably in c.8000BC. Instead of wandering, following wild animals, and gathering seasonal berries, farming meant domesticating animals, protecting them and their grazing land, forming communities, and trading – arts and crafts.

Cain's Family

In the land of Nod, Cain found a wife, and they had a son called Enoch. Cain built a city and named it after his son. Cain's following generations were:

Cain / Enoch / Irad / Mehujael / Methushael / **Lamech**

Lamech had two wives, Adah and Zillah. He told them he had:

- In the past killed a man for wounding him
- In the past killed a youth for hurting him

He pointed out that if God would avenge anyone seven times for killing Cain, then God would avenge anyone seven times seven if they killed him.

Table 6: Children of Lamech

Wife	Children	Comment
Adah	Jabal	Father of those who lived in tents and raised livestock
Adah	Jubal	Father of those who played harp and flute
Zilah	Tubal-Cain	Artificer of bronze and iron
Zilah	Naamah	Sister of Tubal-Cain

Adam and Eve's Family

Adam and Eve had another son called 'Seth' to replace Abel. Seth later had a son called Enosh, and people began to worship God.

From Adam to Noah

This is the Book of Generations of Adam:

When God created mankind, he made male and female in his likeness. Adam and his offspring had many children. Below is a list of eldest sons:

Table 7: Eldest Sons of Adam's Offspring

Name	Date Born	Date Died	Age died	Age when 1st son born
Adam	0	930	930	130
Seth	130	1042	912	105
Enosh	235	1140	905	90
Cainan	325	1235	910	70
Mahalaleel	395	1225	830	65
Jared	460	1355	895	162
Enoch	622	987	365*	65
Methuselah	687	1656**	969	187
Lamech	874	1651	777	182
Noah	1056	2006	950	500
Shem, Ham, and Japheth***	1556			

Enoch is noted as not dying, but he 'walked' with God. This is picked up in the 'Book of Enoch', which says he was taken to Heaven.

** *This was also the year of the Great Flood - 1656*

*** *Triplets?*

120-year Life Span

As the population began to increase, God's own sons noticed there were beautiful women born on earth. From these, they selected wives for themselves. God said, "My spirit will not remain in humans indefinitely. They are mortal and will live no longer than one hundred and twenty years."

In those days, the Nephilim (sons of Anak) were alive on earth. They were mighty Heroes of old, the famous men.

This mention of 'Nephilim' refers to 'Annunaki' or 'Gods' from the Sumerian culture. The Nephilim were said to have come to the earth to create humans. They came from Nibiru, the 'Planet of the Crossing' where one year, a Sar, equally 3600 earth years. The life span of the Nephilim was 120 Sars. The Sumerian text breaks up history into two ages, divided by a Great Flood. After the flood, the Nephilim decided they were too superior or 'lofty' for Humans. The Sumerians believed their gods punished humans for actions, i.e. sin, that displeased them. The gods then disciplined the wrongdoer with illness or disaster.

The story of Azazel – from the book of Enoch

The angels, the children of Heaven, saw the beautiful daughters of men and lusted after them. They wanted to choose wives for themselves and have children. Samjaza, their leader, believed they would not follow it through, and he would have to pay the penalty of a great sin. But they all said they would swear an oath to bind them to the plan. Having taken an oath, two hundred descended onto Mount Hermon's summit.

Semjaza led them. The chiefs of the tens were: Arakiba, Rameel, Kokabiel, Taniel, Ramiel, Danel, Ezeqeel, Baraqijal, Azazel, Armaros, Batarel, Ananel, Zaqiel, Samsapeel, Satarel, Turel, Jomjael, Sariel. *(Names vary according to the text source)*

They all took themselves wives and taught them charms and enchantments, cutting of roots and about plants. Soon they were pregnant and gave birth to giants who would be some 13.5m tall. They began to eat all the food available. When they ran out of vegetables and fruit, they began to eat birds, beasts, reptiles, fish, men, and each other.

Azazel taught men to make swords, knives, shields, breastplates, metal and the art of working them, bracelets and ornaments, how to beautify eyelids, jewels and colouring paints. Others taught the following:

Table 8: Skills taught by Angels

Semjaza	Enchantment, root-cuttings	Armaros	Resolving of Enchantments
Baraqijal	Astrology	Kokabel	The Constellations
Ezeqeel	Knowledge of the clouds	Araqiel	The signs of the earth
Shamsiel	The signs of the sun	Sariel	The course of the moon
Penemue	Writing with ink and paper	Azazel	Metalwork and makeup

As the men were killed and eaten, their cries were heard in heaven. Archangels Michael, Uriel, Raphael and Gabriel looked down from heaven and saw how much blood was being spilt on the earth, and listened to the souls of men making their case for their cause to go before the God of Ages, Lord of Lords, King of Kings and God of Gods. He made all things and has power over everything.

They pointed out what Azazel had taught on earth, revealing the eternal secrets of heaven. Semjaza had the authority to rule but had allowed the angels to take wives, teaching them to sin and have children who were giants. Those they had killed were now at the Gates of Heaven making their claim. *(The concept here of the gate of Heaven shows it is a much later source)*

A Great Flood

God told Uriel to go to Noah and tell him to hide as a Great Flood was coming to the earth to destroy it. He would escape it, and his seed would be preserved for all the generations of the world.

God told Raphael to bind Azazel hand and foot and throw him into darkness. Make an Abyss in the desert at Dudael Raphael threw him in. Thrown on top of him were rough and jagged rocks to cover him with darkness and leave him there forever.

He will be thrown into the fire on the day of the great judgement. Later the angel of peace took Azazel's host and cast them into the Abyss. Michael, Gabriel, Raphael and Phanuel would take hold of them on the Great day and cast them into the burning furnace as punishment for leading astray those who lived on earth.

NOAH

The Great Flood

The story of the flood, and the building of a boat to save humans and animals, was taken from Chaldean Tablets c. 2500BC.

These were found in UR and tell of the Babylonian God Ea, who decided to kill humans and animals in a great flood. He selected Ut-Napishtm to build an ark to save a few humans and animals. A later Babylonian text, "The Epic of Gilgamesh", c.1800 BC, tells a similar story and matches the story of Noah with 20 major points.

The Evil Earth

God saw that man had become evil and regretted creating them. He decided to wipe out:

- all of mankind
- animals
- creatures that move along the ground
- birds of the air

He would cause a great flood following forty days of continuous rain. *(Note fish and creatures of the seas, lakes and rivers are omitted.)*

God's plan for Noah

This is the account of Noah, who God saw as being good. He walked with God.

He had three sons – Shem, Ham and Japheth.

God saw the earth was ruined and filled with violence. All living creatures were sinful. So God told Noah he would destroy the Earth and all the living creatures.

The Ark and Animals

God told Noah to build an Ark with the following main features:-

- Built of Cypress wood – (Lebonese cedar – not available everywhere – Cypress being from Cyprus. Gopher wood mentioned elsewhere.)
- Lower, middle and upper decks
- Divided into rooms

- Coated inside and out with pitch
- Length, width and height to be 450 x 75 x 45 feet
- Add a roof and finish the ark within 18 inches of the top
- A door in the side
- A window to see outside (omitted from a number of texts, including LXX – but could have been cut-in during the occupation)

God told Noah he had one week to build his Ark; after that time, the earth would flood. Then, all the living creatures that have breath of life in them would drown. Everything would die.

God added, "I will confirm my covenant with you."

God told Noah to fill the Ark with the following:

- Noah and his wife
- Shem, Ham, Japheth, and their wives.
- Two of every kind of living creature made of flesh – male and female
- Two of every kind of Birds
- Two of every kind of cattle
- Two of every kind of creeping thing on the ground.
- Food is required to feed his family and the creatures. *(There could have been more animals unless they were all vegetarians.)*

Noah did all God told him to do.

Noah

God told Noah he considered him godly, so his household would go into the Ark and survive the flood. God told him to take (different to those above):-

- Noah and his household
- Seven of every kind of clean animal – male and its mate
- Two of every kind of unclean animal – male and its mate
- Seven of every kind of bird – male and female – to preserve their offspring on the face of the earth.

God said in seven days he would make it rain for forty days and forty nights, and he would wipe every living thing he had made from the face of the ground, including:

- People
- Animals
- Creatures that creep along the ground
- Birds of the sky

Only Noah, and those with him, survived.

(The difference between clean and unclean animals was not defined at the time but would be later explained in Leviticus. For now, they could be considered as follows:

Table 9: Clean and Unclean animals

Clean	Vegetarian, Tasted nice & smelt good when burnt
Unclean	They ate anything, including other animals.

Entering the Ark

When Noah was six hundred years old, the flood came.

The following went into the Ark:

- Noah, his wife, sons and their wives (8 persons)
- Two of each of the following:
- Clean beasts
- Unclean beasts
- Everything that crept on the earth

God shut them all in on the seventeenth day of the second month, and the flood started after seven days. All the fountains of the deep broke open, and the floodgates of heaven opened.

The flood covered the earth for forty days, with mountains covered by twenty feet of water. Finally, the Ark floated on the water, completely overwhelming the Earth.

The water stayed on earth for some one hundred and fifty days. During this time, God destroyed the following:

Every living thing on the ground, including:

- People
- Animals
- Creatures that creep along the ground
- Birds of the sky

God remembers Noah

God remembered Noah, the cattle, and others living with him in the Ark. He blew the wind over the earth, and the water receded.

The fountains of the deep and floodgates of heaven were closed, and the rain stopped. By the seventeenth day of the seventh month, the Ark came to rest on one of the mountains of Ararat. The waters then receded.

On the first day of the tenth month, the peaks of the mountains became visible.

Forty days later, Noah opened the window he had made in the Ark and sent out a raven. It flew to and fro until the waters had dried up.

Noah also sent out a dove to see if the waters had receded from the surface of the ground. The dove could not find somewhere to land and returned to the Ark. Noah sent it out again seven days later. The dove returned with a freshly plucked olive leaf in its beak. (Some say the dove returned with a leaf from the tree of life in the garden of Eden. Not everything had died!)

Noah then knew the water had receded from the earth. He waited seven more days and let the dove out again. This time it did not return.

It was six hundred and one years, one month, one day since Noah's birth when the ground was dry. Noah removed the covering from the Ark. The Earth was dry by the twenty-seventh day of the second month.

Chronology of the flood

The merging of the different sources causes repetition and variations in the text. How many days in a month? What months?

Table 10: The Chronology of the Flood

Date	Event	Comment
10/02/1656	God tells Noah to fill the Ark	Animals go in two by two?
17/02/1656	Rain starts	It was the 600th year of Noah's life
	Rain stops	after 40 continuous days
	150 days of flood	
17/07/1656	Ark rests on the Mountains of Ararat	
01/10/1656	Waters receded	until the tops of mountains are visible
40 days later	Noah sent out a Raven, followed by a Dove.	Neither could find anywhere to land
40 days later, cont.	Noah sent out the Dove again	Dove returned with olive leaf
	Seven days later, Noah sent out the dove again	Dove does not return
01/01/1657	Water dried up from the earth	601st year of Noah's life
27/02/1657	Ark is emptied	The land is completely dried.

Date is in the format of DD/MM/YYYY since Creation (0000)

Noah leaves the Ark

God told Noah to leave the Ark. He should bring out all the living creatures from within. They should be fruitful and multiply on the earth.

Noah built an altar to God. He then took some clean animals and birds and made a burnt offering on the altar. God smelled the aroma and said,

> "I will never again curse the ground because of mankind, even though the inclination of their minds is evil from childhood.
>
> I will never again destroy everything that lives, as I have just done.
>
> While the earth continues to exist - planting time and harvest, cold and heat, summer and winter, day and night - will not cease."

(No bredding would have taken place if only two clean animals had been taken into the Ark. When sacrified, there would have been none left.

Therefore seven clean animals were to be taken onto the Ark, and the increase covered this point.)

God's Covenant with Mankind through Noah

God blessed Noah and his sons and said,

"Be fruitful, multiply and fill the earth. The following will be terrified of you:

- Every living creature
- Every bird of the sky

You have authority over the following:

- Everything that creeps on the ground
- All the fish of the sea

You may eat anything that moves. Just as I gave you green plants to live, now I give you everything.

But you must not eat meat with its life – that is, blood- in it.

For your lifeblood, I will surely exact punishment.

From every living creature, I will exact punishment.

From each person, I will exact punishment for the life of the individual since the man was his relative.

> "Anyone who sheds human blood
>
> must have his bloodshed by others
>
> I have made mankind in my image."

But as for you, be fruitful, multiply, increase abundantly on the earth and multiply on it."

God's Covenant

God told Noah,

"I now confirm my covenant with you, your descendants, every creature from the Ark, every living creature of the earth. I confirm my covenant with you. Never again will all living things be wiped out by a flood."

The Rainbow

God told Noah he was placing a rainbow in the clouds as a perpetual reminder of the covenant between God and all living creatures.

God said to Noah,

"This is the guarantee of the covenant I am confirming between me and all living things on the earth".

Noah gets drunk

From the sons of Noah - Shem, Ham, and Japheth came the whole earth's population.

Noah planted a vineyard and harvested the grapes, and made wine. However, when he drank the wine, he was unused to its strength and fell asleep drunk and naked in his tent.

Ham saw his father asleep with his genitals exposed and laughed. He told his brothers, Shem and Japheth, who were not amused and quickly covered their father. When Noah awoke, he had a hangover and was very angry. He knew what Ham had said.

The curse of Canaan

Noah told his sons:

Table 11: Noah cursed Ham (Canaan)

Ham, (father of Canaan)	You will be the lowest of slaves to your brothers.
Shem	Canaan will be the slave of Shem. Praise the god of Shem.
Japheth	God will enlarge your territory. You will live in the tents of Shem, and Canaan will be his slave!

This curse on the Sons of Ham was fulfilled when:

- Israel became the ruler of Palestine – (All Cannan)
- Alexander the Great took Tyre– (Phoenician origin city)
- Rome destroyed Carthage – (Phoenician origin city)

(The following Table of Nations sets out Ham's claim to these nations.)

The Table of Nations

Following the flood, this is how Noah's sons, **Japheth, Ham** and **Shem,** became established nations when they spread out over the earth.

The Japhethites – Maritime people

Japheth – His sons **Gomer**, Magog, Madai, **Javan**, Tubal, Meshech and Tiras.

Gomer – His sons Ashkenaz, Riphath and Togarmah.

Javan - His sons Elishah, Tarshish, the Kittim and the Dodanim

From these, the maritime people spread out into their territories.

The Hamites – The Canaan Clans

Ham – His sons **Cush, Mizraim,** Put and **Canaan.**

Cush – His sons Seba, Havilah, Sabtah, **Raamah**, Sabteca and **Nimrod**

Raamah – his sons Sheba and Dedan

Nimrod, son of Cush, was a mighty hunter and warrior.

The first centres of his kingdom were Babylon, Erech, Akkad and Calneh in Shinar.

From that land, he went to Assyria, where he built Nineveh, Rehoboth-Ir, Calah and Resen, the city between Nineveh and Calah.

Mizraim – his sons Ludim, Anamim, Lehabim, Naphtuhim, Pathrusim, **Casluhim** (from whom the Philistines came) and Caphtorim.

Canaan – his sons Sidon (of the Hittites), Jebusit, Amor, Girgash, Hivit, Arkit, Sinit, Arvadit, Zemar and Hamaths.

The Canaanite clans scattered and reached from Sidon towards Gerar as far as Gaza and then towards Sodom, Gomorrah, Admah and Zeboiim, as far as Lasha.

The Semities

Shem – His sons Elam, Asshur, **Arphaxad**, Lud and **Aram**

Aram – His sons Uz, Hul, Gether and Meshech

Arphaxad – his son **Shelah**

Shelah – His son **Eber**

Eber – his sons Peleg and **Joktan**.

Joktan – His sons Almodad, Sheleph, Hazarmaveth, Jerah, Hadoram, Uzal, Diklah, Obal, Abimael, Sheba, Ophir, Havilah and Jobab

Their region stretched from Mesha towards Sephar in the eastern hill country.

The Genealogy of Shem

This is the account of Shem, son of Noah

Adam and his offspring had many children. Below is a list of eldest sons:

Table 12: Shem's offspring – the eldest sons

Name	Date Born	Date Died	Age died	Age when 1st son born
The flood	1656			
Shem	1568	2068	500	100
Arphaxad	1658	2061	403	35
Shelah	1693	2096	403	30
Eber	1723	2153	430	34
Peleg	1757	1966	209	30

Reu	1789	1996	207	32
Serug	1821	2021	200	30
Nahor	1851	1970	119	29
Terah	1880	2085	205	70
Abram (Abraham)	1950		175	
Nahor, Haran	1950			
Ismael			137	
Isaac			180	60
Esau and Jacob (twins)				

The Tower of Babel

The whole earth originally had a common language and vocabulary.

As the people moved eastward, they found a plain in the land of Shinar (Babylon) and settled there. There they had no stone but found they could make bricks by baking. In addition, they were able to use tar instead of mortar to bind them together.

To make a name for themselves, they started to build a city and a tower that would reach heaven. This would save them from being scattered across the face of the earth.

God came and saw what they were doing. He said:

> "If as one people sharing the common language they can do this, then nothing will be beyond them."

He decided to add confusion to their language so they would not be able to understand each other.

God then scattered them across the face of the entire earth, and the building of the city, known as Babel, stopped.

About the Bible – 1

The Epic of Gilgamesh – 1800BC

This document contains several events which can be seen as providing sources for the stories of Adam and Eve and Noah. It dates from before 1800BC.

The original stories were found on clay tablets at schools located at Babylonian temples and elsewhere. The range of tablets shows how the story was modified and elaborated over time.

Gilgamesh and Enkidu

The gods made Gilgamesh, with a perfect body, the king of Uruk. He would claim *'droit du seigneur'*, the right to take the virginity of brides on their first night of marriage. A goddess then made Enkidu a complete opposite – with a rough hairy body and long matted hair, and he lived with the animals like an animal in the wilderness.

A trapper discovered Enkidu at a water hole. The trapper was shocked and returned home and told his father what he had seen. His father suggested he took a harlot with him and she should expose herself to Enkidu and show him 'the ways of a woman'. For six days and seven nights, Enkidu made love to the harlot. Unfortunately, Enkidu fell for the harlot, and the animals rejected him.

Enkidu was naked, and the harlot shared her clothes with him. They returned to the city of Uruk. The harlot gave Enkidu bread and strong wine, and he became very merry. His face became red and rubbed down his body, finally appearing more like a man. (Note: Noah became angry when drunk).

There Enkidu later confronted Gilgamesh prior to him ravishing a further bride. They wrestled, and Gilgamesh won. But they then became friends, and Gilgamesh gave up taking local brides.

The Flood

Gilgamesh was told to build an ark by a god and fill it with the seeds of all the wild and tame animals. Then, he fills it with his family, relatives, craftsmen, and gold.

The flood occurred, and he opened a hatch after the rain stopped. He sent out a dove, then a swallow which also returned. Then a raven, which did not come back.

When the flood went down, they could leave the ark, and every other creature had been drowned and turned back to clay.

Legitimate Wife

Babylonia practised monogamy, but a man could have a concubine, or his wife could give him a slave as a concubine. However, in the Hammurabi Code, the wife still retained her position and is still seen as the legitimate wife. This was important for property and establishing the rightful heirs. This we see played out in the story of the Patriarchs.

Cedar

Gilgamesh requires cedar to build his city. The Gods have vast beautiful green cedar forests stretching from the Euphrates to Lebanon. Humbaba, a fierce demigod, protected it. Gilgamesh, Enkidu and a number of loggers went to the forest, killed Humbaba and started cutting down trees into transportable sizes. The trees began to cry, and Enlil, the god of the Earth, Wind, and Air, said, 'Why did you do this thing? From henceforth may the fire be on your face, may it eat the bread you eat, may it drink where you drink'.

Mesopotamia obtained timber from high up the Euphrates, Tigris and Karun rivers. The timber was floated downstream to where it was required. Deforestation over some 1500 years removed the ground cover, exposing salt-bearing rocks.

Natural erosion then led to salt and silt travelling downstream. This led to a decline in food production due to increased salinity and silting up of irrigation channels.

So the great empires fell.

ABRAHAM

An account of Terah

Terah was the father of the following:

1st	Haran
2nd	Nahor
3rd	Abram

Haran died while they were in Ur. He left a young son called Lot, Abram's nephew.

Table 13: Terah's sons

	Wife	Comment
Haran		His Son was Lot, and his daughters were Milcah (married Nahor) and Iscah
Nahor	Milcah	Daughter of Haran
Abram	Sarai	She was barren (daughter of Terah? Abram's sister)

Many years later, Terah left Ur for the land of Canaan, taking with him:

- Abram, Terah's son
- Abram's wife, Sarai (also his half-sister)
- Lot, his grandson, Abram's nephew

They came to Haran and lived there. Terah died at Haran aged 205.

(Journey is perhaps a Parallel with the Exile, returning to Israel and Sinai).

Abram lays claim to Shechem

When Abram was 75 years old, God came and spoke to him. He said,

"Leave your country, relatives, and your father's house.

Go to the land that I will show you, and there:

- I will make you into a great nation.
- I will bless you
- I will make your name great
- I will bless those who bless you
- I will curse those who curse you
- All the families of the earth will bless one another by your name."

35

Abram left with his wife and nephew Lot. They moved into the land of Canaan and travelled until they reached the 'Great Oak of Moreh' at Shechem. (At the time, the Canaanites were in the land).

God came to Abram and said, "I will give this land to your descendants". Abram then built an altar to God before moving onto the hill country east of Bethel. He pitched his tent with Bethel on the west and Ai on the east. There he built an altar and worshipped God.

Abram continued his journey by stages down to the Negev in the south.

Sarai the Courtesan

There was a famine in the land. So Abram and his family moved down to Egypt, where there was plenty of food. Sarai was very beautiful, and Abram was concerned that the Egyptians might take her and kill him. So he always told her to say he was her brother and they would not harm him.

Sarai soon came to the notice of one of the Pharaoh's sons in Egypt. She became a courtesan and moved into his palace. There she received gifts for her 'brother', as well as Camels, cattle, donkeys, servants and sheep. (Camels were not domesticated until the 9th Cent BC; therefore, detail of the story were added later). She became wealthy until a sexually transmitted disease infected her whole royal household.

The Pharaoh investigated and discovered that Sarai was Abram's wife. He called for Abram and asked him why he had allowed him to have Sarai and told everyone she was his sister when she was his wife. Abram explained he feared for his life in Egypt. The Pharaoh told Abram to leave Egypt immediately, taking Sarai, his family, and all their possessions. They were escorted to the border. *(Parallel with Moses – giving Egypt the plague and leaving with everything.)*

Abram and Lot

The family went from place to place until they finally returned to Bethel. There they pitched their tents between Bethel and Ai.

Abram was now very wealthy with gold, silver and livestock. He worshipped again at the Altar he had first built there.

Lot

Lot also had flocks, herds and tents. But the land could not support them all. They had too many animals, with Abram and Lot's herdsmen always quarrelling. The Canaanites and Perizzites were there also.

Abram told Lot they should split up to prevent any more conflict. One should go left, and the other should go right. (Jacob and Esau would later part similarly)

Lot saw the whole region of the Jordan; it was well watered like a garden – like Egypt all the way to Zoar.

Lot chose to move into this region of the Jordan and travelled towards the east. So they settled:

- Abram in the land of Canaan
- Lot on the Jordan plains

Lot pitched his tents next to Sodom, one of the cities of the plains. But unfortunately, the people of Sodom did not obey God.

God came to Abram and told him to look around from where he stood. So he turned and looked all around him. God then said all the land he saw would belong to his descendants forever. They would also be as numerous as the dust of the earth. (Abram knew from this point onwards that he would have children).

God told him to walk through the land which he had been given. So Abram took his family and wealth to Hebron and camped under the Great Oaks, which belonged to his friend Mamre the Amorite. There he built another altar.

Abram Rescues Lot

For twelve years, the five kings of the Jordan Plains were subjects of King Chedorlaomer of Elam and his allies to the east. They paid tribune until the thirteenth year when they decided to rebel.

The following year King Chedorlaomer and his allies came and invaded their lands and defeated the following:

- The Rephaities in Ashteroth Karnaim
- The Zuzites in Ham
- The Emites in Shaven Kiriathaim
- The Horites in the hill country of Seir, as far as El Paran, near the desert
- En Mishpat (Kadesh)
- Amalekites
- Amorites living in Hazazon Tamar

Then the kings of Sodom, Gomorrah, Admah, Zeboiim and Bela went out and prepared for battle. They met Chedorlaomer and his allies in the Valley of Siddim. This valley is full of tar pits, and when the Kings of Sodom and Gomorrah fled, they fell into them. Others fled to the hills.

King Chedorlaomer and his allies then pillaged the land. They took all they wanted, including Lot, his family, and his possessions.

Table 14: King Chedorlaomer, his allies, and Kings of the Plains

Chedorlaomer's Allies		Kings of the Plains	
Chedorlaomer	king of Elam	**Bera**	king of Sodom
Amraphel	king of Shinar	**Birsha**	king of Gomorrah
Arioch	king of Ellasar	**Shinab**	king of Admah
Tidal	king of Goiim	**Shemeber**	king of Zeboiim
		unknown	king of Bela (Zoar).

Abram was still living by the Oaks of Mamre when news reached him that Lot and his family had been taken. He immediately asked the help of the Amorite brothers, Aner, Eshcol and Mamre.

He called on the 318 trained men who had been born in his household (The number 318 is a gematria of the name 'Eliezer', Abram's steward).

They pursued King Chedorlaomer and his allies as far as Dan (obviously written after the land division *by the tribes)* on the northern border. That night they ambushed the kings at Hobah, killing them and many of their men. They retrieved all the people and goods taken, including Lot and his family.

After Abram returned after defeating Chedorlaomer and the kings with him, the king of Sodom met him in the King's valley.

(The king of Sodom had fallen into a tar pit, so maybe it was the King of Salem, Melchizedek, who met Abram in the King's valley, as shown in the following section.)

Melchizedek

Melchizedek, King of Salem (a priest of the Most High God), brought them bread and wine. He blessed Abram for his brave action as follows:

> **"Blessed be Abram by the Most High God,**
>
> **Creator of Heaven and Earth.**
>
> **Worthy of praise is the Most High God,**
>
> **who delivered your enemies into your hand."**

Abram gave Melchizedek a tenth of everything he had.

(Melchizedek receives further comments in 'Letter to the Hebrews'. He is seen as the King of Jeru-salem and the Priest of God before the Jewish religion.)

Then the king of Sodom told Abram he could keep all the plundered goods but return the people to him so he could reinforce his army.

But Abram said to the king:

> "I raise my hand to the Most High God, Creator of heaven and earth and vow that I will take nothing belonging to you, not even a thread or the strap of a sandal. That way, you can never say, 'It is I who made Abram rich.'
>
> I will take nothing except compensation for what the young men have eaten.
>
> As for the share of the men who went with me - Aner, Eshcol and Mamre – let them take their share."

Abram's Dream of offspring

God came to Abram in a vision. He said, "Fear not, Abram. I am your shield and the one who will reward you in great abundance."

Abram asked what good this was as he was childless. As God had not provided him with an heir, his estate would be inherited by his steward, Eliezer of Damascus*, born in his house.

(*Story written after the founding of Damascus)

God said, "This man will not be your heir, but instead, you will have a son of your own, from your own body."

God then took him outside and said,

> "Gaze into the sky and count the stars – if you can count them. So will your descendants be."

Abram believed in God, and God considered his response of faith as proof of genuine loyalty. God then said,

> "I am the God who brought you out from Ur of the Chaldeans* to give you this land to possess."

(*Chaldeans were the Dynasty that removed the Jews to Babylon, forming 'The Exile'. A new Ur was built at this time. Therefore these events were written after 538BC)

Then Abram asked God, "God, how do I know I am to possess it?"

God told Abram to get:

- A three-year-old heifer
- A three-year-old female goat
- A three-year-old ram

- A dove
- A young pigeon

God told him to cut the animals in half and lay them opposite each other. The birds were not to be cut. Abram did this and sat and drove away any birds of prey which came down onto the carcasses.

(These birds of Prey were later said to be the fallen Angels, such as Azazel)

Abram fell asleep when the sun went down, and a great terror overwhelmed him.

Then God said to him:

> "Your descendants will be strangers in a foreign country. They will be enslaved and oppressed for four hundred years. But I will execute judgement on the nation that they will serve.
>
> Afterwards, they will come out with many possessions. But you will go to your ancestors in peace and be buried at a good old age.
>
> In the fourth generation, your descendants will return here, for the sin of the Amorites has not yet reached its limit."

(The Amorites worship the Moon-god, who they called 'Sin')

Abram saw a smoking firepot with a flaming torch pass between the animal parts when it was fully dark.

On that day, God made a covenant with Abram:

> **"I will give your descendants the following land :**
>
> **From the river of Egypt to the Great River (Euphrates), the lands of the following people –**
>
> - **Kenites, Kenizzites, Kadmonites, Hittites, Perizzites, Rephaites, Amorites, Canaanites, Girgashites, Jebusites."**

(These lands were therefore known as 'The Promised Lands' but were never achieved. The river of Egypt is not the Nile, but a seasonal river on the north-east Egyptian border)

The Birth of Ishmael

After living in Canaan for ten years, Sarai, Abram's wife, had not given birth to any children. So she suggested Abram should take her Egyptian servant, Hagar, and start a family. Abram accepted, and Hagar became pregnant.

Hagar then began to despise Sarai. Sarai sensed this and told Abram, "I was wrong when I told you to take Hagar. She is now pregnant and despises me. May God now judge between you and me."

Abram said to Sarai, "Hagar is your servant. Therefore, do to her what you think is best."

Sarai then treated Hagar so harshly that she ran away.

An angel from God found Hagar near a spring of water in the desert by the road to Shur. He asked her, "Hagar, where have you come from, and where are you going?"

Hagar replied, "I am running away from Sarai, my mistress."

The Angel told her to return to her mistress and submit to her authority. He added that her descendants would be greatly multiplied, so they would be too numerous to count. The Angel added,

"You are now pregnant and will give birth to a son. You will call him 'Ishmael', for God has heard your painful groans.

- He will be like a wild donkey of a man.
- He will be hostile to everyone, and everyone will be hostile to him.
- He will live away from his brothers."

Hagar called God and said, "You are the God who sees me. Here I have seen one who sees me."

(That is why the well was called Beer Lahai Roi – located between Kadesh and Bered.)

Abram was eighty-six years old when Hagar gave birth to his son, who he called Ishmael.

The Sign of the Covenant

When Abram was 99 years old, God came to him and said,

"Walk before me and be blameless. Then I will confirm my covenant between us. I will give you a multitude of descendants."

Abram bowed down, and God continued,

"This is my covenant with you.

- You will be the father of many nations.
- Your name will be Abraham Instead of Abram.
- You will be highly fruitful, and nations and kings will descend from you.

- I confirm the covenant between you and me. It will extend to your descendants.
- I will be your God. and the God of your descendants.
- I will give the whole land* to you and your descendants as a permanent possession.

(The change of name was again the result of wordplay. 'Abram' meant 'Exalted Father' referring to Terah, while 'Abraham' sounded like the word for 'the father of a multitude'. Therefore once the vast numbers of descendants were promised, the name was changed. Also, yet another covenant.

**The Lands as previously described.)*

Requirement for circumcision

God then said:

"You must keep the covenantal requirement I am now imposing on you and your descendants.

- Every male among you must be circumcised. You must cut the flesh of your foreskins. This will be a reminder of the covenant between you and me.
- Every male must be circumcised when eight days old, whether born in your house or bought with money.
- The sign of my covenant will be visible in your flesh as a permanent reminder.
- Any uncircumcised male will be cut off from his people – he has failed to carry out my requirements."

(There is no medical need for circumcision. The practice became a block for conversions of older males.)

God then told Abraham,

"Your wife Sarai will now be called Sarah. I will bless her and give you a son through her.

She will become a mother of nations. Kings of countries will come from her."

('Sarai and Sarah' mean the same – 'princess or queen', but in different dialects. Therefore as Abram's name was changed, so was his wife's. The change of names is a common occurrence in Bible Stories. It is thought to be due to merging stories and varying dialects.)

Abraham bowed down and said,

"Can a son be born to a man who is a hundred years old? Can Sarah bear a child at the age of ninety? If only Ishmael were to be that son."

God then said,

"No, Sarah, your wife, will bear you a son, and you will name him Isaac. I will confirm my covenant with him as a perpetual covenant for his descendants after him.

As for Ishmael, I have heard you.

- I will bless him, make him fruitful, and give him a multitude of descendants.
- He will become the father of twelve princes.
- I will make him into a great nation.

But I will establish my covenant with Isaac, who Sarah will bear to you at this set time next year."

When he finished speaking to Abraham, God left him.

Circumcision

Abraham took his son Ishmael and every male in his household (whether born in his house or bought with money) and circumcised them just as God had told him. Abraham was ninety-nine, and Ishmael was thirteen when they were circumcised.

The Special Visitors

One hot day at the Great Oaks of Mamre, Abraham sat at the entrance to his tent. He saw God and two others approaching. (*Christians have explained this person as being Jesus*). He ran to meet them and bowed low to the ground.

Abraham said, "God, I have found favour in your sight, do not pass me by. First, I will get water so you may wash your feet and rest under the tree. Then, I will get some food so that you may refresh yourselves. After that, you may go on your way."

They replied, saying they would accept his hospitality.

Abraham rushed into the tent and told Sarah to "quickly take three measures of fine flour, knead it, and make bread."

Then he ran to the herd, chose a fine, tender calf, and gave it to his servant to kill and quickly prepare.

He took some curds and milk, together with the calf which had been prepared, to his guest. Then, while they ate, he stood near them under a tree.

Where is Sarah?

They asked Abraham, "Where is your wife, Sarah?"

He replied, "There in the tent."

One of them said, "I will return to you when the season comes around again, and your wife, Sarah, will have a son!"

Sarah was listening to their conversation and laughed to herself. She and Abraham were now very old, and she had long since passed menopause. She said to herself, "I am worn out! How will I have pleasure, especially when my husband is too old?"

God said to Abraham, "Why did Sarah laugh and say, 'Will I have a child when I am so old?'. Is anything impossible for God? I will return to you when the season comes round again, and Sarah will have a son."

Sarah heard God say this, and she said to herself, lying, "I did not laugh."

God then said, "Yes, you did laugh."

Abraham pleads for Sodom

The three men got up to leave and looked out over Sodom. Abraham walked with them to see them on their way. Then God said,

> "Should I hide what I am about to do from Abraham? Abraham will become a great and powerful nation. All the nations on the earth will pronounce a blessing on one another using his name. I have chosen him so he may command his children to keep my way by doing what is right and just. Then I will give to Abraham what I promised him."

So God said,

> "The outcry against Sodom and Gomorrah is so great and their sin so blatant that I must go down and see if they are as wicked as the outcry suggests. If not, I want to know."

Two men left and headed towards Sodom. Abraham was still standing in front of God. He asked God if he would sweep away the godly and the wicked.

> "What if there are fifty godly people in the city? Will you wipe it out and not spare the place for the sake of the fifty godly people

who are in it? Surely you would not treat the godly the same as the wicked?"

God replied. "He would spare the city if he found fifty godly people."

Then Abraham asked if he would spare the city if he found forty-five godly people, five less than before.

God replied he would spare the city.

Abraham asked the same question each time, reducing - forty, thirty, twenty, and ten. After that, God said he would spare the city each time, and finally, God said he would not destroy the city if there were ten godly people.

Finally, Abraham was happy. God left and went on his way. Abraham returned home.

The Evil of Sodom and Gomorrah

In the evening, the two angels arrived at Sodom while Lot was sitting in the city's gateway. When Lot saw them, he got up to meet them and bowed down with his face toward the ground.

He invited them to his house to stay the night and wash their feet. They refused to say they would spend the night in the town square. But Lot pressed them, and they finally accepted.

At home, he prepared a meal for them, including bread baked without yeast, and they ate.

Before they could sleep, all the young and older men from every part of the city of Sodom surrounded the house. They shouted to Lot,

> "Where are the men who came to you tonight? Bring them out to us so we can have sex with them."

(See also story in the Book of Judges, set at Gibeah concerning the Levite, his concubine, and the Benjaminites)

Lot went outside, shutting the door behind him. He said to all the men,

> "My Brothers, do not act so wickedly. Look, I have two daughters, virgins. You can have them to do with whatever you like. But the men have come under the protection of my roof, and you cannot have them."

The men told Lot to get out of the way. He had come to live with them as a foreigner, and now he dared to judge them. "We will do more harm to you than to them." They added.

Then the two visitors opened the door, quickly pulled Lot back into the house, and shut the door. Then they struck all the men outside with blindness. They still tried to find the door but could not.

The two visitors asked Lot, "Who else do you have here? Do you have any sons-in-law, sons, daughters, or other relatives in the city? You need to get them out because we are about to destroy it. The outcry against this place is so great God has sent us to destroy it."

Lot went and spoke to his future Sons-in-Law, who would marry his daughters. Then, he said, "Get out of this place quickly, as God will destroy it."

They refused because they thought Lot was ridiculing them.

Destruction of the City

At dawn, the angels hurried Lot, his wife, and his family out of the city. They told them they would be destroyed when the city was judged if they did not move quickly. Finally, they took Lot's hands and his family's and led them away. Once out of the city, they told Lot and his family to:

- Run for their lives
- Not to look behind
- Not to stop anywhere in the valley
- Escape to the mountains

If they did not obey, they would be destroyed.

But Lot told them he would not have enough energy to reach the mountains. So he asked if they would spare the distant small town (Zoar), as he believed they could reach there in time.

The angels decided they would not include this small town in their destruction. Instead, they told Lot and his family to run quickly to Zoar, and they would destroy Sodom after arriving.

Just as the sun was rising over the land, Lot reached Zoar. Then God rained down from the sky sulphur and fire onto Sodom and Gomorrah. God destroyed those cities and all the region, including all the inhabitants and the vegetation. Lot's wife looked back longingly and was turned into a pillar of salt.

Abraham saw what had happened

Abraham got up early in the morning and went to where he had stood before God. He looked out towards Sodom, Gomorrah, and all the land of that region. He could see the smoke rising from the land like a furnace.

Abraham realised God had honoured his request. He had removed Lot and his family from the destruction, and they had lived.

Lot and his daughters

Lot and his two daughters left Zoar as they were afraid to live there. So they went up the mountains and stayed in a cave.

One night the older daughter said to her younger sister, "Our father is old, and there is no man anywhere to give us children as is natural in the world. We must, therefore, get our father drunk with wine so we can have sex with him and preserve our family line."

That night they made their father drunk, and the eldest daughter had sex with him. Their father did not know what they did.

The following night the younger daughter got their father drunk, and she had sex with him, again without his knowledge.

Later the daughters gave birth to Moab and Ben-Ammi.

Table 15: Lot's two daughters

Lot fathered a child with	Son's name	Father of the nation of
Elder daughter	Moab	Moabites
Younger daughter	Ben Ammi	Ammonites

Abraham and Abimelech

Abraham travelled to the land of the South and settled between Kadesh and Shur. While he lived as a temporary resident in Gerar, Abraham said to his wife Sarah, "She was his sister."

Abimelech, King of Gerar, sent for Sarah and took her. (*Abimelech is seen as a title, like Pharaoh, for the King of the Philistines*).

God appeared to Abimelech in a dream at night and said, "You are as good as dead because you have taken the woman who is the wife of another."

Abimelech had not yet had sex with her. He asked God if he would slaughter an innocent nation. He said, "Abraham said she was his sister, and Sarah had said he was her brother. Therefore I have done this with a clear conscience and innocent hands."

As the dream continued, God told Abimelech, "I know you have done this with a clear conscience. That is why I have kept you from sinning against me and did not allow you to have sex with her. But now give back the man's wife. Indeed he is a prophet, and he will pray for you, and you will live. But, if you do not give her back, you will die with all who belong to you."

In the morning, he told all his servants what had happened. They were all terrified.

Abimelech then called for Abraham. He said to him,

- *What have you done to us?*
- *What sin did I commit against you that caused you to bring such great guilt on me and my kingdom?*
- *You have done things to me that should not be done?*

Abraham said, "Because I thought no one fears God in this place. They would kill me for her. But she is indeed my sister, my father's daughter, but not my mother's daughter. She became my wife. When we left my father's house, I told her to be loyal to me and say I was her brother."

Abimelech gave sheep, cattle, and male and female servants to Abraham. He then told Abraham and Sarah they could live where they liked in his land.

Abimelech told Sarah he had given Abraham one thousand pieces of silver as compensation to stand vindicated before all who are with you.

Abraham prayed to God, and God healed Abimelech, his wife, and female slaves so that they could have children. (God had caused infertility to strike every woman in Abimelech's household when he took Sarah.)

(This story appears to be a copy of the earlier report told of Egypt. The relationship between Sarah and Abraham is said to be that of a married half-brother and half-sister. Common father and a different mother. This would explain the claim of Abraham being a brother in preference to being a husband.

Abraham's family's wealth came from others paying for Sarah.)

ISAAC

The Birth of Isaac

God visited Sarah just as he promised, and she became pregnant and later delivered a son. Abraham called him Isaac.

When Isaac was eight days old, Abraham circumcised him just as God had told him. (Abraham was one hundred years old when Isaac was born to him.).

Sarah said, "God has made me laugh. Everyone who hears about this will laugh with me. Who would have believed that Abraham and I would nurse children at our age."

(Sarah and subsequent female ancestors are barren, and they and their husbands have to wait for God to provide a child to ensure the continuation of the covenant promise. Any attempt to father children by concubines leads to their rejection from the male line. The male heirs are also threatened – Isaac is almost sacrificed, Jacob is forced into exile, and Joseph is sold! But Joseph was not a male heir!)

Hagar and Ishmael Sent Away

When Isaac was weaned, Abraham arranged a great feast. During this, Sarah realised Ishmael was continually mocking her behind her back. She told Abraham to get rid of Ishmael and his mother, Hagar. She did not want her servant's son to be an heir to her son, Isaac.

Abraham was upset but decided that as both his children were healthy, he should listen to Sarah. So he spoke to God, who said Ishmael would become the father of a great nation. So the following day, Abraham gave Hagar a skin of water and some bread and told her to take Ishmael and leave.

Hagar left and wandered through the wilderness of Beersheba. When the water had run out, Ishmael, who was sixteen years old, started to whine. He got on Hagar's nerves, so she left him sitting under a bush, went about an arrow's flight away, sat down, and cried uncontrollably. She did not want to watch her child die.

God heard Ishmael whining, and the angel of God called Hagar from heaven to ask her what was wrong. The angel added, "Do not be afraid;

God has heard Ishmael's voice from under the bush. Get up, help the boy and hold him by the hand. I will make him into a great nation."

God help Hagar to see a well of water. So she filled the skin and gave Ishmael a drink.

God watched over Ishmael as he grew up in the wilderness of Paran. He became an archer. His mother found him a wife from Egypt.

(Tradition says Ishmael was the father of the Arab people, and they had settled in Mecca.

The Kabah is said to have been built by Adam and rebuilt by Abraham and Ishmael. Muslims are now expected to visit the Kabah once in their lifetime and face its direction during prayers.

Muslims claim Abraham was not a Jew or a Christian but a monotheist who worshipped God and not idols.)

The Treaty at Beersheba

King Abimelech visited Abraham with Phicol, the leader of his army.

He told Abraham that God was with him in everything he did. He wanted Abraham to swear in God's name that he would never deceive his children and descendants. "Show me and the land where you are now staying the same loyalty I have shown you."

Abraham said, "I swear to do this."

Then Abraham complained to Abimelech about his servants who had seized a well. The king said it was the first he had heard of the matter. They both agreed that whoever had dug the well should keep it.

The two men made a treaty, and Abraham gave Abimelech cattle and sheep. Abraham separated off seven ewe lambs, and once Abimelech had agreed Abraham had dug the wells, he gave them to him. (That is why he named Beer Sheba, as the two swore an oath there.)

Abimelech and Phicol returned to the land of the Philistines where they were staying. Abraham planted a tamarisk tree at Beersheba. After that, he stayed in the land of the Philistines for a long time. There he worshipped God.

(The Philistines arrived in the land in the early twelfth century BC.)

The Sacrifice of Isaac

God decided to test Abraham. He told Abraham to take Isaac, his only son (*What of Ishmael?),* who he loved, to the land of Moriah. "There you are to offer your son as a burnt offering on one of the mountains which I will indicate to you." (Muslims believe it was Ishmael).

Early the next morning, Abraham got up and saddled his donkey. He took two of his young servants with him, along with Isaac. Then, after he had prepared some wood for the burnt offering, they set out for the place God had mentioned.

Three days later, Abraham caught sight of the place in the distance. He told his two servants, "Stay here with the donkey while the boy and I go up there. We will worship and then return to you."

Abraham gave the wood for the burnt offering to Isaac to carry. Abraham took the knife and the fire in his hand and walked off together.

As they continued walking, Isaac said to his father, "Here is the fire and the wood, but where is the lamb for the burnt offering." Abraham told him, "God will provide the lamb."

When they came to the place God had told him about, Abraham built the altar and arranged the wood. He then tied up Isaac and placed him on top of the wood. Then Abraham reached out his hand, took the knife and prepared to slaughter his son.

God's angel called from Heaven and said, "Abraham, do not harm the boy. Do not do anything to him, for now, I know that you fear God because you did not withhold my only son from me."

Abraham looked up and saw a ram caught in the bushes by its horns behind him. So he went over and got the ram and offered it up as a burnt offering instead of his son.

(Abraham called the name of that place "God provides")

The Angel of God called Abraham a second time and said, "God swears that as you have not withheld your son, your only son, he will bless you. He will multiply your descendants so they will be countless as the stars in the sky or the grains of sand on the seashore.

Your descendants will take possession of the strongholds of their enemies. Then, because you have obeyed him, all the nations of the earth will pronounce blessings on one another using the name of your descendants."

Then Abraham returned to his servants, and they all returned to Beer Sheba.

(Was Isaac sacrificed? Child sacrifice was common at the time, and the story pointed out to other religions that Child sacrifice was wrong.

However, others in Canaan, including the Phoenicians, practised it. Discoveries in Carthage demonstrate this.

The story also shows the importance of the family line at the time. There was only one 'wife', and children by other women, especially servants, were of no significance, e.g. Ishmael. However, the tribes of Israel later were made up of wives and servants' offspring. Also, later, the redeeming of the firstborn).

Nahor's Sons

Abraham received news from Nahor, his brother, who he had left in Paddan Aram. His family had increased, and Abraham now had many nephews and nieces.

Nabour had eight sons with his wife, Milcah:

> Uz, the firstborn, Buz, his brother, Kemuel (the father of Aram), Kesed, Hazo, Pildash, Jidlaph and Bethuel (the father of **'Rebekah'**).

He also had four sons by Reumah, his concubine:

> Tebah, Gaham, Tahash and Maacah.

The Death of Sarah

Sarah died at Kiriath Arba (Hebron) in the land of Canaan when she was 127 years old. Abraham mourned and wept for her.

Abraham went and spoke to the elders – called the 'Sons of Heth' who were inside the city gate, "I am a temporary settler among you. Grant me ownership of a burial site among you, so I may bury my dead."

The 'Sons of Heth' told Abraham, "You are a mighty prince among us. You may bury your dead in the best of our tombs. None of us will refuse you his tomb to prevent you from burying your dead."

Abraham asked them, "As you agree that I may bury my dead here, can you ask Ephron, the son of Zohar, if he will sell me his cave at Machpelah, which is at the end of his field? Let him sell it to me publicly for the full price so I may own it as a burial site."

Ephron was one of the elders and introduced himself to Abraham. He told him, "I will sell you the field and the cave within it. Let everyone witness this. Please bury your dead."

The field had a cave within it and several trees. A border of trees also surrounded the field.

Abraham bowed before the local people and said to Ephron, "Hear me, if you will. I will pay you the price of the field. Take it from me so that I may bury my dead."

Ephron said the land was worth four hundred pieces of silver, but the money was unimportant to him. So Abraham paid him four hundred pieces of silver according to the standard measurement at the time.

Abraham buried his wife, Sarah, in the cave in the field of Machpelah next to Mamre (Hebron) in the land of Canaan.

Search for a wife for Isaac

Abraham told the steward of his house to go and find a wife for Isaac. He told him:

- Do not find a wife from the Canaanites among whom they were living.
- Go back to my original country and find a wife from among my relatives.

He told his steward to place his hand under his testicles and make a solemn promise to God of Heaven and earth.

(This appeared to be a Hebrew method of making an oath, perhaps promising the loss of his testicles if he failed to keep the promise he had made).

Before the steward did this, he asked Abraham what he should do if the woman refused to return with him. Perhaps he should take Isaac to meet the woman?

Abraham said, "Be careful; never take my son back there. God took me from my father's house and the land of my relatives and promised me with a solemn oath, 'To your descendants, I will give this land.' God will send his angel before you to find a wife for my son. You will be freed from this oath if the woman refuses to return with you."

The steward placed his hand under his master's testicles and gave his solemn promise that he would carry out his wishes. He then left with ten camels for Paddan Aram, where Nahor lived. The steward also took with him all sorts of gifts.

Once outside the city, the steward made the camels kneel by the well. It was evening and the time when women came to draw water. The steward prayed to God,

"God of my master Abraham, guide me today. Be faithful to my master Abraham. Here I am, standing by the spring, and the daughters of the people who live in the town are coming out to draw water.

- I will tell a young woman, 'Please lower your jar so I may drink.'
- If she replies, 'Drink, and I will give your camels water too.'

Then I will know that you have been faithful to my master."

Rebekah

Before he had finished praying, Rebekah arrived with her water jug on her shoulder. She was the daughter of Bethuel, son of Milcah (Milcah was the wife of Abraham's brother Nahor). She was beautiful and a virgin.

Rebekah went down to the well and filled her water jug. The steward stopped and asked her for a drink of water." She let him drink and then said she would also draw water for his camels. She emptied the water into the watering trough and refilled her jug several times to provide enough water for his camels. The steward watched to establish whether God had made his journey successful.

After the camels had finished drinking, the steward took out:

- One gold nose ring – weighing a beka (half a shekel)
- Two gold bracelets – weighing ten shekels

He gave them to her and asked who her father was and whether there was a room in her father's house where he could spend the night.

Rebekah explained who her father was and said there was a room he could use for the night.

The steward bowed his head and said, "Praised be to God, the God of my master Abraham, who has not abandoned his faithful love for my master. God has led me to the house of my master's relatives."

Rebekah ran home and told her mother's household all about the steward. Laban, Rebekah's brother, saw Rebekah with her gold bracelets and heard her speak about the steward. Laban rushed out to meet the steward. He helped him to his home and unloaded his camels for the night. He provided water for him and his men to wash their feet.

When the food was served, the steward told them about Abraham, how Rebekah was his granddaughter, and how he had been sent to find Isaac, a wife.

Then Laban and Bethuel replied, "This is God's doing. Our wishes are of no concern. Rebekah stands here before you. Take her and go so that she may become the wife of your master's son, just as God has decided."

The steward bowed down to the ground before God. Then he brought out gold, silver jewellery and clothing and gave them to Rebekah. He also gave valuable gifts to her brother and mother. Afterwards, the steward and his men ate the food they had been given and stayed there overnight.

The following morning they prepared to leave. But Rebekah's brother and mother asked if she could stay a few more days, perhaps ten, and then leave once they had time to say 'goodbye'.

But the steward wanted to get on his way and said, "Do not detain me. God has granted me success on my journey. Let me leave now so I can return to my master".

Rebekah's brother and mother called and asked if she still wanted to go with the steward. Rebekah said she wanted to go. So they packed her up with her nurse and female servants and blessed her with these words:

> "Our sister, may you become the mother of thousands of ten thousands. May your descendant possess the strongholds of their enemies."

Rebekah and her staff mounted the camels and rode away with the steward and his men.

Isaac meets Rebekah

Isaac was relaxing in a field in the early evening when he saw some camels approaching and recognized his father's steward. So he walked over to the field to meet them all. Rebekah looked up and saw Isaac. As she got down from the camel, she asked the steward. "Who is the man who is walking over to meet us." The steward replied, "That is your new master, Isaac."

Rebekah quickly covered her face with a veil. The steward told Isaac everything that had happened.

Isaac took Rebekah into the tent his mother, Sarah, had used. There he took her and loved her as a wife. Isaac was comforted by this after his mother's death. Isaac was forty years old when he first met Rebekah.

Abraham remarried

Abraham remarried. His new wife was Keturah, and their children were:

> Wife Keturah – Her sons Zimran, **Jokshan**, Medan, **Midian**, Ishbak and Shuah

> **Jokshan** – his sons Sheba, **Dedan**

> **Dedan**, his descendants were the Asshurim, Letushim, Leummim

> **Midian** – his sons Ephah, Epher, Hanoch, Abida, Eldaah.

While Abraham was alive, he gave gifts to the sons of his concubines and sent them away to the east, out of the reach of Isaac.

Death of Abraham

Abraham was 175 years old when he died. He was buried by his sons Isaac and Ishmael in the Machpelah cave near Mamre, next to his first wife, Sarah. He left everything he owned to Isaac, who lived near Beer Lahai Roi.

Ishmael's Sons

Ishmael died when he was 137 years old. He left twelve sons and a daughter called Mahalath.

> Ishmael – His sons Nebaioth the firstborn of Ishmael, **Kedar**, Adbeel, Mibsam, Mishma, Dumah, Massa, Hadad, Tema, Jetur, Naphish and Kedemah.

His sons became tribal rulers in the area from Havilah to Shur, and they were antagonistic to everyone around, including each other.

Kedar

Muslims believe Ishmael, through his son Kedar to be the forefather of Muhammad. Hence the Jewish and Muslim belief splits with Abraham's sons.

JACOB

Jacob and Esau

After twenty years of marriage, when Isaac was sixty, Rebekah finally became pregnant. She started to have terrible pains in her womb. She became concerned and asked God why she was having these pains. God explained to her:

- She would give birth to twin boys
- They would each form a nation
- One would be stronger than the other
- The older one would serve the younger one.

Rebekah finally gave birth to twin boys. The first baby was red and covered in hair when it was delivered. The second baby was holding onto his brother's heel. The first son was called 'Esau', and the second was called 'Jacob'. Jacob became Rebekah's favourite, while Isaac preferred Esau.

The boys were different in temperament. Esau was physical, enjoyed the outdoors and was a skilful hunter. On the other hand, Jacob was quiet and liked to stay in the tents and cook. Esau loved Jacob's stew, saying, "I will faint unless I have some". Because of this, he was often called 'Edom', meaning 'I faint'.

Birthright for Stew

One day as Jacob was cooking some red lentil stew, Esau arrived back from hunting. He was starving and asked Jacob for some of his stew. Jacob looked at him and asked him to sell his birthright for the plate of stew.

Esau said jokingly, "I will shortly die of hunger, and then what will be the use of my birthright to me?"

But Jacob was serious and told him to "Swear that you have given me your birthright, and I will give you this plate of stew".

Esau thought so little of his birthright that he happily swore an oath to Jacob in exchange for the plate of stew and some bread. So Esau happily ate and drank what Jacob gave him.

Isaac & Abimelech – (repeat from Abraham?)

There was another severe famine, and Isaac thought, like his father, of going to Egypt. But God appeared and told him not to go to Egypt but to stay in the Promised Land. He had promised Abraham that his offspring would be in number like the stars of the sky and would not suffer.

Isaac and his household settle in Gerar, in the land of Abimelech, king of the Philistines. The men of Gerar asked Isaac about Rebekah, so he told them she was his sister. (He was afraid to say Rebekah was his wife as she was very beautiful. The men of the place would kill to get Rebekah. – The genuine blood relationship, in this case, was first cousins)

After Isaac had lived there long, King Abimelech saw Isaac caressing his 'sister' and called Isaac to him. He asked Isaac, "Why did you say Rebekah was your sister instead of your wife?"

Isaac said he feared for his life. But Abimelech told him one of his men could have had sex with his 'sister' and brought guilt on them all. The King then ordered that anyone who touched Isaac or Rebekah would be put to death.

Isaac, the farmer, and wells disputes

God blessed Isaac, and this was reflected in his harvests. What he planted increased a hundred times when it was reaped. Isaac became wealthy with a large number of sheep and cattle. His household grew, and the Philistines began to envy him. They decided to block up some of the wells he used, which had been dug in his father's day.

King Abimelech visited him. He told him he had become too powerful and he should move away. So Isaac went to live in the Gerar Valley. He re-opened the wells his father had dug, which the Philistines had filled.

He also had his servants dig a new well in the valley. The herdsmen of Gerar quarrelled with his men, claiming the water was theirs. He called the well 'Esek'. Then his servants dug another well, called 'Sitnah', but the herdsmen quarrelled again.

Finally, Isaac dug another well further away at Rehoboth, and the quarrelling stopped. Isaac saw that God had made room for them, and they would prosper in the land.

Isaac finally moved on to Beer Sheba. God appeared to him that night and said,

"I am the God of your father, Abraham. Do not be afraid. I am with you. I will bless you and multiply your descendants for the sake of my servant Abraham."

Isaac then built an altar there and worshipped God. Next, he got his servants to dig a well and pitched his tent.

King Abimelech Visits – (Repeat from Abraham?)

King Abimelech came from Gerar to visit Isaac. His friend Ahuzzath, and Phicol, the leader of his army, accompanied him. Isaac was surprised to see them, as he thought they hated him. He asked why they had come. The King said they wanted a peace treaty between them. He said they had not harmed each other and should live in peace. Isaac agreed, and they celebrated with food and drink.

The following morning they all swore an oath to each other. Then the king and those accompanying him left in peace.

Later that day, Isaac's servants told him they had found water in the well they were digging. They called the well 'Shebah', and the town became Beersheba, meaning 'Well of Shebah.

Esau marries

When he was forty, Esau married two rough Hittite women.

Table 16: Esau's two wives

Wife	Daughter of
Judith	Daughter of Beeri
Basemath	Daughter of Elon

Isaac and Rebekah hated both of them.

Jacob steals Isaac's Blessing

When Isaac was very old, he went blind. So he called for Esau and told him to go out and hunt for some venison. Then, on his return, he should make him his favourite savoury meal. Then he would bless him before he died. So Esau picked up his bow and went off hunting.

Rebekah had overheard what Isaac had said to Esau. She found Jacob and told him exactly what to do quickly. She said he could get his father's blessing before Esau returned.

Rebekah told Jacob to get two young goats from the flock, and she would make Isaac's favourite meal. When she had made the meal, she dressed, Jacob is Esau's clothes. To make Jacob's skin feel rough like Esau, she covered his hands and neck with the young goat's skin. Then Jacob took the meal to his father.

Isaac was confused when Jacob arrived. "You sound like Jacob and feel like Esau," he said after checking Jacob's arms. Jacob said to Isaac, "I am Esau, your firstborn and I have your favourite meal, venison and wine."

After Isaac had eaten, he asked Jacob to approach him. Isaac caught the terrible smell of the goatskin and said, "Yes, you are Esau. I can tell by the smell". So Isaac blessed him as he would his firstborn son.

Isaac said,

> "My son smells like the scent of an open field
> which God has blessed
> May God give you the dew of the sky
> and the richness of the earth
> And plenty of grain and new wine.
> May peoples serve you and nations bow down to you.
> You will be lord over your brothers,
> and the sons of your mother will bow down to you.
> May those who curse you be cursed, and those who bless you be blessed."

Esau returns for his Blessing

Just after Jacob had left Isaac, Esau returned with a deer and started to prepare a meal. He took the meal to his father, but Isaac was confused again and asked who he was. Esau said he had returned with the meal as he had asked. Isaac trembled violently as he realised Jacob had tricked him.

Esau cried and asked Isaac to bless him as well. But Isaac said, "Jacob had come and deceitfully taken away my blessing."

Esau then said, "Jacob's name suited him. It means 'he holds by the heel.'" He had tripped him up twice; once, he took away his birthright and now, his blessing. Esau then asked if Isaac had kept back a blessing for him.

Isaac told Esau, "I have made Jacob lord over you. All his relatives are now his servants. They have to provide him with grain and new wine. What is left that I can do for you, my son?"

Esau asked his father to bless him as well. So Isaac said:

"Indeed, your home will be away from the richness of the earth

And away from the dew of the sky above.

You will live by your sword, but you will serve your brother.

When you grow restless, you will tear off his yoke from your neck."

Esau hated Jacob because of the blessing. Esau decided he would wait for his father to die, and then he would kill Jacob.

Rebekah concerned for Jacob

Rebekah knew what Esau was thinking and called Jacob. She told him that Esau would plan revenge and kill him. Then, she told him to run away, "Go to my brother Laban in Haran. Live with him for a while until Esau claims down and he forgets what happened between you. Then I will send someone to bring you back from there. I do not want to lose my husband and son in one day."

(God always preferred the younger son in any conflict)

Jacob told to go to Uncle Laban

Isaac called for Jacob and blessed him. Then, he told him not to marry a Canaanite woman.

Rebekah said, "I am also deeply depressed by these daughters of Heth. If you were to marry one, I would want to die!"

Isaac then told Jacob to go to Paddan Aram. Go there to the house of Bethuel, your mother's father and find yourself a wife from among the daughters of Laban, your mother's brother.

"May God bless you. May he make you fruitful and give you a multitude of descendants. Then you will become a vast nation.

May he give you and your descendants the blessing he gave to Abraham so that you may possess the land God gave to Abraham, the land where you have been living as a temporary resident."

Isaac sent Jacob on his way, and he went to Paddan-Aram.

Esau marries Mahalath

Esau heard Isaac had sent Jacob to find a wife at Paddan Aram. He knew Isaac had told him not to marry a Canaanite woman. Canaanite women displeased his father and mother. So Esau went to Ishmael and there married Mahalath, the sister of Nebaioth.

Jacob's 'Ladder' Dream at Bethel

Jacob went from Beersheba towards Haran. When the sun had set, he rested.

He took some of the stones to use as pillows and went to sleep. He dreamed and saw a ladder set up on the earth with the top reaching heaven. On the ladder were angels of God ascending and descending.

God stood over Jacob and said,

> *"I am the God of Abraham and Isaac. I will give you and your offspring the land on which you lie. Your descendants will be like the dust of the earth, and you will spread out to the west, east, north, and south. I will look after you wherever you go and bring you back to this land. I will not leave you until I have done what I promised you!"*

God's place – future temple location

Jacob woke up and thought this was God's place, which he had not realised. He called the place Bethel. (Beth-El = House of God)

He was afraid and said, "What an awesome place this is. This is nothing else than the house of God. This is the gate of heaven."

Early in the morning, Jacob took the stone he had placed under his head and set it up as a pillar, a sacred stone. He then poured oil on top of it (He anointed it)

Jacob made a vow and said,

> "If God looks after me on this journey, giving me food and clothes so that I can return safely to my father's house, then this stone will be God's House, and I will give back one-tenth of all I have."

(This location was the site of the future temple at Jerusalem. Before the Temple's construction, the ladder marked the location of the Holy of Holies, with angels going up and down.)

THE PADDAN ARAM SOJOURN

Jacob Arrives in Paddan Aram

Similar to Isaac Steward's story

Jacob travelled into the land of the people of the east. He looked into a field and saw a well and three flocks of sheep nearby. A great stone covered the mouth of the well. The shepherds would meet and together roll back the stone, water the sheep, and then roll the stone back. This kept the water cool and secure from others.

Jacob spoke to the shepherds and asked where they were from. When they said Haran, Jacob asked if they knew Laban, the grandson of Nahor. They knew him and pointed out Laban's daughter Rachel in the distance with the sheep. They all watered their sheep at the same time. ('Rachel's name means 'Ewe' in Hebrew)

He continued to speak to the shepherds when Rachel arrived with her father's sheep. Finally, Jacob went over to Rachel and rolled the stone off the mouth of the well, allowing her to water her sheep.

He explained to Rachel who he was and then greeted her with a kiss. Rachel ran and told her father, Laban. He rushed out to meet him. They embraced, kissed him and invited him to his house. There he stayed for a month.

Jacob marries Leah, and Rachel

For a month, Jacob worked for Laban. After this time, Laban said to Jacob:

> "I feel I am taking advantage of a relative; tell me, what should I pay you?"

Jacob thought about this. Laban had two daughters:

Table 17: Laban's two daughters

Leah	Oldest	Tender eyes (poor eyesight?)
Rachel	Youngest	Lovely figure and a beautiful appearance

Jacob had fallen in love with Rachel and said, "I will serve you for seven years in exchange for your younger daughter, Rachel".

Laban replied, "I would rather give her to you than to another man. Stay with me."

Jacob proceeded to work for seven years to acquire Rachel, but they seemed just like a few days to him. He was so in love with her. Finally, after seven years, Jacob spoke to Laban, "Give me my wife, for my time of service is up. I want to make love to her."

Laban arranged a wedding feast for all his family and friends. They all had lots to eat and drink. When Jacob was drunk, Laban gave him his daughter Leah and a girl servant called Zilpah as a maid. After a night of love-making, Jacob realised in the morning that Laban had given him Leah instead of Rachel.

He was very annoyed and angry and found Laban and asked why he had swapped daughters. Laban said it was the custom to marry the eldest daughter off first, and that was why he had been given Leah. He then suggested if Jacob finished Leah's bridal week, he would give him Rachel in exchange for another seven years of work.

Jacob agreed, and after a week, he was given Rachel to marry. Laban gave Rachel his servant girl Bilhah as a maid.

Laban was happy, he had got rid of his responsibility of looking after four women in one week, and now Jacob had to support them!

Jacob was happy and worked for Laban for another seven years.

Jacob's Children - Leah

When God saw that Leah was unloved, he enabled her to become pregnant while Rachel remained childless. Leah gave birth to her first son and called him Reuben. She hoped Jacob would now love her, but he did not. God provided her with four sons:

Table 18: Leah's first four Sons

1st	Reuben	3rd	Levi
2nd	Simeon	4th	Judah

Then she stopped having children.

(The etymology of such words as 'Reuben', meaning 'Yahweh has seen my affliction', or Issachar meaning 'God has given my hire', are simply made up as a means of just trying to associate names and events. This lack of reality in the definition of a name is not apparent once translated into a different language.)

Rachel and her maid

Rachel became jealous of her sister and demanded Jacob should give her children or else she would die. Jacob became angry with her, "Am I in the place of God, who has kept you from having children."

Rachel told Jacob, "Here is my servant Bilhah. Have sex with her so she can bear children for me, and I can have a family through her."

Jacob took Bilhah, and she quickly gave birth to a son, Dan. She had a second son and called him Naphtali.

Table 19: Bilhah's sons

1st	Dan	2nd	Naphtali

Leah and her maid

Leah knew she had stopped having children. So she decided to give Jacob her servant Zilpah to have more children. Jacob had two children with her.

Table 20: Zilpah's sons

1st	Gad	2nd	Asher

Leah and Rachel's agreement

At the time of the wheat harvest (later Pentecost), Reuben found some mandrake plants (an aphrodisiac) in a field and brought them to his mother, Leah. Rachel saw them and asked her for some.

Leah said to her, "It was not enough for you to take away my husband, now you want my son's mandrakes as well!"

Rachel replied, "In exchange for your son's mandrakes, Jacob can sleep with you tonight."

Leah agreed and met Jacob as he returned from the fields. She told him he had to sleep with her that night after explaining about Reuben's mandrakes. Jacob took Leah to bed, and God rewarded her. She became pregnant and gave Jacob another son – Issachar.

Leah became pregnant again and gave birth to another son – Zebulun. Finally, she had a daughter and named her Dinah.

Table 21: Leah's sons and daughter

1st	Reuben	5th	Issachar
2nd	Simeon	6th	Zebulun
3rd	Levi	7th	Dinah
4th	Judah		

(The chance of having ten sons in total by four different women is remarkable. Maybe the daughters were not recorded except for Dinah, as she was required to appear in a later story)

Birth of Joseph

Finally, God took note of Rachel, and she became pregnant. She gave birth to a son and called him Joseph. She then asked God for another son.

Jacob's Flocks Increase

After Joseph's birth, Jacob told Laban he had worked hard for him and wanted to take his family back home to his own country.

Laban wanted Jacob to remain. He believed God had blessed him because of Jacob. He asked Jacob what wage he would accept to stay. Jacob said due to his effort, Laban's livestock had significantly increased in number and quality. He now wanted to work for his household and not Laban.

Laban asked him again what he could give him. Jacob replied, "You do not need to give me anything. However, I have one condition, and if you agree, I will continue to care for your flocks and protect them."

Jacob then set out his condition, "Let me walk among all your flocks today and remove from them:

- *Every speckled or spotted sheep*
- *Every dark-coloured lamb*
- *Every speckled or spotted goat.*

These will be my wages. You can then quickly check I have only taken only these animals. Anyone not marked you can consider stolen."

Laban agreed to all that Jacob said. However, that day Laban removed all the marked goats, sheep and lambs and put them in the care of his sons. They took them three days journey away. This was while Jacob was looking after the rest of Laban's flocks.

Jacob saw that Laban had cheated on him again and started to selectively breed the sheep and goats. He found the following method was successful:

> He took freshly cut branches from poplar, almond, and plane trees. He made white streaks on them by peeling the bark. Then, when the ewes were on heat, he set up the branches in all the watering troughs when they came to drink. He then found that when the sheep mated in front of the branches, they gave birth to those who were streaked, speckled, or spotted.

(The types of trees vary with translation. Some consideration is given to the soaking of peeled bark in the water trough for the sheep to then drink – but water would evaporate)

Jacob went through the flock selecting the stronger females to be mated in front of the branches. They produce good strong, healthy lambs with streaks, speckles or spots. These he removed from the flock to form his own. Soon he had developed two flocks:

Table 22: The Two Flocks

Owner	Strength	colour
Jacob	Strong	Streaked, speckled or spotted
Laban	Weak	One colour

Jacob soon became very prosperous. He owned a large flock, male and female servants, camels and donkeys.

Table 23: The difference between the Sheep and the Goats

Sheep	Goats
Ovis Aries	*Cara Hircus*
54 Chromosomes	*60 Chromosomes*
They have a fleece	*They have fur*
Tail points down	*Tail point upwards*
They are grazers – they eat short, tender grass and clover	*They are browsers – they eat leaves, twigs, vines and shrubs*
Only agile when separated from the rest of the flock	*Agile and will stand on their hind legs*
They are mostly stupid, but there are exceptions.	*They are clever*
They flock together	*They form tribes / social groups*
They are naturally aloof of people	*They are curious about people*
They go 'Baaa'	*They go 'Maaa'*

There are many other differences. For example, the 'Jacob Sheep' is a relatively new breed and has nothing to do with the bible era.

Jacob Flees From Laban

Jacob overheard Laban's sons complaining, "Jacob has taken everything that belonged to our father. He has become rich at our father's expense." However, Jacob could also see that Laban's attitude to him had changed.

God spoke to Jacob, *"Return to the land of your fathers and your relatives. I will be with you."*

Jacob sent a message to Rachel and Leah to come to the fields where he was with his flocks. He told them that their father's attitude had changed. He told them,

"I have worked as hard as I could for your father, but he humiliated me and changed my wages ten times. But God has not permitted him to do me any harm. If God said:

> 'The speckled animals will be your wage, and then the entire flock gave birth to speckled animals.'

But if he said,

> 'Streaked animals will be your wage,' then the entire flock gave birth to streaked offspring.

In this way, God has snatched away your father's livestock and given them to me."

> "Once during the breeding season, I saw in a dream that the male goats mating with a flock were streaked, speckled, and spotted. The angel of God said, 'Observe that all the male goats mating with the flock are streaked, speckled or spotted, for I have observed all that Laban has done to you.
>
> I am the God of Bethel, where you anointed the sacred stone and made a vow to me. Now leave this land immediately and return to your native land."

Rachel and Leah asked him,

> "Do we still have any portion or inheritance in our father's house? He has treated us like foreigners. He not only sold us but completely wasted the money paid for us! Surely all the wealth that God snatched away from our father belongs to our children and us. So now do everything God has told you."

(Some wealth must have come from the gifts left by Abraham's steward when Laban's sister Rebekah was taken to marry Isaac.)

Jacob immediately put his children and wives on the camels. He took away all the livestock he had acquired in Paddan Aram and all the moveable property he had accumulated. Then he set out towards the land of Canaan to return to his father, Isaac.

(Note Isaac was old and near death when he left twenty years, or more, before!)

Laban was away shearing his sheep, so **Rachel stole the household idols that belonged to her father**.

Jacob also deceived Laban by not telling him that he was leaving.

He left with all he owned. He quickly crossed the Euphrates River and headed for the hill country of Gilead.

Laban Pursues Jacob

Three days later, Laban realised Jacob and his family had left, taking everything with them. Laban rounded up all his relatives and set off in pursuit. God came in a dream at night and warned Laban not to say anything good or bad to Jacob.

The next day, Laban caught up with Jacob and camped near him. Laban came and spoke to Jacob and said,

> "What have you done? You have deceived me and carried away my daughters like war captives.
>
> Why did you run away secretly and deceive me? Why did you not tell me so I could send you off with a celebration complete with singing, tambourines, and harps? You did not allow me to kiss my daughters and my grandchildren goodbye. You have acted foolishly."
>
> Then Laban said, "I have the power to do you harm, but God told me last night, 'Be careful that you neither bless nor curse Jacob'."
>
> He added, "I now understand that you have gone away because you long for your father's house. But why did you steal my gods?"

Jacob replied to Laban, "I left secretly because I was afraid. I thought you might take your daughters away from me by force."

Jacob did not know that Rachel had stolen the gods from Laban when he said, "**Whoever has taken your gods will be put to death**. In the presence of our relatives, identify whatever is yours and take it."

Laban entered the tents of Jacob, Leah, and the two female servants but did not find the idols. Then he entered Rachel's tent. (Rachel had hidden the idols inside her camel's saddle and was sitting on them) Laban searched the whole tent but did not find them.

Rachel said to her father, "**Father, please do not be angry that I do not stand up in your presence, but I am feeling unwell as I have my period.**" Laban did not search further and did not find the idols.

Jacob angry with Laban

Jacob was furious and argued with Laban. He said,

"What did I do wrong? What made you chase after me in hot pursuit? You have searched through all our goods and did you find anything that did not belong to us?

I have looked after your flocks perfectly for twenty years. You have made me pay for any missing animal, whether taken by day or night.

Guarding your flock, I have been consumed by scorching heat during the day and piercing cold at night. So often, I had to go without sleep. This was my lot for twenty years.

I have worked like a slave for you – fourteen years for your two daughters and six years for your flocks. You changed my wages ten times.

If God had not been with me, you would have sent me away empty-handed. But God saw how I was oppressed and how hard I worked, and he rebuked you last night."

Laban replied to Jacob. He said,

"These women are my daughters. These children are my grandchildren. These flocks are my flocks. All that you see belongs to me."

Laban then added,

"How can I harm these daughters of mine today or the children to whom they have given birth?

Let us make a formal agreement to prove that we have made peace."

Jacob took a stone and set it up as a memorial pillar. Then he told his relatives to gather and put stones in a pile.

Laban said, "This pile of stones is a witness of our agreement today. If you mistreat my daughters or take wives in addition to them, and no one else is with us, then realise that God is a witness to your actions."

May the God of Abraham, the god of Nahor, and their fathers' gods judge between us."

Jacob took an oath to God, offered a sacrifice on the mountain, and invited his relatives to eat the meal. They ate the meal and spent the night on the mountain.

Early the next morning, Laban kissed his daughters and grandchildren goodbye, blessed them, and returned home.

JACOB RETURNS

Jacob Prepares to Meet Esau

Jacob went on his way, and the angels of God met him. Jacob said, "This is God's host", when he saw them. So he called the name of that place 'Mahanaim'. Jacob then sent messengers to Esau, his brother, in the land of Seir, the country of Edom.

He told the messenger to greet Esau and tell him:

> "Jacob has been living with Laban until now. I have oxen, donkeys, sheep, and male and female servants. I have sent this message to inform my lord so I may find favour in your sight."

The messenger returned and told Jacob that Esau was coming to meet him with four hundred men.

Jacob did not know what his brother would do. They had not parted on the best of terms, and it now seemed Esau was coming to meet him with a small army.

He decided to split his family, procession and livestock into two groups. If Esau attacked him, then at least one group could escape.

Then Jacob prayed,

> "God of my father Abraham and Isaac, you told me to return to your land and my relatives. You said you would make me prosper. I am not worthy of all the faithful love you have shown your servant:

- With one walking stick, I crossed the Jordan
- Now I return with two camps.

> Rescue me, I pray, from the hand of my brother Esau. I am afraid he will come and attack me, my wives and children. You said I would prosper and make my descendants like the sand on the seashore, too numerous to count."

Gifts for Esau

Jacob stayed there that night. Then he sent as gifts to his brother Esau:

- Two hundred each - female goats, ewes,
- Twenty each - rams, male goats, female donkeys,

- Thirty each - milk camels and their colts,
- Forty - cows
- Ten each – bulls, foals

(The total number of goats was 220 – a number identified by Pythagoreans as a 'friendly number' mathematically linked with 284. See 'Numbers' in Appendix)

He told his servants to drive them in small groups, with space between each group. They should tell anyone who enquires that they belonged to Jacob and are a gift to his brother Esau. Then say that Jacob is behind us.

Jacob thought he would first appease him by sending gifts ahead, and then he would meet him and accept him.

Jacob sent his servants off with the animals, and he stayed in the camp. That night Jacob took his two wives, two maidservants and his eleven sons to the ford at Jabbok. He helped them over the stream while his servants took over all their possession.

God renames Jacob as Israel – 1st version

Jacob was sitting on his own when a man appeared and started to wrestle with him. This lasted until dawn. When the man saw he could not defeat Jacob, he struck his hip socket and dislocated his thigh. Jacob held onto the man, who then asked to be released. Jacob said, "I will not release you unless you bless me."

The man asked him his name. Jacob told him, and the man said, "No longer will your name be 'Jacob', but 'Israel'. This is because you have fought with God and men and prevailed."*(Isra-El = Struggle with God)*

Jacob asked him again his name. "Why do you ask my name?" the man replied. He then blessed Jacob.

Jacob named the place Peniel, saying, "Certainly, I have seen God face to face and have survived." (Peni-El = see God)

The sun rose over him as he crossed over Peniel, but he was limping because of his hip. That is why to this day, the Israelites do not eat the sinew which is attached to the socket of the hip.

(The story of Jacob's wrestling match with God attempts to explain the tradition of removing the sinew attached near the hip during the 'Porging' of kosher meat).

Israel

When was the name 'Israel' first used? Certainly, in the native language, it is doubtful if such a word was used. The earliest written word, 'Isrir,' believed to describe Israel, is from the Merneptah Stele of the 12th Century BC. However, language and pronunciation has changed considerably over time. Another possibility is the word on the Stele is 'Jezreel' as the Jezreel Valley, home of the tribe of Issachar. We know the bible used the name 'Israel' as taken from the Greek Septuagint. It is said the Greeks made the word from:

ISis	*– one of the goddesses of Ancient Egypt*
RA	*– a primaeval god of Ancient Egypt*
EL	*– a Hebrew word for god)*

(The Greeks habitually played with words, and all the names in the Bible come from Greek words and not Hebrew.)

Therefore, the names used in the bible are traditional, not the words or pronunciations you would have heard.

Jacob Meets Esau

As they walked, Jacob could make out his brother, accompanied by four hundred men in the distance. He quickly divided his family into two groups, one with Rachel and the other with Leah, each led by their handmaids and their children. Jacob fell to the ground in front of them, and as his brother approached, he bowed seven times.

When Esau finally saw him, he ran to meet Jacob. He embraced him, kissed him, and they cried. Then, Esau looked up and asked who all the people were. Jacob told him they were his wives and children and introduced them individually.

Esau then asked what the purpose of all the animals he had passed was. Jacob said they were a present for him. Esau said he had enough animals, but Jacob insisted he kept them as he had welcomed him kindly. Esau reluctantly accepted them.

Esau invited them all to stay with him and offered to lend him men to drive the animals.

Jacob fools Esau again

Jacob realised he had been accepted without a problem and decided to trick Esau further. He told Esau that his family and animals had walked a long way and must take it slowly. He told Esau to leave them and go and prepare for their arrival. So Esau and his men left and went south to Edom.

Jacob waited until they were out of sight and made for Succoth to the west.

When he got to Succoth, he built a house and made a shelter for his animals.

Move to Shechem

Later, Jacob took his family to live near the town of Shechem. The town was named after the son of the local ruler, Hamor the Hivite. Jacob bought land from Hamor for 100 pieces of silver, and there they settled. Jacob built an altar and called it 'El Elohe Israel', meaning 'El, the God of Israel'.

Dinah and the Shechemites

Dinah was Jacob and Leah's only daughter. She decided to visit some of the other young women in the town but was spotted by Shechem, son of Hamor. He grabbed and raped her. However, Shechem fell in love with her. He went home and told his father to get this woman for him as a wife.

Jacob heard about his daughter's rape and remained quiet until his sons returned home. In the meantime, Hamor and Shechem came to talk to him. Hamor explained that Shechem loved Dinah and wanted her as a wife. Therefore, no actual harm had been done. !

Hamor then suggested that more of their sons and daughters should marry, and the families could trade and cooperate more. Finally, Shechem asked Jacob to name the size of Dinah's endowment, and he would pay for it.

But when Jacob's sons return and learnt of Dinah's rape, they are very angry. So they played along with Shechem and Hamor while planning revenge.

They said to Hamor they could not allow their sister to be given to a man who was not circumcised, as it would be a total disgrace. So the whole family had to be circumcised – all the males in the town. If they refused, their family would leave the area.

Hamor and Shechem were both pleased by the offer. They went to the city gates and spoke to the men of their tribe. They explained what had been agreed. They all thought they would get their hands on Jacob's possessions by marriage.

Circumcision of Shechem

All the men assembled at the city gate and were circumcised.

Three days after all of Shechem had been circumcised, the men were still in pain. Finally, two of Dinah's brothers, Simeon and Levi, took their swords and attacked the unsuspecting city, killing all the men and boys, including Shechem and Hamor.

Then Jacob's other sons plundered the city and took the flocks, herds, donkeys and everything else of value. They took the women and girls alive as slaves.

When Jacob realised what his sons had done, he was shocked and thought the other tribes of the land, the Canaanites and Perizzites, would now attack them.

Simeon and Levi said to him, "They should not have treated our sister like a common prostitute".

Jacob Returns to Bethel

God told Jacob, "Go to Bethel and settle there. Make an altar to God, who appeared to you when you fled from your brother Esau."

Jacob told his family, "Get rid of the foreign gods you have among you. Purify yourselves and change your clothes. Let us go up at once to Bethel. Then I will make an altar there to God, who responded to me in my time of distress and has been with me wherever I went."

They gave Jacob all their lucky charms, idols of other gods, rings and bracelets. Jacob took all their items and buried them under the oak near Shechem before leaving for Bethel to the south.

The surrounding cities were afraid of God and did not pursue them.

Jacob and his household arrived at Luz (Bethel) in Canaan. He built an altar and named the place El Bethel – because God had revealed himself to him when he fled from his brother – The location of Jacob's Ladder.

Nurse Deborah dies

While at Bethel, Rebekah's old nurse, Deborah, who had come with them from Paddan Aram, died. They buried her under the nearby oak tree. The tree was called the Oak of Weeping.

God renames Jacob as Israel – 2nd version

God appeared again to Jacob after he returned from Paddan Aram and blessed him. Then, God said to Jacob, "Your name is Jacob, but your name will no longer be called Jacob. Instead, it will be 'Israel'.

God named him Israel and said, "I am the sovereign God, Be fruitful and multiply. A nation – even a company of nations – will descend from you.

Kings will be among your descendants. The land I gave to Abraham and Isaac, I will give to you. To your descendants, I will also give this land."

Then God left, and Jacob set up a sacred stone pillar in the place where God spoke with him. He poured out a drink offering on it and then oil.

Jacob named the place where God spoke with him, Bethel.

(Bethel has been named three times so far.)

The Death of Rachel / Birth of Benjamin

They travelled on from Bethel, and when Ephrath was still some distance away, Rachel went into labour and was distressed. However, the midwife told her, "Do not be afraid, for you have another son."

With her dying breath, she named her new son Ben-Oni. But Jacob called him Benjamin instead. Rachel was buried on the way to Ephrath (now Bethlehem). Jacob set up a marker over her grave.

Reuben upsets Jacob

Then Jacob and his household travelled on and pitched camp beyond Migdal Eder. While there, Reuben took to bed Bilhah, his father's concubine. Jacob was not very happy when he heard about it.

1Ch 5:1 says Reuben was the firstborn, but when he defiled his father's bed, his rights as firstborn were given to the sons of Joseph, Israel's son. So Reuben is not listed as firstborn in the genealogical records.

Jacob's twelve sons

Table 24: Jacob now had twelve sons as follows: -

Sons of Leah	Reuben (Jacob's firstborn), Simeon, Levi, Judah, Issachar, Zebulun
Sons of Rachel	Joseph and Benjamin
Sons of Bilhah (Rachel's handmaid)	Dan and Naphtali
Sons of Zilpah (Leah's handmaid)	Gad and Asher

(There is no mention of daughters or how many)

Death of Isaac

Jacob and his family returned to his father Isaac in Mamre, Hebron. This was where Abraham and Isaac had stayed.

Isaac lived to be one hundred and eighty years old. Then Isaac breathed his last and joined his ancestors. His sons Esau and Jacob buried him.

(Isaac was near death when Jacob stole the birthright some 20 years or more ago. So the Twins Esau and Jacob had finally made up to be together for the burial?).

Esau's descendants
Table 25: Esau's Wives and offspring:

Wife	Daughter of	Esau's Sons	Son's wife	Grandsons
Adah	Elon the Hittite	Eliphaz	?	Teman, Omar, Zepho, Gatam, Kenaz
			Timna Eliphaz's concubine	Amalek
			?	Korah
Oholibamah	Anah, grand-daughter of Zibeon the Hivite	Jeush		
		Jalam		
		Korah		
Basemath	Ishmael and sister of Nebaioth	Reuel	?	Nahath, Zerah, Shammah, Mizzah

Esau (also called Edom) had two wives from Canaan and took a third, Basemath, the daughter of Ishmael. He left Isaac, as the land could not support them all, and took his families, livestock and possessions to the land of Edom. There they lived and grew in numbers. They later selected a king to rule them before Israel did the same. Esau was the father of all of them.

These are the sons of Seir the Horite who lived in the region

Seir the Horite – his sons **Lotan, Shobal, Zibeon, Anah, Dishon, Ezer, and Dishan**. Timna, their sister

> **Lotan** – His sons Hori, Homam
>
> **Shobal** – His sons Alvan, Manahath, Ebal, Shepho, Onam
>
> **Zibeon** – His sons Aiah and Anah (Anah discovered the hot springs in the desert while grazing his father's donkeys.
>
> **Anah** – His son Dishon and his daughter Oholibamah
>
> **Dishon** – his sons Hemdan, Eshban, Ithran, Keran
>
> **Ezer** – his sons Bilhan, Zaavan, Akan
>
> **Dishan** – his sons Uz, Aran

These were the kings of Edom who reigned before any Israelite king reigned:

Table 26: Kings of Edom before any Israelite King

	King	Son of	Comment
1	**Bela**	Son of Beor	His city was named Dinhabah
2	**Jobab**	Son of Zerah	From Bozrah
3	**Husham**		From the land of the Temanites
4	**Hadad**	Son of Bedad	He defeated Midian in the country of Moab. His city was named Avith.
5	**Samlah**		From Masrekah
6	**Shaul**		From Rehoboth on the river
7	**Baal-Hanan**	son of Achbor	
8	**Hadad**		His city was named Pau. His wife's name was Mehetabel who was the daughter of Matred, the daughter of Me-Zahab

These were the chiefs descended from Esau, by name, according to their clans and regions:

> Timna, Alvah, Jetheth, Oholibamah, Elah, Pinon, Kenaz, Teman, Mibzar, Magdiel and Iram.

Judah and Tamar

Judah decided to leave his brothers and go and stay with Hirah of Adullam. There he married Shua and had three sons:

> Er, Onan, Shelah

Judah found a wife, Tamar, for his first son, Er. God decided that Er was wicked, and Er died.

Judah told his second son, Onan, to take her for a wife. But he did not want his brother's children, so when making love, he withdrew prematurely and spilt his sperm onto the floor. God decided Onan was evil, and he also died.

Judah told Tamar to remain a widow in her father's house until his third son, Shelah, had grown up and was able to marry her. So Tamar went home and lived with her father. After a few years, Judah's wife, Shua, died, and he forgot about Tamar and his promise to her.

One day Tamar heard that Judah was visiting some sheepshearers nearby and would pass through the town. So she took off her widow's clothes, covered herself with a veil to disguise herself, and sat at the town gate.

When Judah saw her sitting there, he thought she was a local cult prostitute because of her covered face. He went over and offered her a young goat from his flock. As he did not have the goat with him, she asked for a pledge. They agreed on his seal, cord, and the staff in his hand. The arrangement was a goat would be delivered later in exchange for the return of his possessions.

Judah then had sex with her and left, still not recognising her. Tamar returned home and put on her widow clothes.

Judah sent a young goat back with his friend, Hirah, in order to get his possessions back, but he could not find her. So he asked all the men where he could find the local cult prostitute, but they angrily told him there was none. So Hirah returned to Judah and told him he could find no trace of a cult prostitute in the town. Judah was surprised.

Tamar found she was pregnant. News spread and reached Judah, who was horrified that his daughter-in-law, a widow, was pregnant. He was waiting to give her to this third son. He said she must be a prostitute and should be fetched and burnt to death.

When she was fetched, she told Judah that she was pregnant by the man who had left these items, his seal, cords and staff. Judah recognised them and realised how wrong he had been as he had not kept his promise and given her Shelah, his son, as a husband. He was very sorry and did not sleep with her again.

She gave birth to twin boys. The midwife had marked the firstborn by tying a scarlet thread around the first arm (belonging to Zerah) to appear out of Tamar. But the baby pulled it back in, and his brother Perez was born first.

Tamar twins by Judah – Perez and Zerah.

(Perez will occur in the genealogy of Jesus in both Luke and Matthew)

About the Bible – 1

JOSEPH

The Story of Joseph is considered a 'Diaspora Novel' along with Esther and Daniel Part 1, added during the Persian period c.400BC. The story moved the Hebrews from the Bedouin environment to that of the Egyptian permanent organised society faced with a serve famine. The story is perhaps placed after the Hyksos period of Egyptian History.

There would have been no real reason to move from their land to Egypt during a drought. There would have been plenty of water in the Jordan, and the sea was nearby for fish and shellfish. Unless both were obstructed and springs/wells were not available.

The latter two 'half-tribes' of Ephraim and Manasseh (Joseph's sons) made up numbers following Levi's appointment as local Priest Ruler within every tribe.

Joseph's Dreams

Jacob had a seventeen-year-old son called Joseph. He would take care of the flocks with his brothers but would often bring back adverse reports and tell his father.

Jacob loved Joseph more than all his sons because he had been born late in his life. When his brother saw their father loved him more than any of them, they hated Joseph and could not speak to him kindly.

Jacob made a unique tunic for Joseph (*a coat of many colours*), and they then hated him even more.

Joseph then had a dream and told his brothers all about it. Finally, they could stand no more.

He told them, *"We were all binding sheaves of corn, and suddenly my sheaf rose and stood upright, and all your sheaves gathered around mine and bowed down."* They all asked sarcastically whether it meant he would reign over them. They hated him even more.

The following night he told them of another dream, *"Listen, I dreamed the sun and moon, and eleven stars all bowed down to me, the earth."* Jacob heard this and asked, *"What is this dream you had? Will I, your mother, and your brothers really come and bow down to you?"*

His brothers really hated him now, but his father kept in mind what Joseph had said.

Joseph Sold by His Brothers

The brothers had taken the flocks to graze near Shechem, and Jacob sent Joseph to check upon them.

When Joseph reached Shechem, a man found him wandering in the field. He asked Joseph for who he was looking. Joseph said, "I am looking for his brothers. Please tell me where they are grazing their flocks."

The man told him they had left the area, and he had heard them say, "Let us go to Dothan." So Joseph went after his brothers and found them at Dothan.

When Joseph's brothers saw him from a distance, they plotted to kill him.

They said to one another, "Here comes the master of dreams. Let's kill him, throw him into one of the cisterns and then say a wild animal ate him. Then we'll see how his dreams turn out."

When Reuben heard this to said, "We will not take his life. Do not shed blood. Thrown him into this cistern that is here in the wilderness, but do not lay a hand on him." (*Reuben said this so he could rescue Joseph from them, and take him back to his father.*)

When Joseph arrived, they all set on him and stripped him of his special tunic. Then they took him and threw him into the cistern – which was empty without any water in it.

When they all sat down to eat a meal, they saw a caravan of Ishmaelites from Gilead going to Egypt with camels loaded with spices, balm and myrrh. Judah suggested they could sell Joseph to them, and so they got twenty shekels of silver for him.

When Reuben returned, he noticed Joseph was not in the pit and thought his brothers had killed him. But they told him they had sold him. They explained what had happened and showed him Joseph's coat which they had torn and dipped in goat's blood.

When they returned to Jacob, they told him graphically, with the remains of the coat, how Joseph must have been attacked by a ferocious animal which tore him into pieces and devoured him.

Jacob wept for many days and refused to be comforted by anyone.

Joseph was taken to Egypt and sold by the Midianites to Potiphar, the captain of the Pharaoh's guard. He was seventeen.

Joseph and Potiphar's Wife

Down in Egypt, Joseph got on well with his new master Potiphar and became the steward of his household. He was put in charge of the household and trusted with everything. Joseph was good-looking and attractive, and Potiphar's wife wanted him for her own pleasures. Joseph refused her again and again, but she planned to get him into bed.

One day when none of the other servants were around, she cornered him and told him to go to bed with her. As he tried to run away, she held onto his cloak, which slipped off. Then, angry at the insult of being refused, she screamed, and when other servants appeared, she told them Joseph had tried to rape her.

When Potiphar heard the story, he was so angry that he put Joseph in the Pharaoh's prison. However, Joseph soon came to the notice of the prison governor, who then put him in charge of running the prison.

The Cupbearer and the Baker

The Pharaoh was angry with his Chief Cupbearer and Master Baker. So he put them both in prison. After some time, they both had dreams, but nobody could tell them what they meant. When Joseph heard, he asked them to tell him.

Chief Cupbearer's dream	Joseph's interpretation
He saw a vine with three branches, which budded, blossomed and ripened with grapes. He squeezed the grapes into the cup and put the cup into the Pharaoh's hand.	The three branches were days, and the Pharaoh would restore him to his position within three days.

Joseph told him to mention him to the Pharaoh and get him out of prison because he had done nothing wrong.

Then Master Baker told Joseph his dream.

Master Baker's dream	Joseph's interpretation
He dreamed of carrying three baskets of bread on his head, and birds were eating all the bread.	The Pharaoh would, in three days, cut his head off. Then, his body would be stuck on a tree for the birds to eat the flesh.

On the third day, it was the Pharaoh's birthday, and he gave a feast for all his officials. He restored the chief cupbearer to his position but hanged the Masterbaker just as Joseph had said.

Sadly the Cupbearer also forgot to tell him about Joseph's ability to read dreams.

Pharaoh's Dreams

Two years later, the Pharaoh had a dream. In the morning, he sent for all the magicians and wise men of Egypt and asked them to interpret the dream, but nobody could. Finally, the Chief cupbearer remembered Joseph and told the Pharaoh about him.

Joseph was washed, shaved, and brought before the Pharaoh, who told him about his dreams.

Pharaoh's dream	Joseph's interpretation
He saw seven skinny cows eat seven fat cows, and seven thin ears of corn swallowed up seven full ears of corn.	Egypt would have seven good years of harvest, followed by seven years of famine.

He then suggested that the Pharaoh should put a wise man in charge and appoint commissioners. Then, they should take one-fifth of the harvest during the years of plenty and store the food, under the authority of the Pharaoh, to use during the years of famine.

This advice made sense to Pharaoh and all his officials, and he thought about whom to put in charge. Pharaoh asked his officials, *"Can we find a man like Joseph, one in which the spirit of God is present?"*

So the Pharaoh said to Joseph, *"Because God has enabled you to know all this, there is no one as wise and discerning as you are. Therefore, you will oversee my household, and all my people will submit to your commands. Only I, the king, will be greater than you."*

The Pharaoh placed his signet ring from his hand onto Joseph's. He clothed him with beautiful linen clothes and put a gold chain around his neck. The Pharaoh then gave Joseph the chariot previously used by his second-in-command. Everyone was told to kneel as he approached.

Pharaoh told him, *"I am Pharaoh, but without your permission, no one will move his hand or foot in all the land of Egypt."*

Joseph was given the name Zaphenath-Paneah (possibly meaning – a revealer of secrets).

So Joseph took charge of all the land of Egypt.

Joseph in Charge of Egypt

Joseph was thirty years old when he began serving the Pharaoh.

The land has seven years of plenty which produced abundant, bountiful harvests.

Joseph collected all the excess food and placed it in grain stores built in the cities. Every city gathered food from the fields around it. There was so much grain, too much to measure, indeed like the sand of the sea.

After seven years of abundance, a famine began, just as Joseph had predicted. There was a famine in all the other lands, but throughout Egypt, there was food. So Pharaoh told his people to "Go to Joseph and do whatever he tells you."

Joseph opened the grain stores and sold grain to the Egyptians.

While the famine was over all the earth, people from every country came to Joseph in Egypt to buy grain. (*Egypt was always famous for its grain – it later supplied Rome*).

Joseph's Egyptian Family

The Pharaoh gave Joseph a wife, Asenath, daughter of Potiphera, priest of On. They had two sons who were born before the famine came. Joseph named them as follows:

Table 27: Joseph's Sons

1st	Manasseh
2nd	Ephraim

These two sons were, therefore, half-Egyptian.

Joseph's Brothers Go to Egypt

There was also a terrible famine in Canaan. Jacob heard grain could be purchased in Egypt and sent his ten sons to buy some. He kept Benjamin, Joseph's brother, at home because he was worried about losing him.

The brothers and many others arrived in Egypt and asked how to buy grain. They were directed to Joseph. Joseph's brothers came and bowed down before him. When Joseph saw them, he recognised them, but they did not recognise him. So he pretended to be a stranger, spoke to them harshly, and asked why they had come from Canaan to buy food.

Joseph remembered his dreams through an interpreter and said to them, "You are spies, coming to see how to invade the land."

They replied, "No, we are not.

- We have come to buy grain.
- We are all the sons of one man.

- We are honest men

Your servants are not spies."

Joseph repeated his accusation, "You have come to see if our land is vulnerable."

They replied, "Your servants are from a family of twelve brothers. We are the sons of one man in the land of Canaan. The youngest is with our father now, and one is no longer alive."

Then Joseph said to them, "I still believe you are spies. I will test you. As long as the Pharaoh lives, you will not depart from this place unless your youngest brother comes here. So one of you must go and get your brother while the rest of you remain in prison. I will then be able to test you and see if you told me the truth or are spies."

The brothers are put in prison

He put the brothers in prison for three days. Then, on the third day, Joseph said to them, "Do as I say, and you will live, for I fear God. If you are honest men, leave one of your brothers in prison while the rest go and take grain back to your hungry families. But you must bring your youngest brother back to me. Then your words will be verified, and you will not die."

The brothers did as Joseph told them.

They spoke to one other, not realising Joseph could understand their language, "Surely we are being punished because of our brother because we saw how distressed he was when he cried to us for mercy, but we refused to listen. That is why this distress has come on us."

Reuben said to them, "I told you, 'do not sin against the boy,' but you would not listen. So now we must pay for shedding his blood."

Joseph turned away from them and wept. Then he turned back around and spoke to them again. Finally, he had Simeon taken and tied up in front of them.

Joseph told his servant to fill the brother's sacks with;

- Grain
- The money they had given for payment was also hidden inside.

Each brother was given provisions for the journey and told to load their donkeys and leave.

At a resting place, one of them opened his sack to feed his donkey. He saw the money and called his brothers to him. "My money was returned. Here it is in my sack."

They were very worried and asked, "What in the world has God done to us?"

The brothers return to Jacob

When they returned to Jacob, they told him everything that had happened. They said they needed to take Benjamin back with them to release Simeon. If they proved they were honest, then they would be allowed to trade in Egypt for grain.

As they began to empty their sacks of grain, they all found their money had been placed in their sacks, and they were very worried.

Jacob said to his sons, "First, you deprived me of Joseph, then Simeon, and now you want to take Benjamin?" Reuben told this father that he could kill his two sons if they did not return with Benjamin.

But Jacob refused to let Benjamin go. His brother is dead, and he is all alone. If anything happened to him, then I would die of sorrow.

The Second Journey to Egypt

As the famine continued, Jacob's family ate all the grain from Egypt and needed more. So Jacob told them to go again to Egypt.

Judah told him they had to take Benjamin. Jacob said, "Why did you bring this trouble to us? You should not have mentioned your youngest brother."

Judah suggested Jacob should allow him to take Benjamin. If they had done this in the first place, they would have been there and back by now. Judah pledged himself to Jacob, and finally, Jacob consented.

Jacob then told them also to take some gifts for the Egyptians. They should take some of their best products with them – some balm, honey, spices, myrrh, pistachio nuts and almonds (*perhaps not the best items to prove there was a famine at home!*) Also, he told them to take twice the money they had taken before. They must return the money they found in their sacks, as it must have been a mistake. Judah told Jacob he would be responsible for Benjamin and return him.

They arrived in Egypt and met Joseph, and when Joseph saw Benjamin, he told the steward of his house to take them home and prepare dinner for them. The brothers were frightened when they were taken to Joseph's house. They thought they would be attacked because of the money and put in slavery, and their poor donkeys would also be taken.

They tried to explain everything to Joseph's steward and told him about the money. The steward told them not to worry and said, "Do not be afraid. Your God and the God of your father have given you treasure in your sacks. I did receive your money." Then he brought Simeon to them.

He gave them water to wash their feet and food for their donkeys. In the meantime, the brothers prepared their gifts for Joseph.

When Joseph arrived, they gave him their gifts and bowed before him. Joseph asked about their father and asked if Benjamin was the one they had told him about. Joseph became very upset at the sight of his real brother Benjamin, and he left to weep and wash his face.

Then he returned and told the servants to serve the food. The Egyptians all sat away from the brothers because they found their manners detestable.

As the brothers looked around, they saw they had been sat in order of their age, which astonished them.

Whenever Benjamin was served food, he was given more than anyone else. So they all ate, drank and became very merry.

The final Test

Joseph told his steward to fill his brother's sacks with as much food as they could carry and again secretly put the money back in the mouth of each sack. Then to put his silver cup in Benjamin's sack with his money.

In the morning, the brother left to return home. Before they had gone far, Joseph's steward caught up with the brothers, and they said they had stolen a silver cup from his master's house, the one he used for divination. The brother boldly said that if anyone had the cup, he would die, and the rest would become slaves. The sacks were searched, starting with the eldest, and the cup was finally found in Benjamin's sack.

The brothers were stunned. They reloaded their donkeys and returned with the steward to Joseph's house. They threw themselves onto the ground before Joseph, and he asked them what they had done.

"Did you not know that a man like me can discover things like this by divination?"

Judah said to Joseph, "What can we say? How can we clear ourselves? God has exposed the sin of your servants. We are now your slaves."

Joseph then told them only the man who had the cup would become his slave. The other could return to your father in peace.

Then Judah approached him and said,

> "Please do not get angry with me. We have an aged father; my young brother was born when my father was old. The boy's

brother is dead. He is the only one of his mother's sons left, and his father loves him. You told us to bring him down to see you.

My father reminded me of how his wife gave him two sons. One disappeared, torn to pieces, but I will die of sorrow if you take this one from me.

When we go back home, and he sees my brother is not with us, he will die. So I also pledge security for him and will be blamed.

Please let me remain your servant and let my youngest brother return to my father. I cannot return without him."

The Reconciliation of the Brothers

Joseph could no longer control himself and told all his servants to leave. Joseph started to weep loudly as he began to tell his brothers who he was. The Egyptians and Pharaoh's household could hear his weeping.

He said to his brothers, "I am Joseph. Is my father still alive?"

His brothers could not say anything. They were so shocked.

Joseph asked his brothers to come nearer, and he said again,

"I am Joseph, your brother, who you sold into Egypt. Now do not be upset and do not be angry with yourselves because you sold me here. God sent me ahead of you to preserve life!

He explained that there had been famine for the past two years and would last another five years. *(Joseph was, therefore, 39 years old.)* There would be no ploughing or harvesting until it was over. He repeated,

"It is not you who sent me here, but God."

He told them he had become:

- An adviser to Pharaoh
- Lord over all his household
- Ruler over all the land of Egypt

Joseph told them to return to their father and tell him the news. Then you all are to come down to me. You will live in the 'Land of Goshen' and be near me. He said he would provide them with food. If they did not come, they and their households would become poor.

Joseph put his arms around his brother Benjamin and wept. Then, he kissed all his brothers, and they talked with him.

When the Pharaoh heard about the brothers' arrival, he was very pleased for Joseph. So he told Joseph to say to his brothers:

You are to do this:

- Load your animal and go to the land of Canaan.
- Get your father and your household and come to me
- Then I will give you the best land in Egypt
- You will eat from the best of the land.

Then he added

You are also commanded to say:

- Take for yourselves wagons from the land of Egypt
- Your little ones and your wives are to use the Wagons.
- Bring your father and come.
- Do not worry about your belongings
- Best of all, the land of Egypt will be yours.

So the brothers left with:

- Wagons, as Pharaoh had instructed
- Provisions for the journey
- Sets of clothes for each of them

For Benjamin:

- Three hundred pieces of silver
- Five sets of clothes

For Jacob:

- Ten Donkeys loaded with the best products of Egypt
- Ten female donkeys loaded with grain and food
- Provisions for his father's journey

Joseph told his brothers as they left not to be overcome with fear.

They returned to their father Jacob in Canaan and said to him:

"Joseph is still alive, and he is ruler over all the land of Egypt."

Jacob was stunned and did not believe them. Then they showed him everything Joseph had said, and Jacob was incredibly happy when he saw the wagons. He finally believed that his son Joseph was still alive and he would see him before he died.

Jacob Goes to Egypt

Jacob and his family packed up everything and left for Egypt. They travelled south first to Beersheba and stopped there for a night. God spoke to Jacob and told him,

> "I am God, the God of your father. Therefore, fear not to go down into Egypt, for I will make you a great nation there. I will go down

with you into Egypt and bring you up again. Joseph will be the one to put his hand on your eyes when you die."

Jacob and his household left Beersheba. The brothers carried their father while the wives and children travelled in the wagons provided by the Pharaoh.

Sixty-six direct descendants went with Jacob to Egypt. Adding to this number are Joseph and his two sons, both born in Egypt, and Jacob himself, added up to a total of seventy. This number excludes wives.

Table 28: Numbers who went down to Egypt

Father	Son / Daughter	No.
Isaac	Jacob	1
Jacob	Reuben, Simeon, Levi, Judah, Issachar, Zebulun, Gad, Asher, Benjamin, Dan, and Naphtali.	11
Reuben	Hanoch, Pallu, Hezron, and Carmi	4
Simeon	Jemuel, Jamin, Ohad, Jakin, Zohar, and Shaul	6
Levi	Gershon, Kohath, and Merari	3
Judah	Shelah, Perez (who in turn fathered Hezron and Hamul), and Zerah	5
Issachar	Tola, Puah, Jashub, and Shimron	4
Zebulun	Sered, Elon, and Jahleel (	3
Gad	Zephon, Haggi, Shuni, Ezbon, Eri, Arodi, and Areli	7
Asher	Imnah, Ishvah, Ishvi, and Beriah (who in turn was the father of Heber and Malkiel)	6
Benjamin	Bela, Beker, Ashbel, Gera, Naaman, Ehi, Rosh, Muppim, Huppim, and Ard.	10
Dan	Hushim	1
Naphtali	Jahziel, Guni, Jezer, and Shillem.	4
Jacob	Dinah (mother Leah)	1
Asher	Serah	1
	Total	67
Jacob	Joseph – in Egypt	1
Joseph	Ephraim, Manasseh – In Egypt	2
	Total	3
	Grand Total	70

Jacob arrives in Egypt

Jacob sent Judah ahead to ask Joseph to meet him at Goshen. So Joseph harnessed his chariot and went to meet his father. When they met, they hugged each other and wept for a long time.

Jacob said to Joseph, "I am now ready to die. I have seen your face and know you are still alive."

Joseph spoke to his brothers and their households and said he would go and speak to the Pharaoh and tell him they had all arrived.

Jacob said it was vital that they told everyone they were shepherds, especially the Pharaoh, as Egyptians always found shepherds detestable. He will then let you settle permanently in the region of Goshen, where there is the best pasture and water.

(The reference to 'Detestable Shepherds' is perhaps a reference to the Hyksos – meaning 'Shepherd Kings'.)

Jacob settles at Goshen

Joseph, accompanied by five brothers, went to see the Pharaoh. Joseph told him that his father and brothers, with their flocks, herds and everything they owned, had come from the land of Canaan. They were now in Goshen because of the severe famine in Canaan.

The Pharaoh asked the brothers what their occupations were. They said they were Shepherds, just as their fathers had been.

The Pharaoh told Joseph his father and brothers could settle in the best part of the land at Goshen. Then Pharaoh said they could be put in charge of his livestock if they had any very capable shepherds.

Joseph later introduced his father to the Pharaoh. He told the Pharaoh he was one hundred and thirty years old. Jacob thanked and blessed the Pharaoh.

Joseph and the Famine

The famine continued in Egypt and Canaan. Joseph sold grain to everyone and took all the money into Pharaoh's palace. When the money ran out, the Egyptians asked for food. "Why should we die before your eyes because the money supply has stopped?"

Joseph told them he would exchange their livestock for money and grain. So they brought him all their horses, sheep, goats, cattle and donkeys. By this means, they all survived another year.

The famine continued, and the Egyptians had nothing but themselves and their land. They begged the Pharaoh to buy them and their land for food. They would become servants to him in exchange for grain so they could survive.

Joseph bought all the land in Egypt for Pharaoh, except the Priests, because they received regular payment in grain from the Pharaoh. As a result, all the people throughout Egypt became slaves to Pharaoh.

Joseph gave all the Egyptians seeds to plant and told them to cultivate the land. Then, when the harvest came, they should pay the Pharaoh one-fifth of the crop as a tax. The other four-fifth they would keep and plant and feed their household.

The Egyptians were happy with this arrangement as they believed Joseph had saved their lives. The statute, which taxes the population on their harvest to the value of one-fifth of the crop, is still in effect today.

Jacob's family increased in numbers

Jacob's family owned the land at Goshen and increased rapidly in numbers. (*Despite the famine!*)

Jacob lived there for seventeen years until he was one hundred and forty-seven years old. (7x7x3 = 147)

In the last days of his life, Jacob asked his son Joseph to come to him and said, "Are you happy to do a favour for me?" Joseph agreed. Then Jacob told him he wanted him to swear an oath that when he died, they would not bury him in Egypt but take him and bury him in the cave of his ancestors. Joseph said he would do this.

Jacob told him to swear to it. Joseph placed his hand under Jacob's testicles and then made his promise. (Patriarchal Oath – Gen 24:2, 47:29)

Joseph's sons - Manasseh and Ephraim

Later, Joseph heard his father was weakening and took his two sons, Manasseh and Ephraim, to see him. Jacob sat up on his bed when they arrived.

Jacob said, "Joseph, when I was at Luz (Bethel), in Canaan, God appeared before me and blessed me.

He told me, "I am going to make you fruitful and will multiply you. I will make you into a group of nations and give this land to your descendants as an everlasting possession."

He then said to Joseph, "Your two sons, Ephraim and Manasseh, who were born before I came to Egypt, will be regarded as my children, the same as Reuben and Simeon. Any children after these that you father will be yours. They will be listed under the names of their brothers in their inheritance."

Jacob then told him about his mother's death. He said, "When I was returning from Paddan, Rachel died – to my sorrow – in the land of Canaan. This happened along the road, some distance from Ephrath. So I buried her there on the way towards Ephrath – (Bethlehem)".

When Jacob saw Joseph's sons, he joked and asked who they were. Then, he added, "I never expected to see you again, but God has allowed me to see your children as well."

Joseph made his two children bow down in front of Jacob. Jacob stretched his right hand out and placed it on Ephraim's head (Ephraim being the younger) and said,

"My God, who has been my shepherd all my life, bless these boys.

May my name be named in them, and may they grow into a multitude on the earth."

When Joseph saw his father place his hand on Ephraim instead of Manasseh, his firstborn, he tried to correct him. But his father said, "I know my son, they will both become a nation, but the younger brother will be even greater, and his descendants will become a multitude of nations."

He then blessed them both and said, "You will in the future bless Israel saying, 'May God make you like Ephraim and Manasseh,'"

Then Jacob said to Joseph, "I am about to die, but God will be with you and bring you back to the land of your fathers. As one above your brothers, I give you the mountain slope I took from the Amorites with my sword and bow."

Jacob Blesses His Sons

Jacob called for all his sons to bless them. Then, he spoke to them one by one, saying what their future would be:

Table 29: Jacob's blessing of his sons.

Names	N/S	L/R	Comment
Reuben	N	L	My firstborn, strong, outstanding in dignity and power. But you are as destructive and took my concubine in my bed.
Simeon and Levi	S	L	You are like twins and use knives as weapons. For your pleasure, they have hamstrung oxen and killed men in anger. You are cruel, angry and very fierce. They will be scattered over the land.
Judah	S	L	Your brothers will praise you and bow down to you. The sceptre will not leave your hand until the arrival of its owner.
Zebulun	N	L	Your border will extend to Sidon, and you will live by the sea.
Issachar	N	L	You are like a strong-boned donkey between two saddlebags.
Dan	N	R	You will judge your people. You are like a snake beside the road that bites the heels of horses, so the riders fall off.
Gad	N	L	You will be raided by marauding bands but will attack them at their heels.
Asher	N	L	Your food will be rich, and you will provide delicacies to the royalty.
Naphtali	N	R	You speak well and are like a free running doe
Joseph	N	R	You are like a fruitful bough near a spring whose branches climb over the wall. They will oppose you and archers will attack you, but your bow will remain steady, and your hands will be skilful. You will be protected by: • The hands of the mighty One of Jacob • The Shepherd • The rock of Israel • God of your father, who will help you • Sovereign God They will bless you from the sky above; from the deep, that lies below, from the breast and the womb. The blessing of your father will be greater than those from the eternal mountains or the desirable things of the age-old hills.
Benjamin	S	R	You are like a hungry wolf. In the morning, you devour the prey, and by the evening, you divide it up.

N/S – Future North or South Kingdom

L /R – Tribe from Leah or Rachel side

The Death of Jacob

Jacob told them he would die shortly and wanted to be buried in the cave purchased by Abraham in the Machpelah field near Mamre in Canaan. Currently buried there were:

- Abraham and his wife, Sarah,
- Isaac and his wife, Rebekah,
- Jacob's wife, Leah

Jacob then pulled his feet up onto his bed and died.

The Burials of Jacob and Joseph

Joseph wept when his father died. He told the Egyptian physicians to anoint him, which took them forty days. The Egyptians mourned for seventy days, and after the days of mourning, Joseph spoke to the Pharaoh and told him of his father's desire to be buried in Canaan. The Pharaoh told him to go and bury his father as he had wanted.

Joseph left with Jacob's body, accompanied by all his and his brother's household members. Only the children were left in Goshen. Pharaoh's officials and dignitaries of his court also went.

They first travelled to the threshing floor of Atad, near the Jordan, and mourned for a further seven days. Then Jacob's sons carried him to the land of Canaan and buried him in the family cave in the field of Machpelah at Hebron. Finally, Joseph, his brothers and everyone who accompanied them returned to Egypt.

Joseph Reassures His Brothers

When Joseph's brothers realised their father was dead, they were concerned that Joseph might still hold a grudge against them. So they decided to tell Joseph that Jacob had left him a message before he died: "I ask you to forgive your brothers for the wrongs they did to you." Upon hearing this, Joseph cried, and his brothers felt at his feet. Joseph told them not to be afraid because while they had meant him harm, he had managed to save so many lives because of them.

The Death of Joseph

Jacob's family stayed in Egypt, and Joseph saw his son's and brother's families increase.

As his life ended, he told his brothers that in the future, God would take the Children of Israel from Egypt and take them to the land of Canaan as he had promised. He also made them and their offspring promise to carry his bones away from Egypt when the time came.

Joseph finally died. He was embalmed and placed in a coffin in Egypt. He was 110 years old.

(His bones would be taken and buried in 'The Promised Land' alongside his father in the family cave at Hebron.)

SUMMARY OF GENESIS

Genesis sets up the extended family of the Patriarchs and their move to Egypt. For some four hundred years, they stayed and prospered.

Food and water storages were the main driving forces in the family's mobility. Their primary food source appears to be sheep (21 mentions) or goats (6 mentions), and the watering of the herds at wells provided to be a sociable activity.

Some areas of the land occupied by the Patriarchs were excellent for supporting the stock but would be fought over later by others.

The Garden of Eden and the creation story would appear later, as it formed the basis of the main temple ritual in Jerusalem.

Magic signs and dreams provide reasons for events to unfold in a particular way. Joseph's ability to read dreams helped him to get on and form the basis of the unfolding story of the tribes of Israel.

While the land was given to Abraham by God, it is surprising how the continuation of the claim can be established some four hundred years or more later. But we see written into the final sections the portability of the remains of Jacob and Joseph.

However, it is surprising that the Genealogy of Jesus does not pass through Joseph, but Judah, Jacob's fourth son by Leah.

Ephraim / Manasseh

Jacob's blessing of the younger son in place of the older parallels Jacob taking of the birthright from Isaac, his father, instead of Esau, his brother.

In Ephraim's tribe would be Joshua, Samuel, and Jeroboam, the first king of the northern kingdom of Israel.

In Manasseh's tribe would be Gideon.

MOSES

The Israelites Oppressed

Four hundred years or so later, and despite the birth problems experienced by Sarah, Rebekah, and Rachel, Jacob's family had grown in numbers and spread out over Goshen in Egypt. They called themselves 'The Children of Israel' after Jacob, who said God called him 'Israel'. They retained their tribal structure organised through a council of elders. The folk-law traditions of the previous generations continued with Aaron as their leader.

A new Pharaoh saw the number of Israelites as a threat.

- If they increased their numbers, they might side with an enemy.
- Who would do all the hard work if they decided to leave Egypt?

So the Pharaoh put taskmasters over the Israelites to make them work hard. He sent them to build two storage cities at Pithom and Raamses. They were set to work, making the bricks and mortar. Then they built the structures. Their lives were made hard and as miserable as possible, but the Israelite's numbers continued to increase despite this. Finally, the Egyptians began to get worried.

Israelite Midwives

The Pharaoh spoke to two Israelite midwives, Shipharh and Puah, and told them when they were delivering Israelite babies, they should secretly kill any boy babies but let girls live.

(Generally, when populations were controlled, the female babies suffered. This strengthened the labour forces and army power, but the selection was intended to weaken the Israelite population).

They did not do this, and when they were again brought in front of the Pharaoh to explain. They said Israelite women were not like Egyptian women; they were vigorous and gave birth quickly before the midwife arrived.

The Israelites increased in numbers, and even the midwives had families.

Israelite boys to be killed

Finally, the Pharaoh ordered all his people that every Israelite boy born must be thrown into the River Nile for the crocodiles, but not the girls who could live.

The Birth of Moses

Amram married his father's sister Jochebed, from the house of Levi. She gave birth first to a boy, Aaron, and then a daughter, Miriam. Finally, after Pharaoh's edict, she gave birth to a boy. He should have been thrown into the Nile, but she hid him.

Moses floated in a basket

After three months, Jochebed could not hide him any longer and decided to put him in the Nile in a papyrus basket, which she coated with tar and pitch to make it waterproof. *(This story probably comes from the Babylonian period, where it was common to use pitch to waterproof items – see Noah's Ark)*. She placed the baby in the basket and hid him in some reeds along the banks of the River Nile.

Pharaoh's Daughter

Her daughter, Miriam, watched from a distance and saw the Pharaoh's daughter go down to the Nile to bathe with her attendants. Pharaoh's daughter saw the basket and sent one of her slave girls to get it. On opening it, Pharaoh's daughter saw the baby and felt sorry for him, knowing it was one of the Israelite babies.

Miriam approached and asked Pharaoh's daughter if she wanted an Israelite woman to feed and nurse the baby. Pharaoh's daughter thought and said, "Yes, go and find a woman." So the Girl went and fetched her mother, Jochebed.

Moses grows up in the Palace

Pharaoh's daughter said to Miriam, "Take this baby and nurse him for me, and I will pay you". So Jochebed took the baby and nursed him. Then, when the child was older, she gave him to Pharaoh's daughter, and he became her son. She named him Moses, and he grew up learning all.

Moses Kills

After Moses had grown up, he witnessed an Egyptian beating a hard-working Israelite. When no one was watching, he attacked the Egyptian. After killing him, he hid the body in the sand.

The following day he saw two Israelites fighting and asked them why they were fighting. They asked, "Who made you a prince and judge over us? Do you plan to kill me like you did the Egyptian?" Moses then realised that what he had done was not a secret, and perhaps the Israelites would be blamed for the death of the Egyptian. So he fled.

Moses flees to Midian

When the Pharaoh finally heard that Moses had killed an Egyptian, he wanted him put to death. By this time, Moses had left Egypt and its controlled land and made his way east to Midian. (*Parallel here this Jacob and his sojourn in Paddan Aram, where he marries*)

Moses meets Jethro and his daughters

Near the village of Reuel, he rested at a well. He saw some women watering a flock being driven away by other shepherds who had arrived. He helped the women draw water and filled the water troughs for their flocks. The women told him they were all the daughters of Jethro, the local priest.

When the women got home, their father asked them why they had come home early. The girls explained how an Egyptian had rescued them from the shepherds. Jethro told them to go and invite Moses to eat with them.

Moses married Zipporah

Moses stayed with Jethro and fell in love with his daughter Zipporah. They married and had a son who was called Gershom.

Pharaoh died

Meanwhile, the Pharaoh died, and the Egyptians continued to mistreat the Israelites as slaves. But the cries of the Israelites were heard by God. He had promised Abraham, Isaac and Jacob that he would look after their offspring.

Moses and the Burning Bush

Moses looked after his father-in-law's flock, and he led them to the far side of the desert to a mountain they called 'Horeb'.

As he looked around, he saw a fire in a bush. An angel appeared in the flames of the fire. Moses thought it strange and went for a closer look. As he approached, God called to him from within the burning bush.

'Moses? Moses!

Moses replied, "Here am I". God told him to stay where he was and to take his shoes off, as the ground he stood on was Holy.

God introduces himself

God then introduced himself, saying,

"I am the God of your ancestors, the God of Abraham, Isaac and Jacob."

When Moses heard this, he hid his face as he was afraid to look.

God told Moses he had seen the continuing suffering and misery of the Israelite slaves, and now he was going to rescue them from the Egyptians, take them out of Egypt, and lead them to their Promised Lands.

The land of Milk and Honey

God described it as a land flowing with milk and honey but currently occupied by the Canaanites, Hittites, Amorites, Perizzites, Hivites and Jebusites.

God's plan for Moses

God told Moses he wanted him to lead the Israelites out of Egypt. However, those who wanted him dead had themselves died, and it was now safe for him to return.

Moses started to make excuses:

- He told God how happy and pleasant his life was.
- How could he see the Pharaoh and ask him to let the Israelites go?

God said:

- He would be with Moses all the time
- He would guide the Israelites out of Egypt.
- He would bring them back here, to Mount Horeb.
- They would then plan the next move to the land flowing with milk and honey in detail.

Moses then asked God if he went and spoke to the elders of the tribes and offered to help them. They would ask which god he was talking about.

God told him to say,

> "God said, I am who I am. My name does not matter."

They would know what I mean.

God's Plan for a series of plagues

God told Moses to take the elders to the Pharaoh. They should say to him:

- They had met their God
- He wants them to walk into the desert for three days
- He wants them then make a sacrifice

This would stop a series of plagues that would affect and destroy Egypt.

Once they were in the desert, they would secretly leave Egypt.

God knew the Pharaoh would not let the Israelites go unless he was forced. So there was a plan to hit Egypt with plagues. This would finally force the Pharaoh to let them all go.

Israelites plunder Egypt

They would not leave empty-handed. They would all plunder Egypt.

The women would steal pieces of gold, silver, and clothing from their Egyptian neighbours and employers and hide it all on their children.

Done correctly, the Egyptians would not realise they had been robbed until it was too late.

It would be regarded as payment for their labour over the years.

Magic tricks

Moses said nobody would believe that God had appeared to them.

God told Moses he could show them some magic tricks to help them believe.

Rod to snake and back

God asked Moses what he had in his hand. "A Shepherd's Staff", replied Moses. So God told Moses to throw it onto the ground.

When he did, it turned into a large snake. Moses was surprised. God then told Moses to pick the snake up by its tail. When Moses did this, it turned back into a staff.

Hand turn to leprosy and back

Then God showed Moses another simple trick. By putting his hand in his cloak, he could withdraw it, so it looked like leprosy. Then by putting it back in the cloak, it could be withdrawn again, looking totally normal.

God told Moses if they did not react to the first magic trick, he should do the second to get a reaction.

Water to blood

If they still do not react, he should perform another trick, making the water look like blood. He showed Moses how to take some fresh, clear water from the Nile and then pour it onto the dry ground so it looked like blood.

Moses' speech impediment

Moses said he had never been able to speak successfully in public and found it difficult because of his hair lip. However, God said all he needed was confidence, and he would be fine.

But Moses was nervous and asked if someone else could speak for him. *(However, despite this, Moses would often address a crowd!)*

Moses' brother Aaron to help

God said that Aaron, Moses' elder brother, could speak very well in public. He was the Elder of the Levite tribe and was on his way to meet them to help with the plans.

God suggested:

- Aaron could take the role of the Prophet, speaking about what was to happen,
- Moses could represent the Israelite God and speak for God to Aaron.

This would make perfect sense.

God told Moses to try hard to persuade the Pharaoh to allow the Israelites to leave Egypt. But he thought the Pharaoh would not want to let them go.

Israelites are God's firstborn child

God told Moses to tell the Pharaoh

"The Israelites only have one God, and he viewed his children of Israel as a firstborn child, special to him. Therefore, if the Pharaoh did not let them all leave, then their God would kill all the children of Egypt in return."

Moses leaves God

The time had come for Moses to leave God. As Moses left, God reminded him to take his new staff so that he could perform the various tricks he had been taught.

Moses tells Jethro he is off to Egypt

Moses returned with the flock to the village of Reuel and spoke to Jethro, his father-in-law. Then, he said he would meet his brother and travel to Egypt to see how many Israelites were still alive.

Jethro wished him well and told him to go in peace.

Moses packs and sets off for Egypt

Moses and his family packed up, loaded their donkeys and set off for Egypt. Along the way, they met other Israelites who had escaped from Egypt. They were suspicious of Moses because they noticed his son Gershom was not circumcised. *(This would not have been normally obvious!)*

Gershom is quickly circumcised

Moses' wife, Zipporah, quickly took out a flint knife, cut off her son's foreskin, and threw it at Moses' feet, saying, "Now our son's penis looked like a bridegroom's on his wedding night". (i.e. after making love and breaking the hyman of a virgin)

The traditional flint knife was used before an iron blade was available.

Moses, Aaron and God meet

Moses had arranged to meet Aaron on his way to Egypt. They sat and discussed how they should proceed and what they needed to do. Aaron told Moses of his meeting with the elders of the Israelites, and they refined their plans and timescale.

They had to consider how to leave Egypt, their possessions, and food. They certainly would not want to be taken as slaves again. They would have to move into a land they could defend. All the materials they needed would have to come from Egypt.

The Elders meet Moses

Aaron arranged a meeting with the other Elders of the tribes and introduced Moses to them.

Moses explained his background and knowledge of Egypt, Midian, Canaan and the various trade routes. This knowledge would be invaluable to them.

They discussed the outline of their plan to leave Egypt.

Then having got their agreement, Aaron said they would go and speak to the Pharaoh.

Aaron and Moses visit the Pharaoh

Aaron and Moses arranged an audience with the Pharaoh.

Israelite's history explained

Aaron told the Pharaoh the history of the Israelites, Joseph, their arrival into Egypt, and why they were called 'The Children of Israel'.

Aaron explained they had to go on a three-day journey deep into the desert to sacrifice to their God. They had to take with them all their:

- Families,
- Possessions
- Livestock

Aaron told the Pharaoh that there was a series of plagues, or the sword, shortly to fall on Egypt. The only way these could be stopped was by the Israelites making their sacrifice.

The Pharaoh just did not believe them

But the Pharaoh had never heard of their god, did not believe them, and would not let them go.

The Pharaoh asked why the Israelites wanted to go so far into the desert. Aaron explained their food needed to be prepared in a particular way. The Egyptians would find it horrible and stone them if they saw them doing it.

Then the Pharaoh asked why everyone needed to go. Could only the men go? Aaron said they all had to go to make the sacrifice.

Then he asked why they needed to take all their flocks and herds. Aaron said the animals were required to make hand sacrifices and burnt offerings to God and had to go with them. They would not know what they needed until they arrived.

Aaron told the Pharaoh, "The Israelites only have one God, and he views his 'Children of Israel' as a firstborn child, special to him. Therefore, if the Pharaoh did not let them all leave, their God would kill all the 'Children of Egypt' in return."

No Straw for Bricks

The Pharaoh had heard enough and was very angry. He accused both of them of trying to stop his workforce from making bricks and dismissed them.

The Pharaoh ordered the taskmasters in charge of the Israelites not to supply any more straw for their brickmaking. If all they can think about is going on a seven-day holiday in the desert, then they should be made to work harder. Then, they can make the same number of bricks and find their own straw.

Building Work falls behind

After a couple of days, the Israelites had fallen behind. So the Taskmasters took a couple of Israelite Foremen to Pharaoh to explain. The Pharaoh told them they were idle, good for nothing, and had nothing better to do than dream about sacrificing to their God. Therefore, they had to work harder and make the same number of bricks as before without fail. If they did not, his taskmasters were given orders to kill the lazy ones.

Moses had made matters worse

The Israelite Foreman realised they were in trouble, left the Pharaoh, and returned to speak to Moses and Aaron. The Foreman said the Pharaoh was very angry.

Moses realised they had put pressure on the Pharaoh, and eventually, he would let all the Israelites leave. Then, he would drive them out.

God spoke to Moses and told him he had appeared to Abraham, Isaac and Jacob as 'God Almighty' but did not make himself known to them as 'God'.

Aaron and Moses then spoke to the Elders and reminded them of the history of the Promised Land and how God would help them. Sadly, they said their workforce was not very receptive to leaving because all they could see was their problems worsening. But they would get over it. So they proceeded to wait for the arrival of the first plague.

Aaron's Staff Becomes a Snake

Moses gave his new staff to Aaron, and they practised the snake trick God had shown Moses.

The following day they both went to see the Pharaoh again. They told him their God wanted the Israelites to leave. The Pharaoh asked for some sign to demonstrate the power of their God. Aaron performed the trick by throwing the staff onto the ground, turning it into a big snake.

The Pharaoh laughed and called his wise men and magicians.

(According to Paul in his second letter to Timothy, the magicians were called Jannes and Jambres – how did he know?)

They also performed the same trick dropping their staff onto the floor. Each of these turned into a snake.

As they looked, Aaron's snake ate the others. Aaron smugly said that his God was bigger than all their little Gods. The Pharaoh got angry, and they left.

The Plagues

A series of plagues next appear. Many people have tried to explain these by natural events, but they were a collection of terrible events intended to frighten any nation into submission. The plague themselves were based on past events, but it is unlikely they would all occur one after another. It is also unlikely that geographic restrictions would happen in the application of a plague, other than watercourses and disease immunity of certain races.

The plagues, as described below, contain some logical thoughts about how they could have occurred.

Plague No 1: Water

Just as Moses and Aaron had predicted, the first natural disaster arrived that September. The tidal River Nile turned blood red with algae that made the water undrinkable and smell bad. All the fish in the river died and floated on the surface. The Egyptians had to dig holes to find water clean enough to drink. The water around the Israelite land of Goshen was unaffected.

Plague No.2: Frogs

After seven days, the frogs and crocodiles came out of the river to die. The banks of the rivers and streams were covered in dead frogs. The Egyptians collected them into heaps, but as they rotted in the heat, they created a terrible smell.

Plague No.3: Mosquitoes and Midges

Due to the death of frogs and fishes, there was nothing to control the mosquito and midge populations. They increased rapidly and bit both humans and animals. But the area around the Israelites remained clear.

Plague No.4: Flies

The piles of dead frogs and fish caused the flies to breed. Maggots and larvae were everywhere. More flies hatched, and soon swarms of flies were everywhere apart from Goshen. The Pharaoh received reports of the plagues and noted the Israelites did not suffer as the Egyptians did.

Plague No.5: Livestock

The flies next infected all the cloven-hoofed livestock in the fields, and they started to die. The Egyptians lost horses, donkeys, camels, herds, and flocks. (*Camels arrived in Egypt after 1000BC*)

Plague No.6: Boils

The flies also brought a plague of boils to both animals and humans. Then Pharaoh called his Physicians to try to cure the sickness, but they could do nothing.

Plague No. 7: Hail

A great hailstorm occurred during the following February when the fields were full of flax and barley. It was the worse Egypt had ever seen. Moses had seen signs of this occurring and had told the Egyptians to get their families, servants and stock undercover to protect them from the giant hailstones.

The next day the storm arrived, and it damaged:

- All the trees and their fruit.
- Flattened the flax and barley crop.

The wheat was not damaged as it has had not seeded.

The storm missed the Israelite land, and the Pharaoh noted this.

Plague No. 8: Locusts

Following the great storm, the locust population significantly increased, and a plague was carried in on the east wind. The locusts eat everything they could in the fields and on the trees.

Food supplies were now being severely affected. So the Pharaoh's advisers suggested Moses and Aaron should be recalled.

The Pharaoh again heard the Israelite lands were not affected, so he called Moses and Aaron to speak to them. But, first, he asked them if this was the work of the Israelite God.

Moses said it was a natural disaster that could have been stopped if the Pharaoh had allowed the Israelites to leave to make sacrifices.

The Pharaoh then gave permission for only the men to leave to make the sacrifice. But Moses refused and left.

Plague No.9: Darkness

In early March, the locusts had left, but a terrible sandstorm arrived, forcing everyone undercover. For three days, the storm caused darkness in Egypt. At the end of this time, the Pharaoh again called for Moses and Aaron. He said Egypt had suffered enough, and they would die the next time he saw either of them. Moses replied, "Just as you say."

Plague No.10: The Children of Egypt

God told Moses he would send one more plague through Egypt, and afterwards, the Pharaoh would force the Israelites to leave Egypt.

He then said that during the night, his angel of death would pass throughout Egypt, and every firstborn Egyptian male would die, including cattle and other animals.

The Egyptians would wail loudly, but nothing would happen during this night to the Israelites. Not even a dog would stir. Therefore, God will separate the Israelites from the Egyptians.

The Egyptians will beg Pharaoh to let the Israelites go.

God had hardened Pharaoh's heart, so he would not let the Israelites leave before this plague.

The Masterplan

The timing was critical, as they needed to travel quickly at night during a full moon. The event was therefore planned for mid-month. Moses called the elders and told them what was going to happen. They should spread details by word of mouth (*How else?*) and make sure everyone knew what to do.

Mark their house with Lamb's blood

On the tenth day of the month, the Israelites should select an unmarked one-year-old male lamb, or goat, for their families. Then, it would be slaughtered on the evening of the fourteenth day. The blood from the lamb would be used to mark the Israelite houses. A bunch of hyssop would be dipped into the blood of the lamb. It would then be used to paint on the top and both sides of the doorframe.

God would then send his angel of death who could see, by the marking made by the lamb's blood, that Israelites lived at that house and would not enter and kill the firstborn. No one should then leave the house until the morning.

The Egyptians who would die

As the angel passed, every Egyptian first-born male would die. Moses listed the type of people who would die:

- The Pharaoh's son,

- Egyptian children,
- the children of their servants
- young animals not killed by the previous plagues.

But as long as the Israelites were careful, none of them would die.

Pharaoh would drive them away

Once the Pharaoh heard of the illness in his land and realised the Israelites were not affected, he believed their God was protecting them and making them leave. He believed this would stop the plague in Egypt.

When told to leave, they would need to travel quickly. That night they should remain fully dressed and ready to go. All their possessions were packed, and enough simple unleavened bread for seven days. Their water supplies would be critical, and Moses had planned the route for them.

The Passover

Moses told Aaron this last plague would mark the first month of the Israelite Year. It would be like a new beginning. The Israelites would remember this night with a simple meal and yearly recital.

When their children ask, 'Why do we do this?' They would be told,

> 'It marked the night of the God passed over the houses of the Israelites in Egypt, but struck down the Egyptians'.

About the Bible – 1

THE EXODUS

During the night of the fourteenth, the Pharaoh and his advisers were aware of the plague killing vast numbers of Egyptians but no Israelites. So his advisors told him to make the Israelites leave so the plague would stop.

He called Aaron and Moses and told them the Israelites had to leave immediately with all their possessions and livestock and never come back. May your God bless us also.

Word spread amongst the tribes that they were to leave, and they quickly plundered the Egyptian houses while they were dealing with their dead.

They took all the gold, silver, clothes and other materials they could carry for their future life. The Egyptian Officials kept pressing the Israelites to leave, so they gathered all their goods and the unleavened dough and left.

The Israelites left on the fifteenth day of the first month, the day after the Passover.

They all marched out of Rameses in full view of the Egyptians early in the morning and made their way Southeast to Succoth.

There were twenty thousand of them, with livestock flocks and herds.

The Israelites had lived in Egypt for about 430 years.

What did the Israelites take with them?

Leaving Egypt would require the Israelites to take all their possession and supplies/provisions for their new life. Indeed they could only assume such items would be of use.

How would they carry them? We know timber was rare in Egypt, as it was mostly imported.

Metal in the form of Gold and Silver is mentioned, but no Copper, Bronze or Iron.

Beasts of burden would have also been very limited. These would have set the speed of the travelling mass but would later be used for moving the tabernacle.

Dedication of the Firstborn

God told Moses the Israelites would in future dedicate all the firstborn sons of Israel and every firstborn male animal to him. The firstborn must be present to God and then redeemed with a lamb.

This will mark the Passover day when he took them out of Egypt and their journey to the Promise Land.

This land was flowing with milk and honey. It was currently occupied by the Canaanites, Hittites, Amorites, Hivites, and Jebusites.

Route to Midian

As they walked, the Israelites noticed a a considerable distance in front of them a column of smoke; at night, it turned into a column of fire. Nevertheless, God was guiding them on their way.

They went first to Succoth, where Moses collected the bones of Joseph. The Israelites had promised under oath to take them if they left Egypt and would bury them with his forefathers.

From there, they travelled onto Etham and erected their tents on the edge of the wilderness.

They avoided the Philistines

They could have gone directly on the road to the Philistine country, but the Israelites were armed but untrained. They feared attacks not only from Egyptians but also from the Philistines. Moses believed the Israelites might want to return to Egypt if attacked.

They camped by the Sea

As they made their way, Moses led them towards Pi-Hahiroth, between Migdol and the sea just before Baal Zephon. They all camp that night by the sea. Moses thought if Pharaoh decided to pursue them, their route would confuse him, and the Israelites could set a trap if they attacked.

The Egyptians approach

The Pharaoh was coming to terms with what had happened in Egypt. He heard the Israelites had left and plundered Egyptian properties. He realised all his slave labour had gone, and getting food was a problem. Even worse, his army horses had died, so more were being brought up to his army from the south.

He decided to attack and destroy the Israelites, as they were to blame.

As soon as his fresh horses arrived, he asked for his chariot to be ready.

He led an army of over six hundred chariots and men in pursuit of the Israelites.

The Egyptian found the Israelites while camped at Pi-Hahiroth by the sea opposite Baal-Zephon. The Israelites began to panic, but Moses told them this would be the last time they would see the Egyptian army. After that, God would fight for them.

Crossing the Sea

God told Moses to get the people to move into the sea quickly. If he held up his shepherd's staff, a path would open up through the sea. The Egyptians would see this and follow you across.

The column of smoke moved from in front of the Israelites to a position between them and the Egyptians. It illuminated the Israelite camp at night but blinded the Egyptians, so they could not see the Israelites.

Moses raised his hand over the sea, and God opened a path to the other side using a strong east wind. The wind blew all night until the seabed was dry as the land. Then, the Israelites were able to walk on dry land to the other side.

The Egyptian army followed them into the sea using the same path. Then, the chariot wheel started to come off, making it impossible for them to move. Once the Israelites had reached the other side, Moses raised his staff again, and the seawater rushed back, covering the Egyptian army.

Not one member of the Egyptian army survived. The following day the Israelites saw all their bodies on the seashore.

They saw the power of their God and Moses' leadership.

What happened?

Many people try to explain this event through natural and mystical events. Those living beside the Nile did not know about tides. They did not occur on the Nile river. The Gulf of Suez is tidal but only has a range of some 0.9m, perhaps more during the Spring tide.

The northern shore of the Gulf has receded over time. It was initially located on the Bitter Lakes. What can be seen today is not what would have faced the Israelites.

The Gulf has not been formed by erosion by a large river feeding into the Gulf. Instead, continental drift has created it, with Africa splitting from Arabia and slowly widening.

The Israelites were able to select their crossing point and time. Whereas the Egyptian forces probably did not. This would have been well 'upstream' of the Gulf and on a well-trod trading route.

The passing of many people and carts over a body of water would have churned up the sediments. Chariots were perfect for firm land without ruts, but problems would have occurred in water with an irregular running surface.

Another thought is the Pharaoh's replacement horses were untrained for Chariots. When the tide returned, it caused panic, and the Egyptian army were drowned.

If the Egyptian army had travelled quickly on horseback instead of on foot, the horses might have caused the demise of the Egyptian Army.

Perhaps it was a rare natural phenomenon. The drawing of water away to allow the Israelites to cross and the seawater rushing over the Egyptian army describe a tsunami. These follow an earthquake and would have been a series of tidal waves.

Finally, is it necessary to find a detailed explanation of an event which is probably a myth?

The Song of the Israelites

Then the Israelites sang this song to God:

> Sing to God and his victory glee.
>
> As horses and riders were lost in the sea.
>
> He is our leader and our rescuer
>
> The Pharaoh's chariots and army were lost in the sea
>
> His best officers were drowned in the Red Sea
>
> The deepwater covered them, and they sank like a stone
>
> The Egyptians boasted they would catch, rob, and kill us
>
> But Moses made them go the wrong way
>
> They were all lost in the spray.
>
> All nations will hear and tremble,
>
> the people of Philistia will panic
>
> The chiefs of Edom and Moab will be terrified
>
> The people of Canaan will melt away
>
> Terror and dread will fall on them all.

The Song of Miriam

Then Miriam, Aaron's sister, gathered the women and danced with tambourines.

Miriam sang to them:

> 'Sing to Moses and his victory glee.
>
> As horses and riders were lost in the sea.'

The Waters of Marah

Moses led the Israelites from the Gulf Sea into the Desert of Shur. They travelled for three days in the desert without finding water.

When they came to Marah, they could not drink its water because it was salty. Moses knew what to do from his experience in the area. He told them to make the water fresh with charcoal from a fire. This means the Israelites were able to freshen the water they found in the local well where they were salty.

Moses told them in exchange for obeying God's commands and laws, God would not inflict any of the diseases or plagues from Egypt. *(This method of purifying water is also mentioned in The Laws.)*

The Waters of Elim

They moved onto Elim. There they found seventy palm trees and twelve springs of fresh water. They were all able to relax for the first time since leaving Egypt.

No Food

The Israelites set out from Elim and followed the sea southwards. They camped finally by the Red Sea before turning inland to camp in the Desert of Sin on the fifteenth day of the second month after leaving Egypt.

As their food ran out, they all started to grumble about Moses and Aaron, saying:

> "We wished we had died in Egypt; at least we had round pots of meat and all the food we wanted. But, instead, they have brought us out into the desert where there is no food to die."

Eat off the land - Quails

Moses showed the Israelites how to live off the land, as he had done while looking after Jethro's sheep. They could find enough food each day to eat.

Moses told Aaron to tell the Israelites,

"Stop grumbling about us, as God will provide food for you. At dusk, you will eat meat, and in the morning, you will find more. Then you will know that God is looking after you."

That evening an enormous flock of migrating birds, quails, flew low and landed in the camp exhausted. They were all quickly caught as they realised this was 'meat'.

(Quails were very common, and there are a number of other records noting the catching of migrating quails.)

Manna

In the morning, there was a layer of dew around the camp. The Israelites saw small round objects on the ground when it evaporated. They asked, "What is it?" Moses told them it was the bread God gave you to eat. The Israelites called it 'Manna'. It was white, small like coriander seeds and tasted like a wafer with honey.

(Manna could have been derived from 'snow' - its method of arrival and disappearance)

The Manna had to be gathered quickly in the early morning because it would melt in the hot sun.

The Israelites should gather as much as they needed each day. The manna, when collected, would last the day, but became mouldy, attacked insects and worms if kept overnight, and would have to be thrown out. So instead, they could preserve it by baking or boiling it.

The Sabbath

Aaron told them to gather twice as much as normal on the sixth day of the week as they could not work on the seventh day and would eat manna which they had preserved.

(This is the first mention of the Sabbath in the bible – it appears that Moses invented the idea first! Maybe it was really a curfew.)

Aaron stores a sample of Manna

Moses told Aaron to put an omer of manna in a pot and keep it for future generations to see what they found to eat in the desert. They survived on manna until they crossed the river Jordan into Canaan and were able to find grain some forty years later. (*Note an omer is approx.. 2 litres*)

Water from the Rock

The Israelites left the Desert of Sin, camped at Aliush, and then made their way to Rephidim. But when they found no water, they were very angry with Moses. Some wanted to stone him.

Moses decided he needed to find water quickly for them and asked God for his help. God told him to take the staff he had in Egypt and hit a rock with it, and water would pour out. He should do this in front of the elder so they would value him.

Moses led the tribal elders to a nearby sandstone rock face. Then he hit the rock's surface violently with his staff, shattering the hardened surface and releasing the stored water from within the pores of the rock. The water flowed out, and Moses said:

"Is God amongst you or not?"

The Israelites drank quietly.

The Amalekites Defeated by Joshua's army

The nomadic Amalekites were worried they would lose access to nearby grazing land, so they came and threatened the Israelites at Rephidim.

Moses told Joshua to select men to form an army and go and fight them. *(Note Joshua means in Greek Jesus)*

While Moses watched from a hilltop, Joshua fought the Amalekites below. Aaron and Hur joined Moses as he watched. During the day, the fight was even, but slowly Joshua's army using swords* overcame the Amalekite army, and they were defeated. Moses wrote all the events in a book, so everyone in the future would remember. He also built a monument to mark the site of their victory.

*(*first mention of swords since Eden)*

Jethro Visits Moses

Jethro, Moses' father-in-law and priest of Midian, came and visited them all. He had heard from others all that had happened in Egypt and their journey. Jethro first met his daughter Zipporah and his grandsons Gershom and Eliezer.

As Moses was camped some distance away at Mount Horeb, Zipporah took her father to see Moses. Moses was happy to see him. They greeted each other with a kiss, and Moses invited him into his Tent.

Moses told Jethro all that had happened, the events in Egypt, and how God had treated the Israelites. Jethro said the God of the Israelites must be greater than all other Gods due to their good fortune. So they made a sacrifice and burnt offerings to God.

Later Aaron came with the elders of the tribes, and they all shared a meal and talked about their plans.

Jethro tells Moses to appoint Judges

The next day, Moses acted as a judge to the people to sort out their disputes. He had people standing around him from morning till night.

Jethro told Moses he was wasting his time. The workload is too heavy for one person, and he would wear himself out. Jethro told him he had no time to sort out more important matters.

Moses listened to his wisdom as a priest. He said that his role was to represent the people before their god. You need to teach them the statutes and laws and show them the way to live and the duties they are to perform.

He should select capable, trustworthy men from all the people and appoint them as judges over the thousands, hundreds, fifties and tens. They will serve the people and only bring you complicated cases. This will make your workload lighter.

(Therefore, it was a priest's ideal to use 'Judges')

Moses and the Elders appoint Judges

Moses considered what Jethro had said with his brother and the Elders and decided to do what he said. He set about drawing up a list of laws and decrees for them. Before completing this, he selected able men from the tribes and set them up as Judges for all but the most complicated cases.

Jethro helped Moses set up the system. He later went back to his town.

At Mount Sinai

In the third month, the Israelites left Rephidim and came and camped in the desert of Sinai before the mountain. Then, finally, Moses climbed the mountain, and God called for him.

God told Moses to tell the people of Israel,

> "You saw what I did to the Egyptians. I have now carried you on an eagle's wing to my mountain. I ask you to obey my voice and keep my laws. In exchange, I will treat you as my possessions. You will be a holy nation, a kingdom of priests."

Moses went down the mountain, called the elders, and told them what God said. Moses looked to the Elders and said: "Do you all agree?" With one voice, they all agreed.

Moses returned to speak to God and told him of the people's answer. Then God told Moses he was going to come to him. He would come as a thick cloud so people could hear him and speak directly to him.

Moses to prepare Israelites

God told Moses to go and prepare the Israelites for his visit:

- Purify them today and tomorrow
- Tell them not to have sex
- Wash their clothing

Make them ready for the third day when I come down onto Mount Sinai as everyone watches.

Boundary stones set out

Moses arranged for stones to be set up to mark a boundary around the base of the mountain. Everyone was told not to pass or touch this boundary because they would be immediately put to death. They would be either stoned to death or shot with arrows – but human hands must not touch them.

The people must keep away from the mountain until they hear a long blast from a ram's horn. Then they must gather at the foot of the mountain.

The People Prepare

Moses went down the mountain and told the people what to do for the days before God appeared. So the people prepared as they had been told.

God descends

On the morning of the third day, there was powerful thunder and lightning. A dense cloud came down on the mountain. Moses led the people to the base of the mountain, and they heard a long blast on a ram's horn.

Everyone stood and looked.

Mount Sinai was covered with smoke as God descended onto the top. It shook, and the horn grew louder and louder.

(The description here is of a volcano. This could reference the memory of Mount Etna in Sicily, which the Greeks saw erupt in their travels. It was written into their Greek Myths and associated with Zeus when he overcame Typhon.)

God calls Moses

God called Moses to go up the mountain. God told him to tell the people they could not pass the boundary markers, or else they would die. Even priests must consecrate themselves before they approach the holy ground.

God told Moses to go and collect Aaron and bring him up the mountain.

The Ten Commandments

Then God spoke to the people. He told them he was their God and had guided them out of the land of Slavery, Egypt, to their new life in the Promised Land.

He then lists the Ten Commandments as follows:

1). You shall have no other gods before me

2). You shall not make an idol or image of anything in heaven, earth, or water and worship them. (in the shape of birds, animals or fish) never worship or bow down to them, as I am a jealous God who will not share your affection with any other god. I do not leave unpunished the sins of those who hate me, but I punish the children for the sins of their parents to the third and fourth generations. I give all my love to those who love me and obey my commands even for a thousand generations.

3). You shall not swear or use God's name in vain. I will not let you go unpunished if you misuse my name.

4). Remember the seventh day of the week and rest. You, your wife, son, daughter, man or maid servant, or your animals or any alien within your gates shall work six days a week and rest on the seventh.

5). You will respect your father and mother.

6). You shall not murder

7). You shall not commit adultery

8). You shall not steal

9). You shall not lie

10). You shall not be jealous of your neighbour's possessions. Be it his wife, house, servants, ox, donkey, or anything else he owns.

(The Ten Commandments - The 'Decalogue' are slightly different in the other version set out in Deuteronomy.)

The people were terrified. Moses told them not to be afraid as God showed the extent of his power. Moses told them to remember their fear of him, as it keeps them from sinning.

As the people stood at a distance, Moses entered the dark cloud from where God had spoken.

Idols and Altars

God told Moses to tell the people not to make any Gold or Silver idols of gods to worship as I am a very jealous God.

God then told Moses to make an altar of sun-dried mud bricks and make offerings of burnt food of sheep, goats or cattle on it. Therefore, I will come and bless you whenever you honour my name.

They should make the altar of stone but not dressed stone as the use of a tool would defile it.

Young priests would look after the altar and deal with the sacrifices. It was important not to locate the altar high up, as people watching would see their bare bums etc.

They would sort out details shortly, but in the meantime, no one should approach an altar without a gift.

Moses states various laws for Israelites to follow

God provided them with a collection of laws, rules, and covenants, which needed to be fashioned into a code. They should then be told to the people, and this would provide the laws for them to live by.

They decided it would be best to write these in a book so they could refer to them. So Moses wrote them down in his book, adding to them as he considered best. See Appendix

Redeeming the Firstborn

God told them how to tax the Israelites to pay for their administration. The method would be by giving up the firstborn male from every womb, whether man or animal.

The firstborn male would be held for ransom until it could be redeemed for payment. For example, a firstborn donkey should be redeemed by giving a lamb, or its neck should be broken.

All the firstborn sons would be redeemed for payment of a half Shekel and would mark the saving of his life from Egypt.

Similarly, each person would offer the 'first fruits' from a harvest.

They plan the way forward to the Promised Land

God said he would send an angel to help them take the Promised Land. They should follow his commands and not rebel against him. By following his commands, their enemies would be God's enemies. He would help them invade the 'Promised Land', now occupied by the:

- Amorites,
- Hittites,
- Perizzites,
- Canaanites,
- Hivites
- Jebusites.

He would help plan the invasion.

They knew they would not drive the enemy out in one year, as there were not enough of them. If they did, the land would become occupied with wild and dangerous animals. So instead, they would drive the enemy out bit by bit as their numbers increased. Their population would increase quickly because their lives and food would be healthier than in Egypt.

The Promised Land Boundaries

The borders would have to be set from the Red Sea to the Mediterranean Sea and from the Wilderness to the Euphrates River.

(This land was never occupied)

The current residents of the Promise Land

The people occupying these lands would be driven out.

They would have to break up all their altars, sacred stones, idols, and Poles to their God, Asherah. The people of these lands made prostitutes of themselves and sacrificed to their gods. It would be impossible to make a treaty with these people as they were wicked and would tempt the Children of the Israelites with their wicked ways.

All the men would appear at a celebration three times a year to show their military strength and help keep other nations away from their lands. This will help their territory and nation grow.

Moses and Aaron returned to the Israelites

Moses and Aaron returned to the Israelites and gathered together seventy of the elders of the Israelites and Aaron's two eldest sons, Nadab and Abihu.

The Covenant Confirmed

Moses told them God wanted him as the sole intermediary. Then he told them of the various laws they had to follow and agreed to abide by. After he had finished reading them out aloud, they all agreed with them. Finally, he told them they must worship from afar while he went up the mountain to speak to God.

They were all still terrified.

The next morning Moses got up early and built an altar with twelve stone pillars representing the twelve tribes of Israel. Then he got some young men who were about to prepare burnt and peace offerings to collect the blood from the animals. He took half of the blood and sprinkled it on the altar.

Then he took the book in which he had written the laws and read it to the people. When he finished, they all agreed to obey. He then took the remaining blood and sprinkled it on them, and said,

"Look, this is the blood of God's covenant with you."

God calls Moses to fetch the two tablets

God told Moses to come up the mountain and wait while he wrote out the Laws on some stone tablets. Moses took his servant Joshua with him and told the elders what he would collect. While he was away, Aaron and Hur would look after them. If there were any disputes, they would sort them out.

So Moses and Joshua left, went up the mountain and waited for God to tell them what to do.

After six days, God called for Moses from within a cloud. Moses and Joshua walked into the cloud and were gone for another forty days. They took no food or water.

The Planning of the Tabernacle

God told Moses and Joshua to make a Tabernacle, a sanctuary for him on earth so he could live with them.

Levi to take charge

They discuss how such a large number of people could be controlled and governed. But, first, they needed some focus to draw the twelve tribes into a unified group. So drawing on their joint experiences, they decided it would be sensible to appoint one tribe to control the rest.

The focus could be a tabernacle to celebrate God and introduce a system of offerings to support the administration. But instead, Moses decided his tribe, the Levi, should take control, as he could trust them and his brother Aaron.

(This is the planning of the coup d'état. Moses' family would now be the elite with Moses as ruler. The Tabernacle would be the means of taxation to support the Levi family. Laws and punishments established.)

The Tabernacle details

They discuss the detailed planning of the tabernacle and its method of operation based on their knowledge of Egyptian practices.

Many items stolen from the Egyptians before they left would be used in the Tabernacle construction. The group planned the Tabernacle and decided it would be based on a frame of acacia wood covered with a tent. Inside it would be split into two rooms. Around it would be a screen to form a courtyard with an Altar for Burnt and other offerings. It would need to be portable until they were settled. If they needed any additional materials, they could always trade for them.

The Priests

God decided that Aaron would make a perfect High Priest, with his sons Nadab, Abihu, Eleazar and Ithamar should serve him as priests. The young sons needed to be fit and healthy to perform the sacrifices.

They would need clothes and jewellery to suit their new status.

They would run the tabernacle and administer all the tribes until they settled in the Promised Land. Moses would anoint them to their new roles

Items for the Tabernacle

God told them the Tabernacle should be of the highest quality and workmanship. Then, God listed out the materials he believed they needed.

The Israelites would donate gold, silver, copper and bronze.

Other items on his list were yarns dyed blue, purple and scarlet, fine linen, goat hair, ram's skins dyed red and hides of dugongs, a species of seal. Acacia wood, olive oil for the light, spices for the anointing oil and the fragrant incense, onyx stones and other gems.

In the inner room of the Tabernacle, they would keep a chest (the Ark) made of acacia wood. The Book of Law and the stone tablets currently being carved would be in it.

In the outer room, God said they would place a table of acacia wood with Plates, dishes, pitchers and bowls of pure gold. A gold lampstand would illuminate the table, and the Priests would provide clear oil to keep the light burning from evening to morning.

Bezalel and Oholiab

Their finest craftsmen would carry out the design of all these items. So Moses would select from the tribe of Judah, Bezalel, son of Uri (and grandson of his friend Hur), to make the artistic designs. He was very experienced at working in gold, silver and bronze, cutting and setting stones, working in wood, and all kinds of craftsmanship.

He would also appoint Oholiab, son of Ahisamach, of the tribe of Dan, to help him. He was a craftsman and designer of fabrics. He would embroider blue, purple, scarlet yarn fabrics and fine linen.

Moses believed there was adequate skill amongst the Israelites to make all the items required.

Atonement Money - Taxes

God told Moses to take a census of the Israelite men to count them. Each one must pay a sum of half a Shekel in exchange for the life he saved from Egypt. They would pay as they were counted. The money collected would go to the Priests for the upkeep of the Tent and all its fittings, equipment, and clothes.

The Sabbath

God wanted the Israelites to strictly observe the Seventh Day, or Sabbath, as it would be a valued day of rest for all. God had created Heaven and Earth in six days, and on the seventh day, he rested.

Anyone who desecrates the seventh day by working, or other activities, even during the ploughing and harvest season, would be put to death.

Moses finishes making the tablets of stone

The many days of planning came to an end. Moses and Joshua picked up their two new stone tablets carved on both sides with the words of the law and carried them carefully back down the mountain.

Moses and Joshua come down the Mountain

Moses wondered what the Israelites had been doing while they had been away.

The Golden Calf

The people thought that Moses had deserted them. As Moses nor Joshua could be found, they asked Aaron to lead them. Despite Moses telling them not to make any idol or image of a God, they asked Aaron if he would make a statue for them. It could precede them on their entry to the Promised Land.

Aaron was receptive to the idea and told them to give him the gold earrings from their wives, sons, and daughters. He then cast it all into the shape of a calf and engraved some decorations. The Israelites were very pleased and said this represented their God, who had brought them out of Egypt. Next, Aaron built an altar in front of the statue and declared the following day would be the 'Feast of God' and a holiday.

So that next day, everyone got up early. First, they made burnt and peace offerings on the altar and shared the cooked food. Then, they all sat down, ate, drank, then danced and played party games.

Moses decides to discipline the Israelites

Moses could see all that was happening from the mountain. Joshua looked and thought the camp was being attacked. But Moses explained what was happening and how the Israelites were disobedient.

He needed to discipline them and make them fear him as they were stubborn. He thought he could kill them all, with a few exceptions. Those that are left would form the basis of a new nation.

Then he remembered the stories of his forefathers, Abraham, Isaac and Jacob, and their wish to make their children as numerous as the stars in the sky. They had said their children would return to their land, which would be theirs forever.

Moses enters the camp

Moses went down from the mountain with the two tablets carved back and front with his laws in his hands.

As Moses and Joshua approached the camp, Moses grew furious. He could see the dancing and the calf.

He threw the stone tablets to the ground and broke them.

He grabbed the gold calf and burned it in the fire. Then he ground the remains into dust, threw them into the water, and made the Israelites drink it.

Moses questions Aaron

He asked Aaron why he had permitted the Israelites to behave badly. Aaron told Moses that he knew what they were like. They outnumbered him and asked him to make an idol as an emblem to follow, as they did not know what had happened to Moses.

> "I asked them if they had any gold, so they gave me all the jewellery from their ears. So I threw it all into a fire, and out came this calf."

Moses looked at him in total disbelief. He needed to take firm control.

Moses takes control of The Levi family

Moses realised that Aaron had lost control of the people, and they were running wild, so he went to the camp entrance and shouted for his tribe to come to him. When all the Levites had come to him, he told them:

> "The God of Israel wants you to punish these sinners. You are to get your swords and kill those out of control".

So the Levites proceeded to cross the camp, killing other Israelites behaving badly. By the end of the day, over 3,000 people had been killed.

That evening Moses called the Levites together. He thanked them for their loyalty and told them God wanted them to serve him forever, in preference to their brothers, sons and families.

Moses addresses the Israelites

The following day, Moses called the Israelites and told them they had behaved despicably, and God would decide how to punish them unless he could persuade God otherwise.

So Moses returned to the mountain to reflect and finally decided it was partly his fault for being away too long. He returned to the camp and found that many people were ill due to the number of dead bodies they were trying to deal with.

It was perhaps time for the tribes to move on.

Time to move on

God told Moses that it was time the people should leave this place and go to the 'Promised Land', the land of Abraham, Isaac and Jacob. They would have to drive out the:

- Canaanites,
- Amorites,
- Hittites,
- Perizzites,
- Hivites,
- Jebusites.

God decided he would not go with them because they made him cross. They were a 'stiff-necked' people, like a horse or Ox that could not be steered.

He told the people to take off their jewellery while he decided what to do. So they took off their jewellery at Mount Horeb.

The Meeting Tent

While God reflected on what to do, Moses had a tent pitch some distance away from the camp and called it the 'Meeting Tent'. He would go there to talk to God and ponder on matters. His young assistant Joshua, son of Nun, lived in the tent all the time. Whenever Moses went to the tent, all the people rose and stood at their tent's entrances, watching as he walked past until he entered the tent. A pillar of smoke rose from the tent whenever Moses was in it, and they could see a small fire at night.

Finally, Moses decided the people needed a leader and clear laws to live by. So he set about replacing the two broken stone tablets.

God's Glory

Moses said to God, "Be my people's guide on their journey, but you have not made clear who you will send with me. Let me see you so that I can know your ways".

God then said he would go with Moses and the people. Moses asked if he could see God. But God told him no one could see his face and live. He then said that if Moses were to shelter in a hole in the rock nearby, then as he passed, he would put his hand over the hole so no harm would come to him. Then, once God had passed, he could remove his hand, and Moses could see his back.

The New Stone Tablets

God told Moses to carve two stone tablets and to take them back up the mountain, and he would write on them again. So Moses went back up the mountain and into the cloud. God then came down in front of Moses and passed before him.

God told Moses that he was compassionate and understanding, slow to anger, abounding in love, and forgiving wickedness, rebellion and sin. He would punish the guilty and ensure their children and their children's children were punished. This would make them think twice before doing anything bad.

Then God said:

> "I will do wonders before your people such has never been seen on earth before. Your people will see the work of God, and what I do will terrify many people.
>
> You must do exactly as I say, as I will send you out before the Amorites, Canaanites, Hittites, Perizzites, Hivites and Jebusites. Please do not make any agreements with these people, as it will be a cause of sin to you. Destroy their altars, images and pillars."

God decided he should provide further laws based on the Tabernacle and the Levi administration.

The Radiant Face of Moses

Forty days later, he returned to camp with the carved tablets. Everyone saw that his face was very sunburnt, but Moses did not know.

He got Aaron to round up the Elders and told them what had happened. He said he had not eaten all the time they were away. But, like before, he had sat with God while he carved the Laws onto the stone tablets.

He showed the Elders the carved tablets, and they were happy that the 'Ten Commandments' were now set into stone. But they were concerned that his sunburnt face might attract some infection or disease. So he was given some lotions, and his face bandaged until it was healed.

The second set of Commandments
Table 30: The outline of these laws were as follows :

1	You will not worship any other god
2	You will not make any molten gods.
3	You will keep the feast of unleavened bread - Passover
4	You will give the first fruit of every womb to god – firstborn, redeem as necessary
5	You will keep the feast of weeks – 50 days after barley harvest on completion of wheat harvest
6	You will keep the feast of ingathering at the year's end – General Harvest Festival
7	You will not offer the blood of my sacrifice with leavened bread
8	Do not keep the fat of my festival offerings until the morning
9	Only the best of the first fruits of the harvest should be given to God
10	Do not cook a kid in its mother's milk

THE TABERNACLE - 1

Moses assembles the masses

Moses decided it was time to make an announcement to the tribes concerning the Tabernacle's construction. But, first, he reminded them of the Sabbath day and said anyone working that day would be put to death. "You cannot even light a fire."

Moses then told them in detail about the Tabernacle, its furniture, fittings, robes, and all the materials required for its construction. The Israelites were then asked to donate all these materials to make their God a ceremonial centre for sacrifices and offerings. He explained that Bezalel had been selected to make the finer items with Oholiab to assist him. *Good job, they had robbed the Egyptian before leaving!*

Materials for the Tabernacle

The tribes returned to their camps and found all the materials required for the Tabernacle. They returned with the materials and many offers of help that Moses had to stop them from making further donations.

Moses summoned Bezalel and Oholiab, gave them all the materials, and told them of all offers of skilled labour. Then, he explained exactly what he wanted and told them to go and make the Tabernacle.

The Tabernacle, Ark and equipment

Bezalel and Oholiab organised the skilled men among their workforce to make the acacia frames, silver bases, covering, and curtains for the tabernacle.

Bezalel made Moses an Ark which was a chest of acacia wood for the stone tablets and a jar of manna. He also made a lid with two winged cherubims. Finally, he overlaid the chest and lid with gold.

The skilled men then made a table and an incense altar out of acacia wood overlaid with gold.

They made gold plates, dishes, bowls and a pitcher for pouring. They then hammered out one piece of gold to make a lampstand.

Next, they made an Altar for Burnt Offerings out of acacia wood overlaid with bronze, complete with bronze utensils and grating.

They made a bronze basin and its stand from bronze mirrors donated by the women who served at the entrance to the Tent of Meeting.

Finally, they made acacia frames, bronze bases and tent pegs, silver hooks, bands and caps, and curtains for the courtyard enclosure.

The Materials Used

Moses had asked Ithamar, the priest, to record the amount of metal used for the Tabernacle. So he recorded the following in Talents and Shekels.

Table 31: Amount of metal used for the Tabernacle

Metal	Value	Used on	Obtained	Shekels	Kg
Gold	29 Talents and 730 shekels	the sanctuary	Wave Offering	87,730	1,584
Silver	100 talents and 1775 shekels	the bases, hooks, caps and bands.	Census	301,775	5,450
Bronze	70 talents and 2400 shekels	for bases, altar, utensils, and tent pegs	Wave Offering	212,400	3,835
Total				601,905	10,870

One Talent = 3000 Shekels

There was a standard Sanctuary Shekel used to assess payments.

The amount of metal, nearly 11 tonnes, which had been amassed for the Tabernacle, was considerable.

This excludes other metal items held by the Hebrews themselves, e.g. knives, swords, utensils etc.

The Priestly Garments

The priests' garments in the sanctuary were made from blue, purple and scarlet yarn. The ephod was made of the same yarn, finely twisted linen with fine gold wire. Onyx stones were set in gold and added to the shoulder straps.

Skilled craftsmen made the breast pieces. They used the same materials as the ephod, and four rows of precious stones were mounted onto it.

They made Aaron and his sons tunics of fine linen with sashes and cords.

The Passover

The anniversary of the Passover was approaching while they were in the Desert. So Moses decided they should all celebrate it on the fourteenth day of the first month at twilight. They were to eat the lamb with unleavened bread and bitter herbs and must not leave the food till morning or break any of its bones.

It would be celebrated each year to mark the day they left Egypt and slavery on their way to the Promised Land. It was to remind the Israelites of the Pharaoh and how he stubbornly refused to let them leave Egypt, and in turn, Egypt lost all her children.

Moses Inspects the Tabernacle

Moses looked at what they had done when all the work was complete. He found it was just as he required, and he thanked them all.

Setting Up the Tabernacle

On the first day of the first month of the second year, Moses told them to set up the tabernacle, the courtyard curtains and the equipment.

First, they set out all the bases and inserted the acacia frames, crossbars and posts. They then spread the tent over the tabernacle frames and put the covering over the top. Next, Moses took the stone tablets and the jar containing the manna, placed them in his new chest and put the cover on. Next, the carrying poles were attached and taken to the back of the tabernacle. Finally, the veil to screen the chest was hung across the middle.

To the front of the tabernacle on the north side, Moses placed the table and set bread on it. Opposite it, on the south side, Moses placed the lampstand and filled the lamps. In the middle, by the veil, he placed the gold incense altar and burnt some incense on it. Then he put up the curtain at the entrance to the tabernacle.

Outside he set out the altar for burnt offerings near the entrance to the tabernacle and made burnt and grain offerings. Then, he placed the basin on its stand between the altar and the tabernacle and added water. This was so Moses, Aaron and his sons could wash their hands and feet whenever they entered the Tabernacle or came to the altar.

Finally, Moses set up the courtyard around the tabernacle and altar and put the curtain at the entrance. The building work was completed.

Moses then took the anointing oil and anointed the tabernacle and everything in it. Then he anointed everything in the courtyard. From that time onwards, the people understood the Tabernacle was dedicated to their God, and he lived with them. There was a permanent fire within the courtyard near the tabernacle. During the day, they saw the smoke and, at night, a flame. Then the fire was put out; it was a sign that they would move on.

The Glory of God

A cloud rose over the old Meeting Tent and passed to the Tabernacle filling it. Moses was unable to enter the Tabernacle again because it was filled with God's glory.

LEVITICUS

The Book of Leviticus contains the instructions which God provided for:

- *Making offerings in the Tabernacle*
- *Conduct of the Israelites*

The running of the Tabernacles

God gave Moses various rules for running the Tabernacles so that everyone knew its purposes and how to use them. For example, the Israelites should bring offerings to the priests for good luck or confess to sin. The offering would vary according to the purposes. The priest would be getting a share of the offering, and it should always be the best available.

The Ordination of Aaron and His Sons

Moses gathered all the Israelites at the entrance of the courtyard. He introduced to them Aaron and his four sons and said they would serve God. He washed and dressed them in their formal robes.

Next, he anointed with oil the Tabernacle and everything there. He then dressed Aaron in his sacred garments and anointed him as a high priest. Next, he dressed Aaron's sons in their sacred garments.

Moses then proceeded with the sacrifices, a bull for a sin offering and a ram for a burnt offering.

They put their hands on the bull's head to give it all their sins, and then Moses killed it. This took away their sins. After that, Moses spread the bull's blood on and around the altar.

Next, they put their hands on the head of the ram, again to take away their sins. Then Moses killed it and sprinkled its blood around the altar. And burnt the ram on the altar.

They took another ram, laid on their hands and then Moses killed it. The blood was drained, and Moses put it on Aaron's right ear, thumb and big toe. Then he did the same with each son. Finally, the rest of the blood was sprinkled around the altar.

They proceeded with the ritual, using bread and finished with Moses sprinkling blood and anointing oil onto the garments Aaron and his sons were wearing.

Moses then told them to boil the flesh left by the Tabernacle doorway and eat it with leftover bread. They should stay there before the doorway for seven days as they had now been given to God and made holy. Their male offspring would continue to be the priests for all generations to come.

The Setting Apart of the Levites

Moses separated all the Levites from the other Israelites and made them ceremonially clean after they had washed and shaved their whole bodies. He then told them a man aged between twenty-five and fifty would work performing duties at the Tabernacle. Once they were older, they could help one of their brothers if they wished but had no more formal responsibilities.

The Priests Begin Their Ministry

After the seven days passed, Moses asked the tribal elders to join Aaron and his sons. They took a bull calf, a ram, a male goat, a calf and a lamb, and an ox and a ram and killed them as they made various offerings. Moses guided them so they understood the required rituals they had to perform. Aaron spread blood onto the altar, and when they slaughtered the animals, they cut out the fat portions for burning on the altar. Finally, Aaron lifted his hands and blessed the elders.

Moses and Aaron went into the Tabernacles and returned to the altar to give a blessing. As they did, just like a magic trick, they quietly poured oil onto the fat portions. It suddenly caught fire, and a great flame rose into the sky, and all the people watching were amazed.

And so the Priests began their ministry.

Offerings at the Dedication of the Tabernacle

Then the elders of the tribes made offerings. They brought as their gifts six covered carts and twelve oxen— an ox from each leader and a cart from every two. These they presented before the tabernacle.

Moses accepted them for the use of the Levi at the Tabernacle. He gave:

- Two carts and four oxen to the Gershonite family of Levis.
- Four carts and eight oxen to the Merarite family of Levis, as their work required more effort.

The Kohathites family of Levi required none because they had to carry the special items.

The moving of the Tabernacle would be under the direction of Ithamar, son of Aaron.

When the altar was anointed, each elder brought offerings for its dedication and presented them before the altar. Each brought the same offering comprising:

- Grain Offering: A silver plate and sprinkling bowl weighing two hundred shekels (2.2 Kg), filled with a mixture of fine flour and oil. A gold bowl weighing ten shekels (110 grams) filled with incense.
- Burnt Offering: A young bull, a ram and a one-year-old male lamb.
- Sin Offering: A male goat
- Fellowship offering: Two oxen, five rams, five male goats and five male lambs a year old.

The Death of Nadab and Abihu

Aaron's sons, Nadab and Abihu, took their censers, filled them with oil and incense and then set light to them. This was contra to how God had said it should be done. A flame came out from the presence of God, and they were both burnt to death.

Moses told Aaron that they should have been more careful. As Aaron remained silent, Moses called his cousins, Mishael and Elzaphan (sons of his uncle Uzziel) and told them to carry the bodies of Nadab and Abihu outside the camp.

Then he told Aaron and his sons Eleazar and Ithamar that they must not let their hair become unkempt or tear their clothes, or they would die if the flame caught them. He also told them the dangers of wine and fermented drink, as it would kill them in the Tabernacle.

Moses then told Aaron and his two remaining sons to take the leftovers from the Tabernacles and eat them by the altar. But Aaron said he did not feel like eating anything.

The Day of Atonement

Following the death of Aaron's two sons, Moses decided they would have strict rules to prevent it from happening again. He decided that only the High Priest would enter the inner sanctuary area once a year to put blood on the Ark. They would call that day 'The Day of Atonement', and it would mark the day that Aaron's two sons died. It would take place on the tenth day of the seventh month, and no work would be done on that day like a Sabbath.

On that day, sin offerings would be made, including two goats, one of which would be selected as a scapegoat to be sent into the countryside.

A Blasphemer is Stoned

A fight broke out in the camp between two men. One was an Israelite, and the other was the son of an Egyptian and Shelomith, daughter of Dibri, of the tribe of Dan.

Shelomith's son had sworn and blasphemed against the tabernacle and God. So he was taken to Moses so he could decide what to do with him.

Moses said he should be taken outside the camp, everyone who heard what he said should place their hands on his head, and then everyone should stone him to death.

He told them that if anyone blasphemes or curses in the name of their God, then that person must be put to death. The same rules applied to a foreigner and an Israelite.

Moses reminded them of the law, "Fracture for fracture, eye for an eye, tooth for a tooth". If a man wrongly kills another, then he must be put to death. A life for a life.

After Moses finished speaking, they all took the blasphemer outside and stoned him to death.

NUMBERS

The Census

The tribes needed to be organised for travelling and to defend themselves against any enemies they encountered. An army of men over the age of twenty had to be established.

On the first day of the second month of the second year after they had left Egypt, God told Moses he needed to take a detailed census. This was to record the number of men who were twenty or more years old and would make up the army. They would record the men by clan and father's house. While in the desert of Sinai, Moses and Aaron, helped by the Leader of each tribe, carried out the census.

The total number of men aged twenty or over was 6098 during the first census and, for comparison, some 6305 during the later second census. *The population during the first census was probably no more than 21,000 rising to some 22,000 during the second census.*

The tribe of Levi was not counted, as it was not to be part of the army. The tribe was in charge of the tabernacle, striking it before moving, carrying it to its new location and its re-erection. They provided a guarding, judicial, and civil service function and had standing instructions to put any non-Levi to death who wrongly went near the Tabernacle. This was to prevent God from getting angry.

Table 32: Numbers of Levites from 1st and 2nd Census

Tribe / Order of birth	1st Census Males over one-month-old		2nd Census Males over one-month-old		Tribe Leader during 1st Census	Camp / order of march
	Troops	Men	Troops	Men		
Levi - Gershon	7	500*			Eliasaph, son of Lael	Center
Levi - Kohath	8	300*			Elizaphan, son of Uzziel	Center
Levi - Merari	6	200*			Zuriel, son of Abihail	Center
Levi Total	**21**	**1000***	**23**	**1000**	**Aaron, son of Amram**	

* total adjusted from those mentioned in Numbers to allow for error. Levite numbers are from one month old.

The tables below show the Tribal numbers, including those from the second census:-

Table 33: Number of the Tribes from 1st and 2nd Census

Tribe / Order of birth	1st Census men over 20		2nd Census men over 20		Tribe Leader during 1st Census	Camp / order of march
	Troops	Men	Troops	Men		
Reuben (1st)	46	500	43	730	Elizur, son of Shedeur	South / 2
Simeon (2nd)	59	300	22	200	Shelumiel, son of Zurishaddai	South / 2
Gad (7th)	45	600	40	500	Eliasaph, son of Deuel	South / 2
Judah (4th)	74	600	76	500	Nahshon, son of Amminadab	East / 1
Issachar (9th)	54	400	64	300	Nethanel, son of Zuar	East / 1
Zebulun (10th)	57	400	60	500	Eliab, son of Helon	East / 1
Joseph / Ephraim (11th)	40	500	32	500	Elishama, son of Ammihud	West / 3
Joseph / Manasseh (11th)	32	200	52	700	Gamaliel, son of Pedahzur	West / 3
Benjamin (12th)	35	400	45	600	Abidan, son of Gideoni	West / 3
Dan (5th)	62	700	64	400	Ahiezer, son of Ammishaddai	North / 4
Asher (8th)	41	500	53	400	Pagiel, son of Ocran	North / 4
Naphtali (6th)	53	400	45	400	Ahira, son of Enan	North / 4
TOTAL	598	5500	596	5730		

The Arrangement of the Tribal Camps

Moses planned out the arrangement for the tribal camps around the tabernacle.

The Levites were located in the middle around the Tabernacle, with the other tribe camps to the north, south, east and west.

Each man would be under family and division ensigns and standards.

Table 34: Layout of Tribal Camps and march order

Location	Lead Tribe	Other tribes	March order	Tribe total
East	Judah	Issachar and Zebulun	1	1400
South	Reuben	Simeon and Gad	2	1450
Middle	Levi	-		See below
West	Ephraim	Manasseh and Benjamin	3	1100
North	Dan	Asher and Naphtali	4	1600
Total				5550

* total adjusted from those mentioned in Numbers to allow for error.

The Levites

Moses and Aaron were from the clan of Kohath of the tribe of Levi, so it was natural to look after their family's interests by giving them the best jobs. Moses gave Aaron the tribe to help him in his duties as High Priest. They would look after all of the tabernacle and its administration.

Two of Aaron's sons had been killed following an accidental fire in the Tabernacle, leaving Eleazar and Ithamar to serve as priests during the lifetime of their father, Aaron.

Moses counted every male, one month or older, of the Levites by their families and clans. Later he counted the men between thirty to fifty years old, as they would be working in the Tabernacle. Then, finally, he set them responsibilities for when the Tabernacle was to be moved.

Moses, Aaron and his sons camped east of the tabernacle. They were in front of the Tent of Meeting, towards sunrise. They were responsible for the overall care of the Tabernacle. Anyone else who approached the Tabernacle would be put to death.

When Moses counted the number of Levites aged one month or more, they totalled 1000. He then counted all the firstborn Hebrews who were one month or more, and they totalled 1,273—a difference of 273.

Moses had claimed the firstborn of man, or animal, as a tax and the price for bringing the Hebrews out. So now he exchanged all the Levites for the firstborn male offspring of every Hebrew woman so that the Levites would be his servants. He would also swap all the livestock as well.

He calculated that the 273 men difference would require an extra payment from the Hebrews. So he asked for 5 shekels for each one, making a total of 1,365 shekels.

Moses collected the redemption money from those who exceeded the number redeemed by the Levites. Then, he gave Aaron and his sons the money for the tabernacle.

Table 35: The numbers and responsibilities allocated to the clans.

Clan	Gershon	Kohath	Merari
Names of Clan	Libnites and Shimeites	Amramites, Izharites, Hebronites and Uzzielites	Mahlites and Mushites
Leader	Eliasaph son of Lael	Elizaphan son of Uzziel	Zuriel son of Abihail
Number in clan over one month old*	500	300	200
Aged 30 – 50*	195	117	78
Camp location	West behind the tabernacle	South side of the tabernacle	North side of the tabernacle
Responsible for	Care of the tabernacle and tent, its coverings, The Curtains: <ul><li>at the entrance to the Tent of Meeting,</li><li>of the courtyard,</li><li>at the entrance to the courtyard surrounding the tabernacle and altar,</li></ul> The ropes Everything related to their use	Care of the sanctuary. Care of the ark, the table, the lampstand, the altars, the articles of the sanctuary used in ministering, The curtain, Everything related to their use.	Care of the frames of the tabernacle, its crossbars, posts, bases, all its equipment The posts of the surrounding courtyard with their bases, tent pegs and ropes. Everything related to their use.
Priest responsible	Ithamar, son of Aaron	Eleazar, son of Aaron	Ithamar, son of Aaron

* total adjusted from those mentioned in Numbers to allow for error.

The Kohathites Levites

Aaron and his sons would go into the tabernacle when the camp was to move. They would prepare the contents to be moved as follows:-

Table 36: Packing up of the Tabernacle

Item	Cover	Accessories	2nd Covering	Final wrapping
Ark of Testimony	Cover with shielding curtain		Spread a cloth of solid blue over it.	Cover with dugong skin and put the poles in place.
Table of Presence	Spread blue cloth over.	Place on this the plates, dishes, bowls, jars for drink offerings; the bread that is continually there is to remain on it.	Spread over these a scarlet cloth.	Cover with hides of sea cows and put its poles in place
Lampstands, lamps, wick trimmers, trays, jars for oil.			Cover with blue cloth	Cover with dugong skin and put on a carrying frame
Gold Altar	Spread blue cloth over.			Cover with dugong skin and put its poles in place
Articles used for ministering in the sanctuary	Wrap them in a blue cloth			Cover with dugong skin and put on a carrying frame
The bronze altar	Spread a purple cloth over	Place on it all the utensils used for ministering at the altar, including the firepans, meat forks, shovels and sprinkling bowls		Cover with dugong skin and put its poles in place

After the wrapping had been finished, when the camp was ready to move, Aaron and his sons would allocate each Kohathite an item to carry. The Kohathites were told not to touch or look at special items because they would die.

Eleazar, the priest, was put in charge of the entire tabernacle and everything in it. He looked after the oil for the lamps, the fragrant incense, the regular grain offering and the anointing oil.

The Silver Trumpets

Moses ordered the making of two trumpets of hammered silver. They would be used for calling the Hebrews and for marching out from camp.

The sons of Aaron, the priests, would blow the trumpets, which would be their responsibility forevermore. Different sounds would mean different orders as follows:

Table 37: Trumpet Sounds

Trumpet sound.	Purpose
Both Trumpets blown	All Hebrews to assemble at the entrance to the courtyard of the Tabernacle
One Trumpet blown	The Leaders, Heads of clans, are to come to Moses.
When an Alarm is blown	The tribes camping in the east are to move off.
When a second alarm is blown	The tribes camping in the south are to move off.
Blow the trumpets when in battle	God will remember you and save you from your enemies.
Sound Trumpets at times of rejoicing over offerings at Appointed Feasts.	So they will be a memorial for you.

Hobab the Midianite

Moses' brother-in-law Hobab the Midianite, decided to leave the Hebrews and return to his land and people. Moses said the Hebrews were going to the *'Promised Land'*, and he should join them. He would be able to help them as he knew where to camp in the desert and could be their eyes. We will share with you whatever good things we find. Finally, he decided to stay with them.

The Israelites Leave Sinai

On the twentieth day of the second month of the second year, the fire was put out at the tabernacle, and the Hebrews set out from Mount Sinai. The Ark of Covenant went before them. They travelled from place to place until, after three days, they came to rest in the Desert of Paran. They travelled in the order Moses had told them :

Table 38: Order of March from Mount Sinai

Order of March	Tribe / Division / Duty	In Command
1st	Judah	Nahshon, son of Amminadab
2nd	Issachar,	Nethanel son of Zuar
3rd	Zebulun.	Eliab, son of Helon
4th	The tabernacle was taken down. Gershonites and Merarites, who carried it, set out.	
5th	Reuben	Elizur son of Shedeur
6th	Simeon,	Shelumiel son of Zurishaddai
7th	Gad.	Eliasaph son of Deuel

8th	Kohathites set out, carrying the holy things. The tabernacle was to be set up before they arrived.	
9th	Ephraim	Elishama, son of Ammihud
10th	Manasseh	Gamaliel son of Pedahzur
11th	Benjamin	Abidan son of Gideoni
12th	Dan	Ahiezer son of Ammishaddai
13th	Asher.	Pagiel, son of Ocran
14th	Naphtali	Ahira, son of Enan

Fire at the Camp

The people started complaining about the sudden hardship of living in the desert. A fire started on the outskirts of the camp, and it took some time to put out because of limited water. They called the place 'Taberah' because of the fire. They moved on.

More moaning about lack of meat

The people started to moan about the lack of meat. They talked about their days in Egypt when they had fish to eat, cucumbers, melons, leeks, onions and garlic. But, all they ate was what they found around them and the 'Manna', which they were sick of.

All Moses could hear was their moaning, and he got angry. Why had he burdened himself with all these people? Finally, he got so depressed with the problem he thought he would sooner die than be surrounded by such moaning people.

As it approached the time of year when the migrating quails would pass by, he called together the seventy Hebrew elders to the Tent of Meeting.

At the meeting, he told them he was fed up with all the moaning and that the elders must help him carry the burden of the various problems. He said that over the next couple of days, there would be so much meat for them to eat it would last them a whole month, and there would be so much they would be sick of eating it.

The Elders wondered how Moses intended to feed the people for a month on meat when they did not have enough flocks and herds. Would everyone be going to the sea and fishing? Moses told them to return to the camp and wait and see.

However, two elders, Eldad and Medad, did not attend Moses' meeting. They realised they knew all that had been said there and told others they could prophesy. A young man ran and told Moses of this unusual event, but Joshua thought they should be stopped from saying such things.

Moses looked at him and said, "I wish everyone could do that, as it would make my life easier".

The Quails return

Within a few days, the quail migration arrived, and thousands upon thousands of tired quails flew by just above the ground. The Hebrews went out and caught them and gathered as many as possible. They killed them and dried them on the ground to preserve them. But those who ate them quickly became ill, and a number died.

They called the place Kibroth Hattaavah, meaning *'Graves of the greedy'*.

From Kibroth Hattaavah, the people travelled to Hazeroth and stayed there.

Miriam and Aaron Oppose Moses

Miriam and Aaron began a family argument with Moses about his first wife, from Cush. He had married her when he was young, and now she was a point of conflict with his later wife.

But the argument continued onto other subjects. They accused him of stealing their good ideas and giving the impression to the Hebrews that he was very clever.

Moses decided to confront them and called them to the Tabernacle. The three had a good argument about how the command structure worked and who was in charge of what.

All three of them could not receive different words from God.

- Moses was the leader, and he would be the only one to hear the word of God,
- Aaron and Miriam would have to tell the Hebrews they had dreams, visions, or prophecies.

Miriam becomes ill

Miriam became so stressed she turned pale and was clearly ill with 'Tzaraath'. Aaron was concerned about Miriam's health and told Moses they had been wrong and Miriam needed immediate rest. Moses said she could rest outside the camp for seven days, and the priest would ensure she was well before they moved on.

When Miriam had recovered, they moved on from Hazeroth through the Desert of Sin to the Desert of Paran.

Exploring Canaan

Moses suggested they send scouts to Canaan to learn about the 'Promised Land'. They should bring back reports on the following:-

- The number of people - whether they are strong or weak-natured.
- The type of towns they live in - Are they unwalled or fortified?
- The quality of the land - Whether good or poor for crops
- Are there trees and fruits - Bring some samples back as well, as it was 'September' when first-ripe grapes could be found.

The Scouts were selected

Moses suggested that one senior person from each tribe should go. So the following were selected: -

Table 39: Selected Scouts

Tribe	Name	Son of		Tribe	Name	Son of
Reuben	Shammua	Zaccur		**Zebulun**	Gaddiel	Sodi
Simeon	Shaphat	Hori		**Manasseh**	Gaddi	Susi
Judah	Caleb	Jephunneh		**Dan**	Ammiel	Gemalli
Issachar	Igal	Joseph		**Asher**	Sethur	Michael
Ephraim	Joshua	Nun		**Naphtali**	Nahbi	Vophsi
Benjamin	Palti	Raphu		**Gad**	Geuel	Maki

The scouts went up through the Desert of Zin, passing the Negev, then onto Hebron and as far as north as Rehob and Hamath.

While at Hebron, they saw, Ahiman, Sheshi and Talmai, giants who they thought were descendants of Anak.

(The Hebrews noted that they thought Hebron was built seven years before Zoan in Egypt).

At the end of forty days of exploring the Promised Land, they return to the Hebrews.

Moving camp

In the meantime, the Hebrews had moved onto Kadesh Barnea via the Mount Seir road, which took them eleven days. Then, finally, they travelled from Hazeroth and camped in the Desert of Paran.

They moved and camped at Libnah, Rissah, Kehelathah, Mount Shepher, Haradah, Makheloth, Tahath, Terah, Mithcah, Hashmonah, Moseroth, Bene Jaakan, Hor Haggidgad, Jotbathah, Abronah, Ezion Geber and

Kadesh, in the Desert of Zin. Kadesh Barnea is situated in the hills south of the Promised Lands. The Amorites occupied it.

Report on the Exploration

When they returned to Moses, and the Hebrews then camped at Kadesh Barnea, they showed the people all the fruits they had found.

Near Hebron, at the Valley of Eschol, they cut a branch from a grapevine with a cluster of grapes so large it required two people to carry it with a pole. They also brought pomegranates and figs and said the land flowed with milk and honey.

The land was occupied as follows:

- The Amalekites occupy the lands to the south,
- the Hittites, Jebusites and Amorites live in the hill country,
- The Canaanites live by the sea and along the Jordan River.

One of the Scouts, Caleb, said to Moses, "We should go at once and take the land". But the others explained that the people they had seen were large and powerful, with large and well-fortified cities.

They had also seen Nephilims, giants, descendants of Anak, and in their sight, the Hebrews looked like mere grasshoppers.

The People Rebel

The Hebrews were very upset by what they had heard and began to plot against Moses and Aaron. They were angry because they had left Egypt for a land of Milk and Honey, but it turned out to be full of giants and huge cities with walls up to the sky. So they would all be killed and their wives and children taken as plunder.

They decided they should choose a new leader and go back to Egypt.

When Moses and Aaron heard this, they fell down in despair in front of the Hebrews. But Joshua and Caleb, two of the scouts, again told the Elders how it would be good to live in the land, and they should proceed. But the Hebrews started talking about stoning Moses and Aaron.

Death of the Scouts

Moses and Aaron pondered on the immediate problem. Then, finally, they decided they needed to teach the Hebrews a lesson to prevent them from treating them with contempt.

The ten scouts who came with negative reports would be poisoned, so the Hebrews believed they had suddenly died from a pestilence.

Moses was tempted to kill lots of them but decided otherwise. He thought the Egyptians would hear of it and believe the Hebrew god had killed them because he could not bring them into the Promised Land.

Moses speaks to Caleb and Joshua

Moses decided to speak to the Hebrews the following day. But, first, he promised Caleb and Joshua that they and their offspring would possess the Promised Land.

Ten Scouts are found dead

The following morning, the tens scouts were dead, and the Hebrews were terrified of what they had done to upset their God.

Moses took control and called the people together.

Moses address the Israelites

Moses told them their God would not let them enter the Promised Land because of their attitude, and he could not lead them.

They would have to wait one year for every day the scouts had been away, and they could then enter the Promised Land. (Forty days away would mean forty years).

But by then, anyone over twenty would probably be dead.

Back to the Desert

In the meantime, as the Amalekites and Canaanites were living in the valleys, they should all turn back and go towards the desert along the route to the Red Sea.

The real reason to wait forty Years

Moses and Aaron knew the Hebrews needed to increase in numbers and physical strength before they could attack the Promised Land and take the land.

The land where the Israelites were located was described as a 'Desert' or 'Wilderness'. This was scrubland with areas of pasture. The number of animals required for sacrifice was considerable, as set out in the new Laws. The celebration of the Passover would also require a large number of goats or lambs. The animals would provide meat, milk, skin and bone for clothing. Fertiliser from animal and human waste would help enrich the soil and any available plants and shrubs.

Defeat by Amalekites and Canaanites

However, some Hebrews disregarded Moses and went into the Promised Land. Moses told them they would be defeated without his leadership, but they ignored him.

They armed themselves, thinking it would be easy to walk into the land and defeat anyone living there. But the Amalekites and Canaanites attacked them and chased them like a swarm of bees all the way to Hormah.

The Hebrews stayed near Kadesh for a few days before moving on.

Korah, Dathan, Abiram and On.

A group of some 250 Hebrew men decided to challenge Moses. They were led by the following :

- *Korah, a Levi from the clan of Kohath,*
- *Dathan, and his brother Abiram, both Reubenites*
- *On, another Reubenites*

The group was made up of well-known leaders appointed by the Hebrew Elders.

They approached Moses and Aaron and asked why they had put themselves above the Elders, like Kings and now made all the decisions.

Moses was shocked when he heard this. He told Korah, and his followers, that he would show them tomorrow why he and Aaron were the leaders.

Moses speaks to Korah

He then spoke to Korah and the other Levites in the group and told them they had gone too far. They were all privileged being Levites as they were separated from the rest of the tribes and benefited greatly from this and had an easy life as Kohathites. He just could not understand why they were trying to cause trouble for the priests and upset Aaron.

Moses tries to speak to Dathan and Abiram

Moses then summoned Dathan and Abiram to have a private word with them. They refused and sent a reply to Moses, saying:

- He had promised them a land of milk and honey, and they now saw death in the desert.
- Moses had not given them anything as an inheritance, like the fields and vineyards he had promised.
- Moses had benefited as he had set himself up as a Prince over them.

Moses arranges meeting at Tabernacle

Moses final told Korah and his followers to appear at the Entrance to the Tabernacle the following day, and each man should bring his bronze censer with fire and incense and present it to him. Following this, they would sort the matter out.

Moses and Aaron met Korah and his group

The next day at the Tabernacle, Moses and Aaron stood at the entrance while Korah and his group presented their censers as requested. Moses spoke to the Hebrew onlookers and told them to move away from the wicked men who had challenged their authority. But, he added, "don't touch anything which is theirs". So they all moved away.

Moses tells Dathan and Abiram they will die

Moses went, with the elders, to see Dathan and Abiram, who stood at the entrance to their tents with their wives and families. Moses spoke to them and said,

> "You have all challenged my authority. You will now die as the ground will open up and swallow you. But if nothing happens, you will know that I am not your real leader."

The ground caves in

As he spoke, the ground caved in under the tents of Korah, Dathan and Abiram, and all their families fell into the hole and were covered entirely by running sand. A fire then spread and consumed the 250 men as they stood nearby with their burning censers. The Hebrews saw the ground was unstable and ran away in case it collapsed under them as well.

Eleazar told to overlay the altar with bronze

Later that day, Moses spoke to Aaron's son, Eleazar, the priest and told him to get all the censers he could find from the 250 followers and get the bronze hammered into sheets to overlay the altar to enrich it. In addition, Moses said that nobody but a Levite should, from now on, burn any incense.

Hebrews unhappy with Moses and Aaron

The following day the Hebrews had sorted out the camp but were still grumbling about Moses and Aaron. They accused them of killing fellow Hebrews the previous day. The Hebrews started to gather outside the Tabernacle as Moses and Aaron watched.

Moses poisons more Hebrews

Moses thought he would put an end to them and their selfish attitudes. Instead, water for drinking was poisoned, and the Hebrews started to drop with illness as if a plague was passing through the camp. Moses told them they would all die unless their attitude changed toward him and Aaron.

The Hebrews all fell on their faces and asked him to forgive them and save them from the illness.

On seeing this, Moses told Aaron to take some fire from the altar, burn incense in the censer, and go among the people to kill the plague. Slowly, the 'plague' stopped before more died from illness. This was in addition to those who died due to Korah, Dathan, Abiram and On.

The Budding of Aaron's Staff

Moses decided to finally sort the Hebrews out and show them God would choose who he wished to deal with for himself.

Secretly Moses would perform another magic trick to show them the Levites were special and should be the priests.

He told the leaders of each tribe to bring their staff to the Tabernacle. He then wrote their name on to each staff. Then he added Aaron's staff with his name also written on it. Finally, Moses told them only one staff would sprout with leaves and flowers, and its owner would be the tribe God had selected to be priests.

The staffs were left in the Tabernacle overnight. The following day, Moses brought them out so all the Tribe Leaders could see what had happened.

They all saw that only Aaron's staff had sprouted with leaves, flowers and almonds. All the Elders went quiet, and everyone stopped grumbling.

They thought that if they came near the tabernacle, they would die and were worried about who would be next.

Moses said to the Hebrews that Aaron's staff would now be kept in the Tabernacle as a sign of the rebellion.

The Sabbath-Breaker Put to Death

Some Hebrews spotted a man gathering sticks for a fire on the Sabbath. He was brought before Moses and Aaron because they did not know what to do with him.

Moses told them the man had broken one of the most important Hebrew laws, that of working on the Sabbath. Therefore, he had to be put to death, and all the Hebrews should join in his stoning outside the camp. So he was taken outside the camp and stoned to death for breaking one of the laws.

Then they all felt better!

Death of Miriam

The Hebrews arrived at Kadesh in the Desert of Zin during the first month of the fortieth year since leaving Egypt. Here Miriam died and was buried.

Water from the Rock

The Hebrews found no water for them or their animals, and they again became very angry with Moses and Aaron.

They quarrelled with Moses and said,

> "We wish we had died with our brothers. Why have you brought us to this desert? So we and our livestock can die here? Why did you bring us from Egypt to this terrible place? It has no grain or figs, grapevines or pomegranates. And there is no water to drink!"

Moses and Aaron went into the Tabernacle to think of what to do. Somehow they had to find water for all the people and their animals. Moses knew that the 'Waters of Meribah' famous springs at Kadesh must still be there but somehow covered. So Moses took his staff and went off to look for them.

Moses finds the springs

Later he returned and asked Aaron to gather the Elders and bring them to a nearby area of rocks he had found.

As they gathered, Moses addressed them. He said to them, "Listen, you rebels, shall I bring water out of this rock for you?"

Moses hit the rock face with his staff, and water began to flow from the springs again. Finally, all the Hebrews and their animals could get water to drink.

Were the Hebrews Helpless?

Moses reflected on the Hebrew's inability to find water or help themselves. He could not see them settling in the Promised Land.

Moses asks Edom for passage

Moses decided they had made their way around the hill country long enough and would turn north. They would pass through the land of Edom, occupied by descendants of Esau. So he sent a messenger to the King of Edom to tell the history of the Hebrews in Egypt and to ask permission to cross his land using the King's Highway. They would go quickly straight through without taking water or food.

(The King's Highway was a significant trade route from Egypt, across the Sinai Peninsula to Aqaba, then across Jordan, past Petra to Damascus and onto the Euphrates River.)

Edom refuses

The king was afraid of them because there were so many of them. So he sent an army to the border to prevent them from entering his land and sent the messenger back with his refusal. So the Hebrews had to go around the Kingdom of Edom using the desert road of Moab. The Hebrews from that time disliked Edom.

The Death of Aaron

All the Hebrew set out from Kadesh and came to Mount Hor near the border of Edom. Moses realised his brother Aaron was shortly going to die and would not enter the Promised Land.

Moses got Eleazar to help take his father to the top of the mountain.

There, Moses stripped Aaron of his garments and put them onto Eleazar.*

Aaron died there on top of Mount Hor in the 40th year, on the 1st day of the 5th month.

Moses and Eleazar returned to the Hebrews, and they all mourned for thirty days.

(*We hope the loss of his clothes did not accelerate Aaron's death!)

ONTO THE PROMISED LAND

The Command to Leave Horeb
In the fortieth year, on the first day of the eleventh month, Moses decided they had stayed on the mountain long enough and should break camp and advance into the Promised Land.

Arad Destroyed
When the Canaanite king of Arad, who lived in the Negev, heard that the Hebrews were coming along the road to Atharim, he ambushed them and captured a number of them. The Hebrews attacked the Canaanites at Hormah and destroyed them and their towns.

Hebrews continue moaning
The Hebrews travelled from Mount Hor to the Red Sea to go around Edom. The people were very impatient and again started to grumble about Moses. They again asked why he had brought them out of Egypt to die in the desert. They had no bread or water and hated Manna.

Snake bites
As they grumbled, they started to find poisonous snakes in their camp and many people died from bites. They begged Moses to help them and make the snakes go away.

The Bronze Snake - Nehushtan
Moses made a bronze snake and put it up on a pole. He told them that anyone bitten could look at the bronze snake, which would cure them, and they would live.

(This bronze serpent was later called 'Nehushtan' when placed in the Temple complex. This represented the Serpent in Eden. This story was probably a later insertion to explain the Serpent. King Hezekiah later smashed the bronze serpent when initiating his religious reforms in 715BC. The name 'Nehushtan' means 'a piece of brass')

The Journey to Moab
The Hebrews moved on and camped at Oboth, then Iye-Abarim, in the desert that faces east towards Moab.

Moses told the Hebrews that the Moabites were the descendants of Lot and his incestuous daughters. Their history said the Hebrew god had given them their land. Therefore they could not take any of it. From there, the Hebrews moved on and camped in the Zered Valley.

Moses noted as they crossed the Zered Valley that it was thirty-eight years since they left Kadesh Barnea. The entire generation of rebellious men (twenty years old and over) had died. He would now lead them towards the Promised Land.

They left the Zered Valley and camped on the other side of the River Arnon, which marks the border of the lands between Moab and the Amorites.

(The Book of the Wars of God says, "Veheb in Suphah, the valleys of the Arnon, the slope of the valleys that incline towards the dwelling of Ar, leans on the border of Moab.")

Onto the Well at Beer

From there, they all continued onto Beer, where Moses had heard there was a well.

When they found the well, the Hebrews sang this song:

> *"Spring up Well to our song,*
> *Dug by our elders and leaders,*
> *Using their staffs and sceptres."*

From the wilderness, they went to Mattanah, then onto Nahaliel and Bamoth. From Bamoth, they moved onto the valley, the field of Moab, and then to the mountain range of which the top of Pisgah overlooks the desert.

The Defeat of King Sihon

While in the desert of Kedemoth, Moses sent messengers to Sihon, king of the Amorites at Heshbon. They asked for permission to travel through his lands using the *'King's Highway'*, saying they would not enter a field or vineyard and did not need water from their wells.

Sihon would not let them pass through his lands and took an army to meet the Hebrews at Jahaz. There he was defeated and killed. The Hebrews captured all his land from the Arnon River to the Jabbok River.

Spies go to Jazer

Moses sent spies into Jazer and later captured the town and drove out all the people. Then, they took all the remaining towns and killed all the men, women and children, leaving no survivors. Then, they destroyed the towns taking with them the plunder and livestock.

Moab God did not save Moab People

The Hebrews were not concerned about capturing the land as they knew the Amorites had taken this land from the Moabs. The Moab God, 'Chemosh', had done nothing to save the Moab people.

The defeat of King Og

The Hebrew army then moved north towards Bashan and was met at Edrei by Og, the king of Bashan, with his whole army.

The Hebrews defeated them and captured all of the king's sixty towns. Some had been fortified with high walls, gates and bars.

They killed all the residents, including women and children. They destroyed the towns, including those on the plateau, Gilead, and Bashan, as far as Salecah and Edrei, taking the plunder and livestock with them.

The Hebrews captured the lands of two kings on the east of the Jordon. This land stretched from Arnon Gorge in the south to Mount Hermon in the north.

King Og's Bed

They found King Og's bed and realised it was made of iron and over four metres long by two metres wide. Everyone could see he must have been a giant.

News of his defeat started to worry all the kings of other nations.

Balak Summons Balaam

The Hebrews moved onto the plains of Moab and camped next to the Jordan opposite Jericho.

The King of Moab, Balak, son of Zippor, knew what they had done to the Amorites and was terrified. He told the elders of Midianites that the Hebrews would soon take everything they had, like Oxen eating grass in a field.

Balak decided to send messengers to Balaam, the son of Beor, who lived at Pethor in Mesopotamia on the banks of the Euphrates. Balaam was a man of peace who cursed or blessed people for a fee. Balak wanted Balaam to come and curse the Hebrews so that he could attack and defeat them.

Balaam turns down request

The messengers travelled and met Balaam. They explained what Balak wanted, and Balaam asked to consider their request overnight. The following morning he told the messengers that he could not curse the Hebrews. So the messengers returned to Balak and told him what was said.

Balaam asked again

Balak sent back some elders of the Moabite and Midianites to put another proposal to Balaam. They promised him whatever he wanted as long as he came and cursed the Hebrews.

He told them he could only say what his God told him to do, no more, no less, even if he was offered a house full of silver and gold.

Once they agreed with the term, Balaam packed, ready to travel back with them to meet Balak.

Balaam's Donkey

The following morning, Balaam saddled his donkey, and they set off to travel back to meet Balak.

His donkey knew Balaam was wrong in going and tried to divert him.

- *First, as Balaam rode along with his servants, the donkey walked off into a field. Balaam had to beat her to get her back onto the road.*
- *Then, while going through a narrow path between two vineyards with walls on both sides, the donkey pressed Balaam's foot hard against the wall. So Balaam again beat her.*
- *Then later, the donkey stopped walking and just laid down, and Balaam again beat her.*

Then suddenly, the donkey spoke to him and said,

"What have I done that makes you beat me three times?"

Balaam was very surprised and said to the donkey that she had made a fool of him and he would have killed her if he had a sword.

The donkey said,

"I am the donkey you have ridden every day, so have I been in the habit of doing this to you?"

Balaam said truthfully, *"No".*

Balaam understand the donkey's words

Then Balaam suddenly saw the meaning and realised his path was reckless, and he should go back home.

But he decided, in the end, to go on and meet Balak but only to speak when he needed to.

Balak when out to meet Balaam as he approached. He asked Balaam why he did not come when first requested. Balaam told him he had come now.

Balak and Balaam overlook the Hebrews

The following morning Balak took Balaam and the elders to Kiriath Huzoth, where he sacrificed some cattle and sheep and had a good meal. Then he took Balaam to Bamoth Baal, the highland overlooking the plain of Moab, so that they could look down on the mass of Hebrews.

Balaam's First Oracle

Balaam told Balak to build seven altars and prepare seven bulls and rams to be jointly offered in sacrifice. They made sacrifices in the view of the Moab elders.

Balaam then told Balak to stay by the burning offering and went again to overlook the Hebrews. When he returned, he told Balak he could not curse the Hebrews. The Hebrews did not live as part of Balak nations, and there was no reason to condemn them.

He had looked down on so many Hebrew people. They were like the dust of the earth set out on four sides around their tabernacle.

Balak was very surprised and thought, *"Balaam was hired to curse my enemies, not to praise them."*

Balaam's Second Oracle

Balak asked him to come to another place where only part of the Hebrews could be seen. He wanted to know if he had different opinions there.

Balak took him to the field of Zophim on the top of the Pisgah Hill range, and they again built seven altars and prepared seven bulls and rams for each altar. After the sacrifice, Balaam went again to overlook the Hebrews.

When he returned, he told Balak that their God had blessed them, and it could not be changed. So he has brought them out of Egypt and is with them now. This is because he has the strength of a wild ox.

The Hebrews will destroy the surrounding nations, like a lion who will not lie down until it has eaten its prey and drunk the blood of those it slain.

Balak told Balaam not to curse or bless them, but Balaam said he could only do as his God told him.

Balaam's Third Oracle

Balak then finally took him to the top of Mount Peor. This overlooked the desert, and he hoped Balaam could curse the Hebrews from there. Next, they prepared seven more altars, bulls, and rams for sacrifice.

Balaam looked over the Hebrew camps and thought how beautiful the tribe-by-tribe layout of tents looked. They would stretch out and settle like trees next to a river. Their population would increase, and they will have a king greater than Agag.

They had been brought out of Egypt with the strength of an ox. They will destroy their enemies, breaking their bones in pieces and piercing them with arrows. He will lie down like a lion. Everyone who blesses them will be blessed. Everyone who curses them will be cursed.

Balak got angry and told Balaam he had summoned him to curse his enemies and not bless them. He told him to return home, and his God had prevented him from earning any payment.

Balaam answered Balak and told him he would tell him what the Hebrews would do to his people in the coming days.

Balaam's Fourth Oracle

Balaam now told Balak what the Hebrews would do, in the future, to the Moabites.

- *A king would come from Jacob, and he would strike Moab and kill all the sons of Shut.*
- *The Hebrews would take the lands of Edom and Mount Seir.*
- *The survivors from the town of Ar-Moab would be killed.*

(The Oracle says:

"A star will march forth out of Jacob,
and a sceptre will rise out of Israel."

This is taken as King David beating his neighbours and later as Jesus, the son of David. However, the term 'Star' normally refers to a King.)

Balaam's Final Oracles

Then Balaam looked around and saw an Amalekite and said,

"Amalekites think themselves as the first of nations, but their nation will perish forever".

When he saw a Kenite and said,

"You have built your houses in the rocks, but the Asshurs* will carry you away captive."

Finally, he said, "The isles in the north will assemble ships from the farthest sea, and they will attack Asshur and Eber. But they will themselves suffer destruction."

Then Balaam left Balak and went back home.

(*Asshurs here is a tribe in North Sinai, the neighbours of Kenites. The ship which will attack Asshur and Eber are similar to the Philistine, otherwise known as the 'Sea People'.

Moab Prostitutes seduce Hebrew men

The Hebrews were camped at Shittim on the plain of Moab by the River Jordan. Some men began to enjoy the services of Moabite prostitutes and followed some other Moab practices, including worshipping their god, 'Baal' of Mount Peor. (Baal Peor)

A new plague

The prostitutes started to spread a sexually transmitted disease, a plague, amongst the Hebrew Men. As a result, Moses told the Elders to kill all the Hebrew men who had used one of the infected prostitutes.

Phinehas kills a couple in bed

While Moses was talking outside the Tabernacle, they all saw a Hebrew man bring a Midian woman into the camp. Zimri, a Simeonite, had taken Cozbi, a daughter of Zur, a Midian Chief, to his tent to share her with his brothers.

Phinehas, the priest (Eleazar's son and Aaron's grandson), was enraged by what he saw and took a spear and went to Zimri's tent. There he found Zimri and Cozbi in bed and drove the spear straight through their abdomens in one thrust.

The Plague stops

The plague was soon halted, but many people were now dead.

Moses praised Phinehas for what he had done and told him he, and his offspring, would be blessed with the covenant of peace and everlasting priesthood. In addition, his actions helped make atonement for the plague.

Moses said they should always harass these Midianites and kill them as they had tried to corrupt them with their deceit and wicked ways.

(Note: Moses' wife and father-in-law Jethro are Midianites!)

A further Census

After the plague, Moses and Eleazar, the priest (son of Aaron), decided to take a census of all the Hebrews males by families and organise them again into an army. In addition, they would count those twenty years old or older who could serve in the army of Hebrews. The census took place on the plains of Moab by the Jordan at Jericho.

Only Moses, Caleb, son of Jephunneh and Joshua, son of Nun, remained from those first counted in the Desert of Sinai.

The Second Census

These were the Israelites who came out of Egypt.

Table 40: Numbers of Men over 20 who left Egypt

Tribe	Clan Names of the Tribe	2nd Census men over 20	
		Troops	Men
1). Reuben	Hanoch, the Hanochite; Pallu, the Palluite; Hezron, the Hezronite; Carmi, the Carmite.	43	730
2). Simeon	Nemuel, the Nemuelite; Jamin, the Jaminite; Jakin, the Jakinite; Zerah, the Zerahite; Shaul, the Shaulite	22	200
3). Gad	Zephon, the Zephonite; Haggi, the Haggite; Shuni, the Shunite; Ozni, the Oznite; Eri, the Erite; Arodi, the Arodite; Areli, the Arelite	40	500
4). Judah	Shelah, the Shelanite; Perez, the Perezite; Zerah, the Zerahite. The descendants of Perez were: Hezron, the Hezronite; Hamul, the Hamulite; Er and Onan were sons of Judah, but they died in Canaan.	76	500
5). Issachar	Tola, the Tolaite; Puah, the Puite; Jashub, the Jashubite; Shimron, the Shimronite	64	300
6). Zebulun	Sered, the Seredite; Elon, the Elonite; Jahleel, the Jahleelite	60	500
7). Joseph / Manasseh	Makir, the Makirite (Makir was the father of Gilead); Gilead, the Gileadite. These were the descendants of Gilead: Iezer, the Iezerite; Helek, the Helekite; Asriel, the Asrielite; Shechem, the Shechemite; Shemida, the Shemidaite; Hepher, the Hepherite. (Zelophehad, the son of Hepher, had no sons; he only had daughters. These	52	700

	were named, Mahlah, Noah, Hoglah, Milcah and Tirzah.)		
8). Joseph / Ephraim	Shuthelah, the Shuthelahite; Beker, the Bekerite; Tahan, the Tahanite. These were the descendants of Shuthelah: Eran, the Eranite	32	500
9). Benjamin	Bela, the Belaite; Ashbel, the Ashbelite; Ahiram, the Ahiramite; Shupham, the Shuphamite; Hupham, the Huphamite. The descendants of Bela: Ard, the Ardite clan; Naaman, the Naamite	45	600
10). Dan	Shuham, the Shuhamite	64	400
11). Asher	Imnah, the Imnite; Ishvi, the Ishvite; Beriah, the Beriite; through the descendants of Beriah: Heber, the Heberite; Malkiel, the Malkielite. (Asher had a daughter named Serah.)	53	400
12) Naphtali	Jahzeel, the Jahzeelite; Guni, the Gunite; Jezer, the Jezerite; Shillem, the Shillemite	45	400
	Total	**596**	**5730**
13) Levi*	Gershon, the Gershonite; Kohath, the Kohathite; Merari, the Merarites. These also were Levite clans: the Libnite, the Hebronite, the Mahlite, the Mushite, the Korahite	23	1000

*Levite numbers are from one month old.

Vengeance on the Midianites

Moses was ill and knew he would shortly die. But he wanted the Hebrews to have the best opportunity of settling in the Promised Land.

He decided they should attack the Midianite Army in the area to prevent it from pursuing the Hebrews across the Jordan River. This would also take revenge on them for the sexually transmitted disease their women had spread to the Hebrews.

The army defeats the Midianites

The army made up of all the troops from the tribes numbered over five thousand men. They went into battle accompanied by Phinehas, son of Eleazar, the priest. He brought with him articles from the sanctuary and the trumpets for signalling.

They fought the Midianites and killed:

- All the men of the army
- Five kings of Midian - Evi, Rekem, Zur, Hur and Reba.
- Balaam, son of Beor, was killed with the sword.

They burned all the towns where the Midianites had settled and all their camps.

165

The Hebrews returned to their camps on the plain of Moab with the captured Midianite women and children and took all the Midianite herds, flocks and goods as plunder, intending to present them to Moses and Eleazer.

Hebrew men allowed to keep virgins

Moses became very angry and asked them why they had permitted the women to live. He told them these women followed Balaam's advice and caused the plague on the Hebrew Men.

He told them to kill all the boys and all the women who were not virgins. They could then have these virgins for themselves.

(The test for a virgin was similar to that for a pending bride. But the men might have also taken non-virgins if they liked them.)

Purification of men and plunder

Eleazar, the priest, told the men of war that all those who had killed anyone or touched a dead person would need to go through purification. They must stay outside the camp for seven days, and on the third and seventh days, they must purify themselves and their captives. Anything of theirs that could withstand fire, like Gold, silver, bronze, iron, tin, and lead, must be passed through fire to clean it. Anything else, such as garments made of leather, goat hair or wood that cannot withstand fire, must be purified with water from the priests.

On the seventh day, they would wash their clothes and be clean. They would then be allowed to enter the camp.

Dividing the Spoils

Moses told Eleazar, the priest and the Elders that they should divide the spoils into two equal lots when they counted all the people and animals they had captured. One lot for the soldiers who fought and the rest for the Hebrews.

Spoils for the priests

The Soldiers would give as tribute to the priests, one out of every ten, whether persons, cattle, donkeys, sheep or goats.

The Hebrews would give one out of every five to the Levites, responsible for the care of the tabernacle.

The breakdown was as follows:-

Table 41: Spoils for the Priests

No.	Plunder	Tribute to Eleazar the Priest (10th)	For Levites (5th)	Half share for those who fought in the battle, less Tribute	Half share for the Hebrews, less contribution for the Levites
a		a/10	a/5	a-a/10	a-a/5
6750	Sheep	675	1,350	2,700	2,025
720	Cattle	72	144	288	216
610	Donkeys	61	122	244	183
320	Virgin Women	32	64	128	96
	Gold Handcrafted Articles	1,675			

The officers in charge of the army counted the men who had returned and found no one was missing. Surprised, they took to Moses all the gold articles they had acquired in plunder, armlets, bracelets, signet rings, earrings, and necklaces as a gift to the tabernacle. The total weight of the gold was 1,675 shekels.

The Transjordan Tribes

The tribes of Reubens and Gad were delighted when they saw the lands of Jazer and Gilead. It was perfect for the grazing of their large herds and flocks.

They met with Moses, Eleazar, and the elders of the other tribes - Ataroth, Dibon, Jazer, Nimrah, Heshbon, Elealeh, Sebam, Nebo and Beon.

They asked if they could occupy these lands instead of those in the 'Promised Land'. It would save taking their livestock across the Jordan. More land would, therefore, be available for the other tribes on the west side of the River Jordan.

Moses was concerned. He believed:

- Gad and Reuben were leading another rebellion similar to that at Kedesh Barnea.
- They would discourage the Hebrews from crossing the Jordan into the Promised Land.
- It would be unfair for them to settle while their brothers would fight for the 'Promised Land'.

Moses told them if they settled now and left the other tribes, he would have nothing more to do with them.

(The Promised Land was defined in Genesis as the following: "To your descendants, I give this land, from the river of Egypt to the great river, the Euphrates River —the land of the Kenites, Kenizzites, Kadmonites, Hittites, Perizzites, Rephaites, Amorites, Canaanites, Girgashites, and Jebusites." Therefore the land on the east of the Jordon is already included in the 'Promised Land'. Furthermore, the river of Egypt refers to a seasonal river, not the Nile. Finally, the promise made to Abraham referred to all his descendants, not just this group following Moses!)

Reubens and Gad offer to fight on

The Elders of Reubens and Gad guaranteed the other tribes their continued support. This reassured Moses and the other elders.

If they were allowed to settle, they would arm their men and lead the Hebrews into the Promised Land. They would only return to their land on the east side of the Jordan when the other tribes had settled.

Moses agreed with their offer but warned them that they would only be given land on the Westside among the other tribes if they failed to do this.

Reubens and Gad settle on the Eastside

The Elders of Reubens and Gad wanted to settle their women, children and young and older men on the east side, build livestock pens, and fortify their towns.

Manasseh expresses interest in the Eastside

During their discussions, half of the tribe of Manasseh also said they would like to settle on the east side.

What has to be done with the locals

Moses would tell the Hebrews after they had crossed over the River Jordan to:-

- Drive out all the inhabitants
- Destroy all their stones gods
- Destroy their cast images
- Demolish all their religious site in the mountains.

If they fail, the inhabitants will be thorns in the Hebrew sides and harass them.

Moses agree on arrangements for divisions

Moses then agreed to all the arrangements with the elders of the other tribes, setting out the rules for the division of the new land. First, lots would distribute in proportion to the size of each family.

Moses told the Hebrew Elders that the *'Promised Land'* should be allotted to them based on the numbers in each tribe. The land within each tribal area would be distributed by lot to make it fair for everyone.

The actual assignment of the land would be overseen by Eleazar, Joshua and the following leaders from each tribe.

Table 42: Leaders of Tribes on entering the Promised Land

Name	Son of	Tribe
Caleb	Jephunneh	Judah
Shemuel	Ammihud	Simeon
Elidad	Kislon	Benjamin
Bukki	Jogli	Dan
Hanniel	Ephod	Manasseh, son of Joseph (half)
Kemuel	Shiphtan	Ephraim son of Joseph
Elizaphan	Parnach	Zebulun
Paltiel	Azzan	Issachar
Ahihud	Shelomi	Asher
Pedahel	Ammihud	Naphtali

The land was to be split between nine and a half tribes. Reuben, Gad and Manasseh received land on the east side of the Jordan.

The Levites would receive no inheritance, as each other tribe would give them land for their priestly use.

Towns for the Levites

Moses told the Hebrews that the Levi tribe would not share in the land distribution but would instead be given forty-eight towns in total by the tribes within their allotted lands. Around these towns the other tribes would provide pasture-land for their cattle, flocks, and livestock. This pasture land would surround the town for a distance of some 450 metres to form a square of approximately 900 x 900m, ignoring the town's size.

Cities of Refuge

Six of the Levite towns would be called *'Cities of Refuge'*, three on each side of the Jordan. Anyone who accidentally killed someone without malice aforethought could flee to these cities for protection under the law. This would allow an investigation to be carried out.

The cities on the eastside would be:

- *Bezer in the desert plateau, for the Reubenites*
- *Ramoth in Gilead, for the Gadites*
- *Golan in Bashan, for the Manassites.*

Zelophehad's Daughters

The daughters of Zelophehad of the tribe of Manasseh, Mahlah, Noah, Hoglah, Milcah and Tirzah approached the entrance of the Tabernacle. They stood before Moses, Eleazar, the priest, and the elders, to speak about their concerns about their inheritance.

They explained that their father died in the desert but was not among Korah's followers and had left no sons. They asked by their father's name should disappear from his clan, simply because he had left no son. They asked for his shared to be given to them.

Moses thought about their cases and decided Zelophehad's daughters were right, and his inheritance should be given to them. He told the Hebrews that:

- If a man dies leaving no son, his inheritance should go to his daughter.
- If he had no daughters, then it should pass on to first his brothers,
- Then his father's brothers, or then his nearest relative.

This would be a legal requirement for the Hebrews.

Inheritance of Zelophehad's Daughters

On hearing this, the family heads of the clan of Gilead of the tribe of Manasseh asked Moses a further question. They wanted to know what would happen if a couple married from different tribes. Would the wife's possession be added to the tribe she married into?

Moses thought about this and decided that no inheritance should pass from tribe to tribe, as the Hebrews should keep the land they inherited from their forefathers.

So in time, Zelophehad's daughters married their cousins on their father's side, and their inheritance remained in their tribe.

DEUTERONOMY

Obedience Commanded

Moses called together the Hebrew elders, and they reviewed all events of their journey since leaving Egypt. Moses told them they must not fall and worship false gods. Because of what happened at Baal Peor, he was going to add further laws and decrees. These were not to be changed in any way. He continued:

The Promised Land

The Promised Land has been given to you by your God. He is with you, not far from you, and is watching you.

Tell your Children

Your children, and their children, must be told of the day when you all stood before me at Horeb. I told everyone the laws to be obeyed. These are the same that are written on the two stone tablets in the Ark, and also in my 'Book of Law'.

Idolatry Forbidden

You cannot worship an idol. Anyone who makes an idol of a:

- Man
- Woman
- Animal
- Bird
- Fish
- or any other creature

They will become corrupt.

Planet worship is forbidden

You cannot be enticed, like other nations, to bow down to the

- sky
- sun
- moon
- stars

Moses not entering the land

I brought you out of the iron-smelting furnace of Egypt to be people of the Promised Land.

I will die shortly and will not enter the land with you.

You and your children will take possession of that good land.

If you become corrupt

But if you become corrupt, you will be:

- destroyed and
- scattered among the people and
- only a few of you will survive.

But your God is merciful; if you return to him, he will remember you.

The LORD Is God

God has taken this one nation out of all others and tested you. This is because he loved your forefathers:

- He has chosen to look after their descendants
- He has brought you out of Egypt
- He has given you the strength to drive out other nations from the 'Promised Land.'
- He wants you to take the land for your inheritance.
- He wants you and your children to live long in this 'Promised Land' and has given you laws and decrees to keep.

The Ten Commandments

Moses summoned the Hebrews and told them to listen and learn what he said.

> *"God did not make this covenant at Mount Horeb with our ancestors but with us who are here today, all of us living now. God spoke face to face with you at the mountain, from the middle of the fire."*

At that time, they were afraid of the fire, and he had proclaimed them in a loud voice from the mountain, accompanied by the Elders of the tribes.

> *"God told you, I am the LORD your God. I have brought you from the land of Egypt, from the place of slavery. You all agreed to keep my laws, and in exchange, you and your descendants will enjoy longevity in the 'Promised Land'."*

The Commandments were then written on stone tablets and given to them as follows.

Table 43: The Ten Commandments

1).	You must not have any other gods besides me.
2).	You are not to worship any idol. I will show you love for a thousand generations if you keep these laws.
3).	You shall not swear or take my name in vain.
4).	Remember the seventh day of the week. You shall work for six days a week and rest on the seventh. Neither shall your son, daughter, man or maidservant, your animals or any alien within your gates.
5).	You will respect your father and mother
6).	You shall not murder
7).	You shall not commit adultery
8).	You shall not steal
9).	You shall not lie
10).	You shall not be jealous of your neighbour's possessions. Be it his wife, servants, ox, donkey, or anything else he owns.

Moses then said:

> *"God told me to send everyone back to their tents to teach their children the laws. But he told me to stay so I could learn the additional commands, decrees and laws you must follow before taking the Promised Land. "*

You all must listen to and obey these laws.

Love the LORD Your God

I have told you to observe these commands, decrees and laws in the 'Promised Land'.

You, your children and their children after them must keep all my decrees and commands that I give you so that you all may enjoy a long life.

Be careful to obey so that it may go well with you and that you may increase greatly in a land flowing with milk and honey, for your forefathers promised you.

Love one another with all your heart and with all your soul, and with all your strength.

These commandments that I give you today are to be:

- Taken into your hearts.
- Impress them on your children.
- Talk about them when you sit at home, walk along the road, lie down, and get up.
- Tie them as symbols on your hands and bind them on your foreheads.
- Write them on the door-frames of your houses and on your gates.

Arriving in the 'Promised Land'

The Promised Land you will find will be:

- A land with large, flourishing cities you did not build,
- Houses filled with all kinds of good things you did not provide.
- Wells, you did not dig, and
- Vineyards and olive groves you did not plant

When you eat and are satisfied, be careful not to forget who brought you out of Egypt, out of the land of slavery.

- Do not follow other gods as those around you might do.
- Be sure to keep the stipulations and decrees I have given you.
- Do what is right and good, and all will go well with you as you take over the Promised Land.

Your forefathers have promised this, and you will force out all your enemies.

Future enquiries

In the future, when your son asks you, 'What is the meaning of the stipulations, decrees and laws?' Tell him the following:

- We were the slaves of Pharaoh in Egypt.
- Moses brought us out of Egypt with a mighty hand
- We caused great suffering for Egypt, Pharaoh and his household.
- Moses brought us to land promised by our forefathers.
- Moses gave us decrees, laws and commandments to obey, so we will always prosper and live as we do today.

Therefore, we must abide by all these laws to live righteous lives.

Driving Out the Nations

Many nations occupy the Promised Land:

- Hittites,
- Girgashites,
- Amorites,
- Canaanites,
- Perizzites,
- Hivites
- Jebusites,

They are seven nations larger and stronger than the Hebrews.

- You will defeat them.
- You must then totally destroy them
- You must not make any treaty with them
- You must not show them mercy.
- Do not let your daughters or son take partners or intermarry with them.
- Just destroy them totally.

You may ask how you can drive out nations stronger than yourselves. But do not be afraid. Remember what we did to Egypt. Drive out the nations bit by bit so wild animals do not multiply around you.

If you pay attention to my laws your numbers will increase. This will be by

- the fruit of your womb,
- the crops of your land – your grain, wine, oil, herds and flocks.

You will all be blessed. You will be free of every disease, and no horrible disease will affect you.

Destroy all the people you overcome.

- Break down their altars,
- smash their sacred stones,
- cut down their Asherah poles and
- burn their idols in the fire.

Do not covet silver or gold on them as if you take it for yourselves. It will ensnare you.

Take care and follow the commands, decrees and laws I gave you.

Do Not Forget the LORD

You all had a difficult time in the desert, eating manna which none of you knew how to deal with. You know that man does not live by bread alone, but any find food around them by living off the land. You could survive with the clothes and shoes you had with you.

But when you enter the Promised Land, you will find it is good, with:

- streams and pools of water,
- springs flowing in the valleys and hills.
- A land with wheat, barley, vines, figs, pomegranates, olives, oil, and honey.
- A land where bread will not be scarce, and you lack nothing.
- Indeed the land has rocks of iron and hills of copper for you to dig.

After you have eaten and are satisfied, thank me for the land given to you.

Do not forget me when you become settled and wealthy.

I led you through the vast desert with its venomous snakes and scorpions.

You may say you have produced everything yourself, but remember the one who gave you the ability to produce wealth in the first place.

I brought you out of slavery from Egypt.

Not Because of Israel's Righteousness

You are about to cross the Jordan and dispossess nations greater and stronger than you. They have large cities with walls up to the sky. The people are strong and tall – Anakites, but you will drive them out and annihilate them quickly.

Remember, you are not taking their land because of your righteousness or integrity but their wickedness. You can also be a stiff-necked people at times.

Fear the LORD

It is important you remember who you are and are no longer a stiff-necked nation. You have been chosen from all nations to walk into a new land. You must love your God.

You must defend the fatherless and widows. Love the alien – giving him food and clothes – as you yourselves were aliens once in Egypt. They went to Egypt, seventy in total, and now you are as numerous as the stars in the sky.

Love and Obey the LORD

Remember, your children did not see or experience our hardship in Egypt or at the hands of their army and chariots. Or saw what happened to the followers of Korah. But it was your eyes which saw these things.

You need to observe all the commands I give you so that you have the strength to go and take over the land. This land is not like Egypt. There you can plant seeds and irrigate it, by foot power, as in a vegetable garden.

This land:

- Drinks rain from the sky to feed its mountains and valleys.
- There are both autumn and spring rains to gather new grain, wine and oil.
- You will have grass in the fields to feed your livestock.

But if you worship other gods, the land will become a desert.

You need to remember this:

- Tie them as symbols on your hands and bind them onto your foreheads.
- Teach them to your children, and tell them when you are at home or walking along the road.
- Write them onto the door-frames of your house and on your gates.

This will make your days and your children's days many in this land given by your forefathers.

You will drive out all the nations you see before you. Every place you set foot in will be yours. Your land will extend from the desert to Lebanon and from the Euphrates to the Mediterranean Sea.

I am giving you both a blessing and a curse.

- The blessing if you obey my commands
- The curse is if you disobey and turn away and follow other gods.

When you enter into the land you are to possess, you are to proclaim on:

- Mount Gerizim, the blessing
- Mount Ebal, the curses

These mountains are near the 'Great Trees of Moreh' (Oaks at Shechem).

Keep my requirements, decrees, laws and commands always.

Destroy old places of Worship

These are the decrees and laws you must carefully follow in the Promised Land:

- You must destroy all the places the previous nations worshipped their gods, places on high mountains, on hills, and under every spreading tree.
- Break up their altars and sacred stones and burn in a fire their poles to their goddess Asherah.
- Cut down all idols of their gods and wipe out their names totally.

The One Place of Worship

You will find a place to establish the tabernacle. There you can bring your:

- burnt offerings,
- sacrifices,
- tithes,
- special gifts,
- freewill offerings, and
- firstborn of your herds and flocks.

You and your families will eat and rejoice in everything to which you put your hand.

But first, you must reach your resting place and the land of inheritance.

When you settle, you will have a rest from all your enemies and live in safety.

When you have settled, take everything I have commanded you to bring to the Tabernacle with your sons, daughters, servants and the Levites from your towns and make your burnt offerings.

You may, of course, kill and eat as much meat as you want in your town, as if it were game, like a gazelle or deer. The ceremonially clean and unclean may be eaten, but you must not eat the blood, pour it onto the ground like water.

You must not eat your tithe of grain, new wine, oil, or the firstborn of your flocks and herds in your town. Or whatever you have vowed to give as a freewill offering or special gift. You must eat them in the presence of the Tabernacle with your sons, daughters, servants and Levites. You will rejoice in everything you do. Remember not to neglect the Levites as long as you live in your land.

The Sanctity of Blood

When you enlarge your border and want meat, you may eat as much as you want. Again you must not eat the blood, as blood is the life, and you must only eat the flesh. So pour the blood on the ground like water. You will then only need to take your consecrated items and whatever you have vowed to give to the Tabernacle. Then make a burnt offering as usual.

Do not start inquiring about their gods when you have driven out and destroyed all the people from the Promised Land. Their worship included some terrible things, as they even burnt their sons and daughters in fires as sacrifices to their gods.

Make sure you obey all these laws I am giving you. Do not add to them or take away from them.

Worshipping Other Gods

If there appears amongst you:

- a prophet, or
- a reader of dreams,

He will tell of signs of wonder, and they come true. But, if he tells you to serve and worship other gods, you must not listen to him.

God is testing you to see if you have a strong heart.

The prophet or dreamer must be put to death as:

- He is preaching rebellion against you all.
- He is trying to turn you all away from the ways you have been commanded.

You must purge evil from among you.

(Does this cover St.Stephen? Deu 13, Acts 6-7. This would appear to be a conflict between Hebrew and Christian beliefs.)

False Prophets within the family

Should your own:

- brother,
- son,
- daughter,
- wife, or
- close friend

Suggest you go and worship other gods. Then do not:

- Listen,
- Pity,
- shield or
- spare them.

You must kill them.

- Your hand must be the first to put them to death
- Afterwards, all of the people must join you.

They must be stoned to death because he has tried to draw you away from the god who brought you out of slavery in Egypt. So all of Israel will hear and be afraid and scared.

Punishment of Community Idolatry

Should one of the towns given to you lead another town away, saying, 'Let us go and worship other gods', then you must first check it is true.

- If it is true, then you must:
- Put the inhabitants to the sword
- Kill all the livestock.
- Gather all the spoil and contents of the town in the street, and set it on fire.

It is to be destroyed completely, its people and livestock.

It is to remain a ruin forever

It is never to be rebuilt.

No possessions of those condemned will be found in your hands, or you will suffer also.

Follow the LORD's Commands

Moses told them that from this day to follow and obey all of God's:

- Laws,
- Decrees and
- Commandments

Carefully observe them with all your heart and all your soul. As from this day, you will walk in his ways.

The Altar on Mount Ebal

Moses told them when they had crossed the Jordan into the 'Promised Land', they should set up some large stones and coat them with plaster. Then, onto the stones, they should write all the words of this law.

Then on Mount Ebal, they should set up stones and coat them with plaster. Then, without using iron*, they would build a monument, an altar of stones from the field and make a burnt offering.

Then sacrifice fellowship offerings there, eat them, and be happy. The words of the law should then be written on these stones.

*Iron was seen as a material used to make weapons and should not be used during the construction of an altar. In addition, local stones varied in hardness, which could be a considerable handicap in cutting stones. Although copper and bronze were allowed, the Egyptians had used them for their building work before the introduction of iron.

Curses from Mount Ebal

Moses then told them how to bless and curse the Hebrew people.

Finally, he explained when they had all crossed the Jordan, the Hebrews should split into two groups as follows:

Mount Gerizim - One group would stand on Mount Gerizim and bless the people. They would comprise six of Jacob's sons, the offspring of his wives, Leah and Rachel. The tribes of Simeon, Levi, Judah, Issachar, Joseph and Benjamin.

Mount Ebal - The other group would stand on Mount Ebal and pronounce curses. They would comprise the other six of Jacob's sons, the offspring of Jacob's two concubines, Bilhah and Zilpah. The tribes of Gad, Asher, Dan, Naphtali, Reuben and Zebulun.

Table 44: The Split of the Hebrews at Gerizim / Ebal

Tribe	Order of birth	Mother	Mount
Reuben	1	Leah	Ebal
Simeon	2	Leah	Gerizim
Levi	3	Leah	Gerizim
Judah	4	Leah	Gerizim
Dan	5	Bilhah R	Ebal
Naphtali	6	Bilhah R	Ebal
Gad	7	Zilpah L	Ebal
Asher	8	Zilpah L	Ebal
Issachar	9	Leah	Gerizim
Zebulun	10	Leah	Ebal
Joseph	11	Rachel	Gerizim
Benjamin	12	Rachel	Gerizim

(R/L = Servant of Leah or Rachel)

The Levites would then shout the following curses to all the people, and they should reply, 'Amen.'

Cursed are those:

- *Craftsmen who make an image or idol and set it up in secret.*
- *Who dishonour their father or mother.*
- *Who moves his neighbour's boundary stone.*
- *Who leads the blind astray on the road.*

- *Who withhold justice from aliens, those who are fatherless, or a widow.*
- *Cursed is the man who makes love to his father's wife.*
- *Cursed are those who have sex with any animal.*
- *Cursed is the man who:*
  - *Commits incest with his sister or step-sister.*
  - *Sleeps with his mother-in-law.*
  - *Kills his neighbour secretly.*
  - *Accepts a bribe to kill an innocent person.*
  - *Does not obey these laws.*

Reward for Obedience

If you obey all my commands and worship your God, then you will be set high above all other nations of the earth. Furthermore, you will be blessed and rewarded for your obedience.

- You shall be blessed in the city, in the field, and in your land. When you lie down at night, no one will make you afraid.
- You shall be blessed in the fruit of your body, of your ground, of your animals, livestock, and flocks. All the savage beasts will be removed from your land.
- You will receive rain from the sky on your land to bless the work of your hand.
- You will have food all the year-round, and your threshing will continue until the grape harvest. You will still be eating last year's harvest when you move it out to make room for the new.
- Your basket and your kneading trough shall be blessed.
- Your barns will be blessed with all that you put your hand to.
- You will lend to many nations, but you will not need to borrow.
- You shall be blessed when you come in and go out. You will be the head and not the tail
- You will be at the top and not the bottom
- When your enemies rise up against you, they will fall by the sword before you.
- They will come against you one way and run off in all directions. Five of you will chase a hundred, and a hundred will chase ten thousand.
- No one will invade your land. However, all the people of the earth will see you are a holy people, called 'Israel', and they shall be afraid of you.
- You shall not turn from the words I command you this day, neither to the left nor to the right.
- Do not make any idols.

I am Moses, who brought you out of slavery in Egypt.

I broke the bars of your yoke so you can now walk with your head held high.

Punishment for Disobedience (a prophesy?)

If you do not obey all my commands, you will be cursed in every way. All my blessings will be curses. You will be cursed, confused and rebuked in every way until you are destroyed and perish.

You will suffer:

blight,	blindness,	boils,	consumption,	fever
fiery heat,	inflammation,	itches,	madness	mildew
pestilence,	scurvy,	the sword,	tumours,	

I will multiply your afflictions seven times over.

The sky above you will be copper and the earth like iron, with rain falling on dust and powder.

God will not defend you from your enemies. You will attack them in one direction and flee from them in seven directions. You will be dispersed to all the kingdoms of the earth.

(This particular curse originated the word 'Diaspora' from the Septuagint. The Greek word 'Diaspora' (dispersed) referred to Greek citizens who colonised captured land. Deuteronomy 28:25)

- Your dead body will be food for the birds and animals
- Others will rape your wife. Others will occupy the house you built. Your vineyard will not fruit.
- Your Ox will be slain in front of you.
- Your donkey will be violated before your eyes.
- Your sheep, sons and daughters will be given to your enemies.
- You and your king will be taken by a nation you do not know, and they will make you serve other gods made of wood and stone
- Locusts will eat all your crops in the field, and worms will eat your vines.
- All these curses will come to you, pursue and overtake you until you are destroyed because you did not listen to me.
- A nation will take you to the end of the earth whose language you do not understand.
- They will put a yoke on your neck and have no respect for young or old.
- They will come and eat all your fruits and besiege your cities until they are taken.
- During the siege, you will be distressed and forced to eat your son's and daughters' flesh.
- Men and women of mild temperament will turn on each other and their families in order to survive.

- There will be no rest for you. In the morning, you will wish it was night, and at night you will wish it was the morning.
- You will fear both night and day.
- You will be returned to Egypt by ships and sold to your enemies as slaves, but no one will buy you. (Unsold slaves would be killed due to the cost of support).

But if you confess your father's sins, all the sins that sent you away from your lands, you will have paid for your sins. I remember the promises of Jacob, Isaac, and Abraham and the gift of the Promised Land.

(These curses take the literary form and vocabulary of a seventh-century BC Assyrian treaty – the writer is reinforcing national identity).

Renewal of the Covenant

These are the words of the covenant Moses made with the Israelites on the plains of Moab, which was in addition to that made at Horeb.

Moses had called together the Israelites and told them the following.

You all know what happened to the Pharaoh, his army, and Egypt's people. But until today, you did not understand. You did not have eyes to see or ears to hear.

For forty years, you have been in the wilderness, and:

- *Your clothes and shoes have not worn out*
- *You have not had bread, wine or strong fermented drink.*

When you came here, the following kings came out to attack us:

- *Silhon, king of Heshbon and*
- *Og king of Bashan*

But we defeated them.

We then took their land and gave it as an inheritance to:

- *Reuben,*
- *Gad and*
- *half of the tribe of Manasseh.*

Keep the words of this covenant so you will prosper in all you do. You stand here today with the following:

- *the Elders of your tribe and clans,*
- *your officer,*
- *all the men of Israel,*
- *your wives,*
- *children and*

- *families, and*
- *aliens who cut your wood and draw the water.*

You stand here this day to enter into the covenant, an oath with each other, to confirm that you will have the land as promised by your fathers, Abraham, Isaac and Jacob.

We are making this covenant with each other and those who are not with us today.

Since leaving Egypt, we have passed through many lands and seen their despicable images and idols of wood, stone, silver and gold.

You need to make sure there are no:

- man or woman,
- tribe or clan

who worships other gods so that no root produces a bitter poison.

- Any person who hears the words of this oath and thinks he will be safe will bring disaster to himself.
- All the curses written in this book will fall upon him.
- He will be singled out, and all the curses of the covenant will fall on him as written in the Book of the Law.

The generations to come, your children who come after you, and the foreigner who come from far lands will see:

- All the plagues and sickness that have fallen on the land.
    - It will be like a burning waste of salt and sulphur in which no plant will grow.
    - It will be like the destruction of Sodom, Gomorrah, Admah and Zeboiim.

All the nations will ask what had happened to this land.

They will be told it was turned into this wasteland because the people abandoned their god and the covenant made to each other and their fathers when they came out of slavery from Egypt.

They were all taken to other lands where they live to this day.

Remember this, so you do as the Book of Laws says.

(The text is written after the return from exile and justifies why all the Jews were taken away, and most did not return but spread around the Mediterranean and Orient.)

Prosperity After Turning to the LORD

If you have been cursed and driven too far off-lands, even the most distant, you can return to the Promised Land. You can do this by returning to worshipping your God and following the laws I have given you with all your heart and soul.

- You will then love your God and worship him.
- The curses will be sent to your enemies.
- You will become prosperous in the work of your hand and in the fruits of your body, livestock and land.

The Offer of Life or Death

What I command you to do is not difficult or beyond your reach.

It is not in the sky or beyond the sea.

What I tell you to do is very near you.

It is in your mouth and heart so that you can do it.

I have set before you the choice of either:

- Life and Good, or
- Death and Evil

I have commanded you to follow my laws and decrees so that you can live in the Promised Land and multiply.

But if you do not follow them and worship other gods, you will be destroyed, and your days in the land will be short.

I call this day upon the sky and earth to witness that I have set before you life and death, the blessings and curses.

Therefore choose life, so you and your children can live long and love each other in the land given to you by your forefathers, Abraham, Isaac and Jacob.

Joshua to Succeed Moses

Moses knew he needed to appoint his successor, someone to lead the Israelites. Otherwise, they would be like sheep without a shepherd.

Moses selected Joshua, son of Nun. He laid his hand on him and then made Joshua stand in front of Eleazar, the priest and the elders of the tribes. He said:

- The elders are to obey him as their leader.
- Eleazar to obtain decisions for him by using his Urim.

Moses addresses Israel

Moses then addressed the whole of Israel and said:

- He would not be able to lead them for much longer.
- He would not be well enough to cross the Jordan.
- His successor would be Joshua
- He would lead them into the Promised Land.
- Joshua would do the same to the nations in the Promised Land as he had done to the Kings of Sihon and Og.
- All the nations would be destroyed and their lands given to you as long as the Israelites obeyed Joshua's commands.

Moses told Joshua to be strong and courageous and to divide the land among the Israelites as their inheritance.

Israel's Rebellion Predicted

Moses talked to Joshua in the Tabernacle about his fears of the Israelites soon prostituting themselves to other gods and not following his laws.

Moses said he had written a little song and wanted Joshua to teach the Israelites to sing it. It would help them in times of trouble and difficulty. So Moses gave Joshua a copy of his song, and he went and taught it to the Israelites.

The Reading of the Law

Moses had written down the laws in a book and gave it to the Levites to place beside the Ark so that it would remain a witness and reminder to them all.

He knew how rebellious and stiff-necked the Hebrews had been. He thought if he had suffered all this trouble with them, goodness knows how much trouble they would be after he died.

He told the priests to read the laws to all the people at the end of every seven years, in the years of cancelling debts and the feast of Tabernacles.

The priests should gather the whole of Israel, men, women, children, and aliens, and read aloud the laws so everyone could hear. The children will not know the laws but will learn and understand them.

Final words to Tribe's leaders

Moses asked Joshua to gather together all the elders and officials of the tribes so he could speak to them for one last time. He wanted to warn them not to let the Israelites become corrupt and forget his laws, or disaster would fall on them.

The Song of Moses

Moses and Joshua recited the words of Moses' song to all the Israelites.

Introduction

> Worship your God. His work is set in stone and always right.

Interrogation

> Some of you are corrupt and stupid people.
> You think you do not need him, but he created you!

Recollection

> He gave your forefathers their inheritance.
> He looked after you and led you to a land of milk and honey.

Direct indictment

> But as Israel grew fat, it forgot God.
> They looked for other gods, who were not real, and could not protect them.

The Sentence

> God could not watch them but waited to see their fate.
> You were a foolish nation.
> Your lands were burnt, and mountains were set on fire.
> Evil fell on them, both hunger and thirst.
> Wild animals and snakes will torment your young and old.

Assurance of Deliverance

> You were scattered far, forgotten, a nation without help.
> If only someone would help you.
> Vengeance is mine
> God will judge these people.
> He will have compassion for them when he sees their powers have gone.
> He will ask where their god is, who ate the sacrifices and drank their wine.
> Why not let him protect you now?

God's words of Deliverance

> But, there is no other god but me.
> I kill and make life, wound and heal.
> I render vengeance on my adversaries and recompense those who hate me.
> I make arrows drunk with blood
> My sword devours flesh, and I desire the leaders of my enemy.

Worship God

Rejoice, God's nation. He will avenge the blood of his people. Render vengeance to his adversaries, and make expiation for his land and people.

When they had finished, Moses told them to set their hearts on all the words and command their children to observe them.

Moses Blesses the Tribes

Moses, the prophet, blessed the Israelites before his death and said.

God came from Sinai and rose like the sun upon Israel. He was the guardian of the people, assisted by Moses, the king of the Israelites, who provided the law to the gathered tribes.

- Let Reuben live and not die
- Bring Judah to his people and help him.
- Let Levi use the Thummim and Urim, teach Israel your laws and decrees, and punish those who rise against them.
- Benjamin is always looked after all day long by God.
- The land of Joseph is blessed with all the precious things of the heavens, the dews, the fruits of the sun and moon, the ancient mountains and everlasting hills. Let the blessing come on the head of Joseph, who was separate from his brothers. His military strength is like the horns of a wild ox.
- Zebulun and Issachar must rejoice in the mountains and find treasure in the sand.
- Gad is a lioness who executes the righteousness of God
- Dan is a lion's cub that leaps away from a viper
- Naphtali will inherit the sea of Galilee
- Asher has lots of children to defend the land.

(Simeon is missing from the list!)

All your bars will be iron or bronze, and your day will be like your strength.

Israel, there is none like God, who rides the heavens for your help. He is your refuge, an eternal strength for his chosen people.

Israel can live in safety with grain, wine, and rain.

You are now happy, Israel, saved by God.

A shield and sword to protect you.

Your enemies will surrender to you, and you will destroy their high places.

The Death of Moses

Moses was carried from the plains of Moab to Mount Nebo and to the top of Pisgah. From there, he could see the whole of the Promised Land as far as the Mediterranean Sea. So Moses said, "Now I can see the land promises to the Israelites by their forefathers".

Moses then died and was buried in the valley opposite Beth Peor, but no one knows the location of his grave.

The Israelites grieved for Moses for thirty days, and then Joshua took command of the people.

Joshua was filled with a new spirit of wisdom, due, he thought, to Moses laying his hands on him.

Israel has known no greater prophet than Moses.

Who buried Moses?

"God buried Moses because Satan was fighting for Moses' body so that Moses could not be resurrected as one of the two witnesses to be sent in the days of Revelation. So God descended to Earth to bury the body of Moses."

See Deu 34:5-6 & Jude 1:9

> Deu 34:5 So Moses, the servant of the Lord, died there in the land of Moab as the Lord had said.
>
> Deu 34:6 He buried him in the land of Moab near Beth Peor, but no one knows his exact burial place to this very day.
>
> Jude 1:9 But even when Michael the archangel was arguing with the devil and debating with him concerning Moses' body, he did not dare to bring a slanderous judgment, but said, "May the Lord rebuke you!"

JOSHUA

God commissions Joshua.

Joshua took over as leader and immediately started planning the River Jordan crossing and the 'Promised Land' invasion.

He aimed to occupy all the land from:

- *Lebanon in the north to the desert in the south, and from*
- *The Euphrates in the east to the Mediterranean Sea to the west.*

He knew he had to command his forces well and firmly. Luckily he had been left with Moses' Books and lecture notes which provided the valuable advice he required.

He started by calling all his officers together and told them:

- *They would be crossing the Jordan in three days.*
- *They should return to their tribes,*
- *Organise the masses,*
- *Sort out provisions,*
- *Prepare for the invasion*

The Loyalty of the East Jordan Tribes

The leaders of Reuben, Gad and the half-tribe of Manasseh were asked to a meeting with Joshua. He reminded them of their earlier promise.

- *They reaffirmed their promise to help their brothers until the land was taken.*
- *They would leave their wives, children, and livestock on the east bank.*
- *They would lead the invasion.*

Spies sent to Jericho

Joshua sent two young men from Shittim to spy on Jericho and the land.

The Prostitute Rahab

They were taken in and spent the night in Jericho at a house of a prostitute called Rahab. But they had been seen. So the king of Jericho sent an officer to warn her and ask for the men to be surrendered.

In the meantime, she had hidden the men under stalks of flax drying on her roof.

She told the officer:

- They had arrived from goodness knows where.
- They had left just before the city gates had shut.
- If the king opened the city gates, they could be pursued and caught.

The king then sent men to catch them along the road that led to the fords on the river Jordan.

Rahab went onto the roof and spoke to the spies. She explained that stories of the Hebrews crossing the Red Sea and the defeat of Kings Sihon and Og to the east of Jordan had made everyone very worried and downhearted.

If they were going to invade, in exchange for her help, she wanted to save her:

- Father,
- Mother,
- Brothers and
- Sisters
- all their possessions

The spies agreed and said they would trade their lives for her family.

Rahab's house was built into the city wall, and the spies could leave by means of a red coloured rope lowered from a window. The spies told her that when the Hebrews came to Jericho, she was to:

- Mark her house by tying the red rope to the window.
- Bring her family to her house
- Do not let them leave.
- They would all be rescued.

If she told anyone of the plan, they would all be killed. Rahab agreed and told them to go in the direction of the mountains for a few days, as the king's men would still be looking for them.

When they returned to Joshua, he was delighted with all they told him. He hoped all the land's inhabitants would melt away in fear.

Crossing of the Jordan

All the Hebrews followed orders, left Shittim, and moved to the River Jordan, where they camped for three days.

The officers again went through the camp, giving instructions. They were told to move out and follow the Levites carrying the Ark of Covenant when they saw it pass. They were told to allow a thousand metres gap between it and them. They were not to go close to it.

The Levites carrying the Ark were told to:

- *Go ahead with the people.*
- *When they reached the Jordan, they crossed at the ford to the dry land in the middle of the river. There they waited.*
- *When the people finally crossed downstream, they were to continue to cross the Jordan and come ashore.*

One man from each tribe was to stand in the river to mark the safe passage on the ford to be used, as the river was usually high during harvest time.

So all the tribes cross over the River Jordan.

Twelve large stones

The twelve men who acted as markers were then told to pick up a large stone from where they stood, carry them out of the river, and put them in a heap where they camp the night. Joshua told the Hebrews that when their children asked the meaning of the twelve stones, they could say this was the spot where they crossed into the 'Promised Land'.

Once everyone was across, the Levite carrying the Ark finally crossed over and came ashore.

News spread of the Invading force

News of the invading force spread. The Amorite kings on the west bank and the Canaanite kings along the Mediterranean coast started to get very worried and depressed.

The Hebrews are circumcised

Following the river crossing, Joshua realised that no men or boys were circumcised as Abraham had wished. All the men had died since leaving Egypt, and those born on the journey had not been circumcised.

In order not to bring any bad luck and to be able to identify a fellow Hebrew, he decided to circumcise the lot of them.

He ordered that flint knives should be made and circumcisions carried out immediately. While they were all waiting for the cut to heal, they named the location *'Gibeath Haaraloth'* after the *'Hill of Foreskins'* they would leave.

Passover celebrations in the Promised Land

They celebrated their first Passover in the Promised Land while camped at Gilgal on the plains of Jericho. They made some unleavened bread and roasted grain from the fruits of their new land. It was much better food than the Manna they had been forced to collect and eat.

Notes on Jericho

The city is one of the world's oldest continually occupied towns, on the route out of Africa to the north and Asia. The walled city has a tell at its core of 2.5 hectares, 8 to 12 metres of fill. There appear to have been some 23 layers of civilization. The oldest occupation dates from 10,800-8,500BC and the first walls were built between 8,500-7,300BC.

It's located some 4 miles from a ford by which the River Jordan can be crossed. It is surrounded by very rich fertile farmland. Its ancient name, 'The City of Palms,' was due to the local production of dates. Twenty miles to the east is the 'King's Highway'. The town itself has an ancient spring which still delivers 4.5 M3 of water per minute.

Joshua receives a theophany.

As the Hebrews approached Jericho, Joshua noticed a man waving a sword in the distance. Joshua went over and asked whether he would fight for the Hebrews or their enemy. The man said 'neither, as he was going to fight for himself'. Joshua laughed and asked him if he had any advice on attacking the city.

The man replied, "Take your shoes off, as where you stand is Holy". Joshua returned to the camp, smiling.

The Fall of Jericho

The King of Jericho had completely sealed the city, and no one could escape.

God told Joshua he would defeat Jericho, and a little show of strength might be appropriate. So he told Joshua to march his army, in step, around the city walls for all the residents to see. To keep time, he placed seven priests in the middle of the procession with a ram's horn trumpet and Ark of the Covenant.

They walked around the city once in silence, apart from the priests blowing time on their trumpets. Then they returned to their camp. They did this daily for six days.

The walls of Jericho fall

God told Joshua to get his army up at daybreak on the seventh day. They should then march around the city six times in the same manner. Then on a seventh and final circuit, they should all shout as loud as they can.

When they did this, the city's walls fell down, and they could take the city.

Rahab's family rescued

They had all been told to look out for Rahab, the prostitute, and her family. They had agreed to spare them all. The two spies returned, found her and her family, and took them to a place of safety near the Hebrew camp.

Slaughter at Jericho

In the meantime, the army slaughtered every living thing in the city, every man, woman, child, cattle, sheep and donkey. Finally, they burnt the city and everything in it. Joshua cursed the city and said their children would die if anyone rebuilt it.

Before sacking the city, the army was given strict instruction to keep away from idols of other gods as this would bring them bad luck.

Also, any valuable items of gold, silver, or bronze must be given to the High Priest for his treasury.

Note on taking a Walled City

(It would seem that there were a number of standard methods of capturing a city. After surrounding the city, the attacker would ask for the city to surrender. If it did not, they would cut it off from the outside world and try to prevent it from obtaining water and food to weaken the inhabitants. :-

- *Laying siege to the city and waiting for it to surrender. Perhaps the offer of a payment to the attacker was enough for them to go away.*
- *Attack the city with siege engines. Specialist equipment was developed once cities began to build fortified city walls. Initially, mining under the walls was an option. But soon as timber and iron developed., mobile towers and later catapults (invented in approx 399BC at Sicily) became the necessary accessories. Men were generally killed on capturing the city, and women and children were taken into slavery.*

- *City Gates opened by an insider. A common method to enter the city was someone opening the gates early in the morning while the guard slept. It could be done by disgruntled inhabitants or soldiers climbing over the wall. (also the Trojan Horse method)*

In the case of Jericho, the real option is that the walls have been badly built or increased in height. But more likely, the city fell due to 'spies' re-entering the city via Rehab's window at night when there was no moon, and then when given the signal, e.g. a loud shout, they rushed the gates and opened them. The guards would have been up on the walls watching the procession of the enemy. The killing of everything was required because they had no means of holding them prisoner. The killing of animals would have provided welcome food.

It is also interesting to see in Deuteronomy 20:19 that cutting down fruit trees during a siege is not allowed. Non-fruit trees, however, could be used)

Achan's Sin

Despite clear instructions, Achan, the son of Carmi of the tribe of Judah, took items of value and hid them, bringing bad luck to the Hebrews.

Unsuccessful attack on Ai

Joshua sent spies from Jericho to Ai near Beth Aven, east of Bethel. When they reported, they told Joshua that only a small force would be required to take the city as they had only seen a few people. So three hundred armed men left to take the city. But they had been tricked. They were routed by the men of Ai, who killed about thirty-six of them at the city gate. The rest were chased to the stone quarry at Shebarium and pushed down the incline.

The bad news reaches Joshua

When news reached Joshua, he tore his clothes. He then fell face down on the ground in front of The Ark of Covenant until the evening. Then he and the elders of the Hebrews put dust on their heads to mourn the dead. They asked each other, 'What had gone wrong?' How could they conquer this land if their enemies could route them? Surely the Canaanites would hear of their defeat and attack and destroy them.

They thought it was perhaps bad luck brought about following the fall of Jericho.

Then they thought something might have been taken from Jericho, which was in their camp.

This may have prevented the men from standing against their enemies and made them run away.

Stolen goods from Jericho

The following morning they would ask each tribe whether anyone had wrongly stolen something from Jericho. When they found the person responsible, they would burn them.

Early the following morning, Joshua and the priests worked their way through the tribes, clans, and families until their suspicions fell on Achan, son of Carmi, son of Zabdi, son of Zerah of the tribe of Judah.

Achan confesses

Joshua took Achan and told him to confess to what he had done. He told Joshua how during the fall of Jericho, he had come across a beautiful robe from Babylon, two hundred shekels of silvers and a wedge of gold weighing fifty shekels. These he had kept for himself and buried them in his tent.

Joshua sent officers to collect the items, and they returned shortly with all that Achan had described.

Joshua and the Hebrews collected all Achan's possessions, including his sons and daughters, gold, silver, cattle, donkeys, sheep, his tent and the robe and took him to a nearby valley.

Joshua said to Achan that he had brought trouble on them all and caused the death of the armed men who went to Ai, and now the Hebrews would kill him.

Stoning of Achan

So all the Hebrews stoned them all to death in the valley. Then, when they were all dead, they burnt the bodies and possessions and finally put a heap of stones over the remains. The place is now called the Valley of Achor.

Ai Destroyed

Joshua decided to take the whole army to Ai and attack the city. He told his men they were to kill everyone, but they may keep the plunder and livestock for themselves this time.

The Plan

He set an ambush behind the city and sent out 300 of his best fighting men at night with instructions to go to the west of the city, between

Bethel and Ai, and hide and watch. After that, Joshua would approach the city on the north side with the army and stop near the city gates. When the men of Ai come out of the city, we will run away, and they will chase us like before. Then the ambush should go in and take the city.

The trap was set during the night, and Joshua took his army towards the city gates early the following day.

The Battle

The King of Ai saw the Hebrew army, and the city's men hurried to meet them in battle. Joshua and the Hebrew army allowed themselves to be driven back, and they ran away from the city. All the men in the city were called together to pursue them, and the city was left unguarded.

Joshua then signalled with a spear for the ambush to attack the city. They entered the city and set part of it on fire.

The Hebrew army then turned on the men of Ai and attacked them. They saw their city was on fire and realised there was no escape. The men of the ambush then came out of the city. The men of Ai were all killed except for the King of Ai. He was taken alive and brought before Joshua.

The City of Ai destroyed

When all the men of Ai had been killed, the Hebrew army entered Ai and killed all the women, children and elderly. They plundered the city and took all they found. Then Joshua ordered the city to be burnt. The king was hanged the king from a tree. Joshua had his body taken down at sunset and thrown at the city gates. They piled rocks over it.

The Law read on Mount Ebal.

Joshua had built an altar on Mount Ebal exactly as Moses had described in his Book of Law. It was of uncut stone, made without the use of iron tools. The Priests used it for burnt and fellowship offerings, which the Hebrews provided.

Joshua also copied out onto the stones the Law of Moses. Then he assembled the Men, women and children of the Israelites, aliens, elders, officials and judges. He made them stand on either side of the Ark of Covenant, facing the priests who carried it.

One half faced Mount Gerizim, while the other half faced Mount Ebal. Joshua then read out, so everyone could hear them:

- all the words of the Law,
- the blessing, and
- the curses,

all as written in the Book of Law.

The Kings unite against the Hebrews

News of Jericho and Ai's Hebrew invasion and fall reached the kings of the Hittites, Amorites, Canaanites, Perizzites, Hivites and Jebusites. They held lands in the hill country, the lowlands, and along the entire coast of the Mediterranean Sea as far as Lebanon.

The Kings decided to unite against the Hebrews.

The Gibeonite Deception

However, when the Hivite people of Gibeon heard what Joshua had done to the people of Jericho and Ai, they resorted to a ruse.

They made out they were ambassadors from a distant land and loaded their donkeys with old, worn out and patched sacks, wineskins, sandals and clothes. All the bread in their provisions was dry and mouldy.

They made their way to the main Hebrew camp at Gilgal and told Joshua and the Elders that they were from a far country and wanted to make a treaty with them.

But the elders asked how they could make a treaty with them as they might live near them. The Gibeonites told the elders that they were their servants.

Joshua asked them directly where did they come from?

They said, "We, your servants, have come from a very distant country because of the fame of Moses. We heard all he did in Egypt and to kings Sihon and Og of the Amorites on the east side of the Jordan.

Our elders have told us to take provisions for our journey, meet you, and tell you we are your servants and make peace with you.

Our bread was warm when we left, but now we see how dry and mouldy it is. As for these wineskins, they were new, but now they are torn. Our clothes and shoes are worn out as well."

The Hebrew elders looked at their provisions but did not check them closely.

Joshua decided to make peace with them and let them live, and the Elders agreed, made a covenant, and swore an oath to them.

Treaty sealed with Gibeonites

Three days later, after the treaty had been made, the Hebrews heard that the Gibeonites were, in fact, their neighbours.

So the Hebrew army made their way to the cities of Gibeon, Chephirah, Beeroth and Kiriath Jearim. They arrived there three days later. But they did not attack them because they had sworn an oath to them.

Joshua asked the Gibeonites to explain

Joshua spoke to the Gibeonites again and asked why they had deceived him. They did not live far away. In fact, they lived just down the road.

The Gibeonites explained they knew Moses had ordered the Hebrews to kill all the people in the land. So they were in fear for their lives.

Joshua told them they were now cursed and would now be the Hebrew's servants and would serve them. So they became woodcutters and water carriers for the priest and the entire community.

Battle of Gibeon

When Adoni-Zedek, king of Jerusalem, heard the people of Gibeon had made a peace treaty with the Hebrews, he was very worried. He had heard what Joshua had done to Ai and Jericho and to their kings. The Gibeon people were good fighters, and their city was larger than Ai. They could become a big danger to Jerusalem. So he needed to attack Gibeon and asked the following kings for help:

- Hoham of Hebron,
- Piram of Jarmuth,
- Japhia of Lachish and
- Debir of Eglon

So the five kings joined forces, took their armies to Gibeon, and attacked the city.

The Gibeonites quickly sent a message to Joshua at the Gilgal camp and begged him not to abandon them to the five kings. Instead, they asked for him to come quickly and help save them.

Defeat of the Five Kings

Joshua responded by marching his entire army to Gibeon. He knew no one would be able to withstand them. They marched all night, surprised the five Kings with their attack, and defeated them. The Hebrew army pursued them along the road to Beth-Horon and struck them at Azekah and Makkedah.

The glorious defeat

Joshua praised the army for the glorious defeat and wished the day would never end, as it was written in the Book of Jashar. It was like the sun had stood still in the sky. They all returned to the camp at Gilgal.

Five Amorite Kings Killed

Joshua was told that the five kings were hiding in a cave at Makkedah. He ordered large rocks should be used to seal the mouth of the cave and a guard set. The Hebrews continued to pursue their enemies, killing as they went. They prevented any of them from returning to their cities. Finally, the army destroyed the enemy and returned to Joshua outside Makkedah.

Joshua ordered the cave should be opened, and the five kings were brought out. The kings were of:

- Jerusalem
- Hebron
- Jarmuth
- Lachish
- Eglon

They were taken before Joshua. Joshua summoned the army and told the army commanders to put their feet on the neck of the kings to show how they would always treat their enemies.

The commanders took turns in placing their feet on the kings' necks. Finally, Joshua killed the kings and hanged them on five trees until the evening. At sunset, he ordered that the bodies be taken down and thrown into the cave and the mouth sealed with large rocks.

End of Makkedah

Finally, Joshua captured Makkedah and ordered everyone was to be slaughtered, just as at Jericho and Ai.

Southern Cities Conquered

The army moved from Makkedah to Libnah. There Joshua attacked the city and captured it.

The city was plundered, and the inhabitants were slaughtered. The king was killed in the same way as the King of Jericho.

Help for Lachish against Horam of Gezer

The army moved onto the city of Lachish with the intention of taking it. Horam, king of Gezer, came to help the city but was defeated, and the city was taken and plundered.

The entire army and inhabitants of the city were slaughtered, and there were no survivors.

Eglon, Hebron and Debir Taken

Joshua moved the army onto the cities of Eglon, Hebron and Debir. The cities and villages were taken and plundered, and everyone was slaughtered.

The conquest of the South completed

So Joshua subdued the whole region, including the hill country, lowlands, and slopes from Kadesh Barnea to Gaza and Goshen to Gibeon. All the inhabitants were slaughtered, and their kings were killed in one campaign.

Finally, Joshua returned with the army to the camp at Gilgal.

Conquest of Northern Palestine.

News of the defeat of the southern kings spread.

Northern Kings Defeated

When Jabin, king of Hazor, heard the news, he contacted other northern kings in order to raise an army to defeat the Hebrews. So they raised a vast army with horses and chariots and camped at the 'Waters of Merom' to fight the Hebrews.

Joshua told his army not to be worried by them as they could easily beat them and would then hamstring their horses and burn their chariots.

Joshua planned a sudden attack on the king's army and routed them. They chased them to Great Sidon, Misrephoth Maim, and eastward to the Valley of Mizpah until they had killed them all, and none remained.

King Jabin had been captured, and Joshua killed him with a sword and burnt his body.

The Hebrews burnt only the city of Hazor and captured and plundered the other northern cities, slaughtering everyone there.

The Israelites carried off for themselves all the plunder and livestock of these cities. All the people were put to the sword. No one was spared.

Completion of Conquest.

Joshua took all the land and captured all their kings, who he put to death. He had plundered and destroyed most villages, towns and cities and killed all the inhabitants.

Only the Gibeonites had made a peace treaty with the Hebrews.

Joshua had killed all the giant Anakims from the land, and only those who lived in Gaza, Gath and Ashdod survived.

List of Defeated Kings

The Hebrews had defeated the following kings:-

To the east of the Jordan, Two kings: - Sihon, king of the Amorites, who reigned in Heshbon and Og, king of Bashan, one of the last of the Rephaites, who reigned in Ashtaroth and Edrei.

Moses and the Hebrews had conquered them. Their lands had been given to the Reubenites, the Gadites and the half-tribe of Manasseh.

To the west side of the Jordan, Thirty-one kings: - The kings of Jericho, Ai (near Behel), Jerusalem, Hebron, Jarmuh, Lachish, Eglon, Gezer, Debir, Geder, Hormah, Arad, Libnah, Adullam, Makkedah, Behel, Tappuah, Hepher, Aphek, Lasharon, Madon, Hazor, Shimron Meron, Acshaph, Taanach, Megiddo, Kedesh, Jokneam in Carmel, Dor (in Naphoh Dor), Goyim in Gilgal, Tirzah.

Joshua took all the land, just as Moses had instructed. Now he wanted to give it as an inheritance to the Hebrews. So the land would have a rest from war.

PARTITION OF THE LAND AMONG THE TRIBES.

Land Still to Be Taken

Joshua was now old and realised there was still a large area of land to be captured.

But he decided the tribes should settle in the land they already held.

The tribes of Reubens, Gad and Manasseh held land on the east side of the Jordan.

The Levites received no share of the land but only towns to live in, with pasturelands for their flocks and herds. They receive no inheritance as they were to benefit from the priestly service.

The sons of Joseph had become two half-tribes— Manasseh and Ephraim.

Division of the Land West of the Jordan

These are the areas the Israelites received as an inheritance in the land of Canaan, which Eleazar, the priest, Joshua, son of Nun and the heads of the tribal clans of Israel allotted to them.

As Moses commanded, their inheritances were assigned by lot to the nine-and-a-half tribes.

Hebron given to Caleb

The men of Judah asked Caleb, son of Jephunneh the Kenizzite, to speak to Joshua and remind him of what Moses had promised him.

He was one of the original spies who went with Joshua from Kadesh Barnea to the Promised Land. They had brought back good reports while the others with them, who were all now dead, brought back depressing ones.

He said that Moses had promised them both the land on which our feet had walked would become their inheritance, and our children's, forever.

Caleb asked Joshua to give him the hill country of Hebron, which Moses had promised. They had heard Anakims were there, and their cities were large and fortified. But he was confident he would be able to drive them out.

Then Joshua blessed Caleb and gave him Hebron as his inheritance.

Allotment for Judah

The land given to the tribe of Judah extended to the land of Edom and the Desert of Zin in the south.

The land had 112 towns and villages.

Judah could not dislodge the Jebusites living in Jerusalem, so they continued to live there with the people of Judah.

Allotment for Joseph's Children - Ephraim and Manasseh

The allotment for Joseph began at the Jordan of Jericho, east of the waters of Jericho. It then through the desert into the hill country of Bethel. It went on from Bethel (that is, Luz), crossed over to the territory of the Arkites in Ataroth, descended westward to the territory of the Japhletites as far as the region of Lower Beth Horon and on to Gezer, ending at the Mediterranean sea.

Their land was to be split so that Manasseh and Ephraim could each receive their inheritance.

The Elders of the two half-tribes asked Joshua why they had only received one portion of the land for an inheritance when there were so many of them.

The Elders said the land for Ephraim would be too small for them, and the Canaanites had iron chariots. Joshua said the tribe of Ephraim were numerous and very powerful. They would soon be able to clear the forested hill country and drive out those with the iron chariots.

Allotment for Ephraim

The half-tribe of Ephraim received from Ataroth Addar in the east to Upper Beth Horon and continued to the sea. From Micmethath on the north, it curved eastward to Taanath Shiloh, passing by it to Janoah on the east. Then it went down from Janoah to Ataroth and Naarah, touched Jericho and came out at the Jordan.

From Tappuah, the border went west to the Kanah Ravine and ended at the sea.

This was the inheritance of the tribe of the Ephraimites, clan by clan.

They did not get rid of the Canaanites living in Gezer but made them into servants to do forced labour.

Allotment for Manasseh

The land was first allocated to two groups within the tribe.

- Makir, Manasseh's firstborn, received Gilead and Bashan on the east side of the Jordan because his family were ferocious fighters.
- Moses had promised the daughters of Zelophehad, son of Hepher, inheritance among our brothers.

The territory of Manasseh extended from Asher to Micmethath east of Shechem. The boundary ran southward to include the people living at En Tappuah. The boundary then continued south to the Kanah Ravine. There were towns belonging to Ephraim lying among the towns of Manasseh, but the boundary of Manasseh was the northern side of the ravine and ended at the sea.

Where some Canaanites still remained they made them do forced labour.

The Division of the Promised Land

The remaining tribes meet at Shiloh and set up the Tabernacle.

The Promised Land had been brought under control, and they decided to divide the remaining territory between the seven tribes without their inheritance.

They decided that:

- Judah would remain in its land to the south
- Joseph would stay in the land to the north
- The Levites were excluded because of their priestly service
- Gad, Reuben and Manasseh had received their land on the east side of the Jordan.

Joshua asked the Hebrews, 'How long would they wait until they occupied their lands?'

Survey of the land

They appointed three men from each tribe and sent them out to survey the land. They would survey town by town and write a description of the land, which would then be given to Joshua.

The land would then be divided into seven lots, and Joshua would cast lots to decide who had what.

Joshua cast lots

After the land had been surveyed, the land was divided at Shiloh at the entrance to the Tent of Meeting by Joshua casting lots.

Table 45: Division of the Promised Land

Lot	Tribe	Number of Towns
1st	Benjamin	26 towns and their villages
2nd	Simeon	17 towns and their villages
3rd	Zebulun	12 Towns and their villages
4th	Issachar	16 towns and their villages
5th	Asher	22 towns and their villages
6th	Naphtali	19 towns and their villages
7th	Dan	unknown

The Danites found it difficult to occupy their lands, so they attacked the largest city, Lesham, and killed everyone. They settled there and named their land 'Dan' after their forefather.

Allotment for Joshua

When they had finished dividing the land into its allotted portions, the Hebrews asked Joshua which town he would like as an inheritance among them. This was to thank him for guiding them into the Promised Land.

Joshua asked for Timnath Serah in the hill country of Ephraim, and there he retired and built up the town.

Table 46: Summary of other land given to others

Spy	Joshua	Timnath Serah, Ephraim
Spy	Caleb	Hebron
Priests	Levites	As table 46, below
East	Reubenites	East side of the Jordan
East	Gadites	East side of the Jordan
East	Manasseh*	Bashan, East side of the Jordan
West	Manasseh*	West side of the Jordan to Mediterranean.
West	Ephraim*	Land on West side

*The two Half tribes of Joseph.

Appointment of Cities of Refuge.

Then Joshua told the Hebrews to designate the cities of refuge, as Moses had instructed. These cities were for anyone, Hebrew or Alien, who accidentally and unintentionally killed another. They could flee there for protection.

Towns given to the Levites

The Elders of the Levites approached Eleazar, the priest. They asked him to provide towns for them to live in, with pasture land around for their livestock. The other tribes provided the towns so the Levites could live amongst them. The towns and land were issued to the Levites by means of lots drawn by Joshua, as follows:

Table 47: Towns given to Levites

Lot	Clan of Levites	No. Towns	Town received from Tribe of
1st	Priests - Kohathites	13	Judah, Simeon and Benjamin
2nd	Kohathites	10	Ephraim, Dan and Manasseh
3rd	Gershon	13	Issachar, Asher, Naphtali and Manasseh in Bashan
4th	Merari	12	Reuben, Gad and Zebulun

Forty-eight towns were given to the Levites, each with their own pasture land.

Occupied Land

The Hebrews occupied all their lands as promised by their forefathers. They had no trouble from any of their enemies.

Eastern Jordan Tribes go to their Home

Joshua summoned the elders of the tribes of Reubenites, Gadites and Manasseh. He told them they had done all that was asked of them and could return to the east side of the Jordan to their lands given to them by Moses if they kept his Laws.

Moses had given land in Bashan to the half-tribe of Manasseh. To the other half of the tribe, Joshua gave land on the west side of the Jordan to their brothers.

Then Joshua blessed them and sent them off. So the Reubenites, Gadites and Manasseh left the Hebrews at Shiloh in Canaan and returned to Gilead, their own land.

They returned with great wealth comprising of:

- Large herds of livestock,
- Silver,
- Gold,
- Bronze
- Iron,
- a great quantity of clothing.

They were told to divide it amongst themselves.

The Altar at Geliloth

When the East Jordan tribes came to Geliloth near the Jordan in the land of Canaan, they built themselves a large altar.

But when the other Hebrews heard they had built their own altar, they became very angry. They wanted to go and tear it down as they believed there was only one altar for the Tabernacle.

Phinehas, the priest, son of Eleazar, was sent to the land of Gilead to meet with Reuben, Gad and Manasseh. He was accompanied by ten of the elders for each other tribe.

Conflict over Eastern Altar

When they all met, Phinehas asked why the tribes on the east had built their own altar.

He explained that they had all suffered from the problems of Peor, and the plague had spread because they were not clean. Building their own altar would mean they would become unclean compared to the other tribes.

Phinehas suggested they pulled it down and came back to the land on the west where the Tabernacle stood.

Phinehas pointed out that when Achan, son of Zerah, was unfaithful at Jericho, all the Hebrews suffered because of bad luck and did not want bad luck again.

The Eastern tribes explain the Altar's use

Then Reuben, Gad and Manasseh explained the reason for the altar. It was not to be a cause for bad luck or to be unclean.

The River Jordan makes a boundary between you and us. They had built the altar as a replica of the altar at the Tabernacle. It was not for burnt offerings and sacrifices but as a witness between you and us.

They feared their children might say "What do we have to do with our forefathers and Moses?" They would forget our history and have a problem keeping the Laws of Moses.

The replica altar would help them to teach their children about Laws and history.

Phinehas accepts the Altar's use

They were all pleased when Phinehas, the priest and the Elders heard what the eastern tribes said.

Phinehas said, "Today, we have learned that our forefathers are watching over us all".

Phinehas and the elders returned home and reported to the other elders and Joshua. They were all very pleased and settled in peace.

Those on the East side of the Jordan called their altar "A Witness between us all".

Joshua's farewell address.

After many years, the Hebrews found they had no trouble from their enemies around them, and all was peaceful.

Joshua asked all the Elders, Leaders, Judges and other officials to join him so he could talk to them. He knew he was getting old and would shortly die.

Joshua said they had all seen what had happened to the original nations in the lands. They now benefited and held lands between the Jordan and the Mediterranean Sea to the west.

They needed to be strong and obey all written in the Book of the Law of Moses without turning to the right or the left.

They must not associate with the nations that remain among them, not get involved with their gods or swear, serve, or bow down to them.

As a nation, you are stronger than the rest. But if you intermarry and associate with them, you will become weaker. They become snares and traps for you, whips on your backs and thorns in your eyes until you perish from this good land.

I am about to die. I believe you have been given all that was promised to you.

Joshua and the Hebrews Renewed covenant at Shechem

Joshua then told them the history of the Hebrews and what he had seen:

> *"Years ago, your forefathers, Terah, the father of Abraham and Nahor, lived far away and worshipped gods.*
>
> *Then your father Abraham came to his land and had one son Isaac, who then had two sons called Jacob and Esau.*
>
> *Jacob and his sons went to Egypt, but Esau remained and lived in the hill country of Seir in Edom.*
>
> *Jacob's sons laboured hard for the Egyptians.*
>
> *Then Moses, Aaron and the Elders planned to bring you out from there.*
>
> *When your fathers left, the Egyptians chased after them in their chariots and horseback but were all lost in the Red Sea.*
>
> *After crossing the Red Sea, they lived for a long time in the desert. At first, they were not very numerous, but after many years, they increased in strength and defeated all their enemies.*
>
> *They came to the Amorites' lands on Jordan's east side. They killed them all and took their lands.*
>
> *Next, Balak, son of Zippor, king of Moab, wanted to fight us and called on Balaam, son of Beor, to put a curse on us. But we again killed them and took their lands.*
>
> *Next, we crossed the Jordan and defeated the citizens of Jericho and the Amorites, Perizzites, Canaanites, Hittites, Girgashites, Hivites and Jebusites.*
>
> *We took their lands full of vineyards and olive groves ready to eat, and we took their ready-built cities in which to live.*
>
> *Remember how lucky we have been.*
>
> *Our forefathers worshipped gods from beyond the River and in Egypt. The Amorites worshipped other gods. You can worship whichever god you like!*
>
> *But in my household, we only worship God and thank our forefathers for all they had done to deliver us to this land.*
>
> *Because of them, we are not slaves, but they must have protected us from other nations on our journey here.*
>
> *We have been lucky, but our luck can end for many reasons, so as Moses told us, we must keep to his Book of Laws."*

The people replied to Joshua that they would always keep the Laws of Moses and honour their forefathers. Joshua witnessed their choice and told them to throw away anything related to foreign gods.

On that day, Joshua made a covenant with the people, and there at Shechem, he drew up for them decrees and laws. He recorded these things in the Book of the Law of Moses.

Then he took a large stone and set it up under the Great Oak near Abraham's monument of Shechem.

"See!" he said to all the people. "This stone will be a witness against us. It has heard all the words we have spoken. It will be a witness against you if you are untrue. "

Then Joshua sent the people away, each to his inheritance.

The death of Joshua.

After these things, Joshua, son of Nun, the servant of the Israelites, died. They buried him in the land of his inheritance, at Timnath Serah in the hill country of Ephraim, north of Mount Gaash.

The Elders who outlived him were by then experienced in overseeing Israel.

Death of Eleazer

Eleazar, son of Aaron, died and was buried at Gibeah in the hill country of Ephraim.

Joseph buried in the Promised Land

Joseph's bones had been brought up from Egypt and were buried at Shechem in the tract of land that Jacob bought for one hundred pieces of silver from the sons of Hamor, the father of Shechem.

This marks the end of the foundation period of the nation of Israel.

Summary

It is hard to justify the return of the Hebrews to a land promised to them some five hundred years before.

Indeed, the location of the 'Promise Land' varies. For example, land west of the Jordan was not fully partitioned and occupied by all the tribes.

It is easier to justify the settling of the tribes in the area, followed by folk law created to justify their ownership. But, indeed, why did they need to justify their ownership?

The key was not the land but the people. They were God's possessions.

God himself develops within the various stories. One minute he is living at the top of a volcano, the next, he is living in a tent.

God and Moses appear to put together the various Laws guiding the Israelites over the next thousand years.

From the pieces of folk law that form the Pentateuch's five books, we will move on to establishing the Kingdom of Israel and its final collapse.

THE TABERNACLE - 2

Initially, a 'Tent of Meeting' was set up outside the camp over which a pillar of cloud indicated whether God was present. Reference to the name of this tent also occurs in the 'Laws' after the Tabernacle's construction.

Moses and his team designed the layout of the Tabernacle and its courtyard, including all the fittings. It was to provide a centre for making offerings and sacrifices.

The administration of the Tabernacle was put solely into the hands of the Levi tribes of which Moses and Aaron were part. They benefited from all the gifts. While the other tribes laboured, the Levites profited.

In reality, the layout was scaled up from what you would have expected for any nomadic leader—a tent with an inner section for the women, surrounded by a stock enclosure.

The Layout

The Tabernacle comprised a rectangular courtyard formed by a perimeter fabric wall. Within was a large tent 14 x 5.6m on plan and 4.5m high.

The tent structure called the Sanctuary was divided into two parts, the inner and out Sanctuary. Within the inner sanctuary was located the 'Ark of The Covenant'. The courtyard was furnished with a large altar for the sacrifices of animals. In addition, there was an area where animals were slaughtered and butchered. The Tabernacle was set out on an east-west axis, with the entrance to the courtyard and sanctuary facing east, to the rising sun.

Offerings for the Tabernacle

For the construction of the Tabernacle, Moses asked each Hebrew for an offering in the form of either:

> Gold, Silver, Copper or Bronze.

Other items on his list were:

- yarns dyed Blue, purple and scarlet,
- fine linen,
- Goat's hair,
- tanned ram's skins

- dyed red and hides of dugongs, a species of seal.
- Acacia wood,
- olive oil for the light, spices for the anointing oil, and fragrant incense.
- Onyx stones and other gems must be mounted on the ephod and breastpiece.

The Blue, purple and scarlet dyes.

- *Blue dye source has been lost in history. The Talmud says it comes from a marine creature known as the 'Hilazon' (Hexaplex trunculus), found near Sycamine.*
- *Purple dye was extracted from the murex shellfish. The Phoenicians at Tyre would set up an industrial-scale process in dying fabric of this colour. The Romans later adopted this colour to indicate imperial status.*
- *Scarlet dye came from crushing small insects – scale Kermes echinatus.*

Bezalel and Oholiab

The craftsmen put in charge of making all the items for the Tabernacles were:

- Bezalel son of Uri, from the tribe of Judah. He was experienced working in gold, silver and bronze, cutting and setting stones, and working in wood.
- Oholiab, son of Ahisamach, from the tribe of Dan,
- and others as required.

Atonement Money

Additional materials were required for the construction, which had to be purchased from other nations. Moses raised money by taking a census and charging a half-shekel per person. In addition, he said each Hebrew over the age of twenty must pay a ransom for his life, which was not lost at the time of the plagues in Egypt.

The 'tax' was the same for rich and poor, but at the time, the Hebrews still had all their plunder taken from the Egyptians before they had left.

The Levite Priests collected the money.

(This text is later as coins did not exist at this time. They first appeared about the 7th Century BC and were refined by king Croesus about 550 BC.)

THE STRUCTURE AND COVERING

The Frame

The frame for the Sanctuary tent was formed from forty-eight acacia wooden panels assembled from a timber frame with trellis strips, all overlaid with gold. Each panel was 4.5 metres high by 700mm wide, with two parallel projections linking the panels together. Each panel was to be fitted into two silver bases. (Depending on ground conditions, such bases could be spiked for driving into the ground and later dug out.)

Twenty boards would be required for each long side to the north and south. The west side had six normal panels and two double-thickness corner panels. No panels were provided on the east side.

To add strength, the panels were tied horizontally at about 800mm centres with five acacia wood crossbars on each side. The crossbars were covered with gold and fixed to the outside of the boards with gold rings. The middle crossbar was continuous along each side.

The Curtain of fine Linen

The inner lining of the tent was formed from ten curtains of finely twisted linen; each was decorated by an embroiderer with blue, purple and scarlet yarn and cherubim emblems. Each curtain was 13 metres long and 1.8 metres wide, and they were joined to form two sets of five. The joint had fifty loops and gold clasps on the long dimension. The curtains were dressed up one side, across the roof, and then down the other side to cover the whole of the Tabernacle.

The Curtains of Goats' Hair

The covering over the top of the panels was made from eleven curtains of woven goat hair. Each curtain was 13.5 metres long and 1.8 metres wide and joined to form two sets, one of five and the other of six curtains. The joint was made by means of fifty loops and gold clasps on the long dimension. The curtains are like the inner lining and dressed up one side, across the roof, and then down the other. The tent curtains were to hang over both sides by 470mm to cover the tabernacle completely. To the west side, the extra half curtain was to hang down over the rear.

The Tanned Rams' Skin

Over the Goat's hair curtain was placed a tent of tanned rams' skins, red in colour

The Outer Covering

The final outer covering of the tent is to be of dugong skins, a species of seal which lives in the Red Sea and Gulf of Aqaba.

The Sanctuary

The Sanctuary was a finished size of approximately 13.5m long and 4.5m high x 4.5 m wide. It was divided into two parts by a veil supported on four posts. It was entered from the courtyard. The first room was called 'The Holy Place', and the inner room was called 'The Most Holy Place'.

Sanctuary Entrance.

The entrance to the sanctuary was a curtain of finely twisted linen and decoration by an embroiderer in blue, purple and scarlet yarn. The curtain was hung on gold hooks from five posts of acacia wood overlaid with gold. The posts were set into bases of cast bronze.

The Holy Place

The Holy Place was the first room. It was 9m long x 4.5 wide x 4.5 high. Within this room were placed:

- On the north side, a Table for Showbreads.
- On the south side, a Gold Lampstand.

Between the two and to the west would be placed The Gold Altar of Incense.

The Veil

The veil which separated the two rooms in the Tent was made of finely twisted linen and decorated by an embroiderer with blue, purple and scarlet yarn and a cherubim emblem. It was hung with gold hooks from four posts of acacia wood overlaid with gold and set in four silver bases.

The Most Holy Place

The Most Holy Place was the inner room and was 4.5m long x 4.5 wide x 4.5 high. Within the room was placed 'The Ark of The Covenant' and a few other items over time.

THE FURNITURE

The Ark of The Covenant and Mercy Seat

Moses asked the Hebrews to make him a wooden chest, 1100mm long, 700mm high x 700mm wide. The chest was to be overlaid inside and out with gold and with a gold moulding around it.

Four gold rings were made and fastened to its feet, two at each end on the corner. Through these, two gold-covered poles of acacia wood were permanently fixed to carry the chest.

The lid of the chest, which Moses called a 'Mercy Seat', was 1100mm long and 700mm wide. It was made of pure gold with two gold Egyptian-styled winged Cherubims facing each other at each end. Their wings were spread upwards, overshadowing the cover to form armrests.

The Altar of Incense

The Altar was placed in The Holy Place in the middle in front of the veil. The altar, for burning incense, was 450mm square and 900mm high. It was made of Acacia wood with four projecting horns at each corner.

It was overlaid with gold and had a gold moulding around it. Two rings were fixed to each side for two carrying poles of acacia wood, again overlaid with gold.

The priest was to burn incense on the altar every morning and at twilight.

The Lampstand

The Lampstand was placed on the south side in The Holy Place. The lampstand with its base, shaft, cups, wick trimmers, and trays were made out of a talent of pure hammered gold.

It had six branches, with three on each side of the lampstand. Each branch was to have three cups shaped like almond flowers with buds and blossoms.

On the lampstand were four cups shaped like almond flowers with buds and blossoms, one under each pair of branches. The lamps were for oil lights and were to be kept continuously alight.

The Hebrews were to provide clear oil from pressed olives for the lamps. The priest would maintain the lamps every morning and evening and keep the 'eternal flame' burning all the time.

The Table (for Show bread)

The Table was placed on the north side of The Holy Place. It was made of acacia wood and was 1000mm long, 500mm wide and 800mm high. It was overlaid with gold, with gold moulding around it and a 100mm gold rim moulding. Four gold rings were fixed to the corner legs for gold-covered acacia wooden poles to be fastened for carrying.

On the table were to be put two gold plates, and between them were dishes for incense, pitchers and bowls for the drink offering. On the gold plate were put each Sabbath, twelve bread cakes, 'the bread of Presence', each made of two-tenths of an ephah of fine flour. The bread cakes were to be stacked six per plate. The priest in the courtyard could eat the bread being replaced.

Anointing Oil

The recipe of fine spices for the sacred anointing oil was 500 shekels each of liquid myrrh and cassia, 250 shekels each of fragrant cinnamon and fragrant cane, and a hin of olive oil. It was blended by a perfumer and used to consecrate items to make them holy.

It was used to anoint:

- The Sanctuary,
- Ark of The Covenant,
- The Table and its articles,
- the Altar of Incense,
- the Lampstand and its accessories,
- the Altar of Burnt Offering and all its utensils, and
- the basin with its stand.

The oil was not to be made for any other purpose, and if anyone made oil using the same recipe, they risked being put to death.

Incense

The recipe for fragrant spices was simpler.

> Sweet spices, stacte, onycha and galbanum were to be mixed in equal amounts with pure frankincense and then salted. It was to be the work of a perfumer.

The priest was to grind it into a powder and place it in front of Moses' Chest in the Sanctuary.

The incense was not to be made for any other purpose, and if anyone made incense using the same recipe, they risked being put to death.

THE OUTER AREAS

The Courtyard

The Sanctuary was set within a courtyard some 46 metres long and 23 metres wide on an east-west axis. The courtyard's perimeter was formed of finely twisted linen, some 2.3 metres high, suspended between 60 acacia wood posts. The posts had silver caps and four silver hooks at their top. Two more silver hooks were towards the foot.

The posts were set in bronze bases and were held in place by two guide ropes. First, the ropes were secured to bronze 'tent' pegs inside and outside the courtyard. Next, two silver rods were fixed to the hooks between the posts at the top and bottom of the post. From this, the perimeter curtain was suspended and tied.

The courtyard entrance was in the middle of the 23m wide east end, facing towards the sunrise. On either side of the entrance, three posts were set in line to take the perimeter curtains, some 6.9 metres long. The actual entrance curtain was 9 metres long and of finely twisted linen decorated by an embroiderer with blue, purple and scarlet yarn. It was set on four posts and bases.

All the other articles used in the service of the tabernacle, whatever their function, including all the tent pegs for it and those for the courtyard, were of bronze.

The perimeter curtain formed the division between the normal world and the tabernacle. It provided some form of control over those who were in the courtyard.

The Altar of Burnt Offering

The altar was a hollow square frame 2600mm, 160mm high, made of acacia wooden boards. Inside was a ledge 800mm above the ground to hold a bronze grating through which the ashes could drop. The top of the altar frame was carved, and a horn in each corner was overlaid in bronze. A bronze ring was located on each corner so two acacia wooden poles overlaid with bronze could be used for carrying it.

All the altar's utensils were made out of bronze— its pots for removing the ashes, shovels, sprinkling bowls, meat forks and firepans.

The five offerings (Burnt, Cereal, Peace, Sin, and Guilt) were to be made at this altar.

Basin for Washing

There was a large bronze basin with a stand for washing.

It was to be placed in the courtyard between the Sanctuary and the Altar of Burnt Offerings.

The priests were to wash their hands and feet with water from it when they either entered the Sanctuary or presented an offering on the altar. They would die if they did not follow this rule.

Outside the Courtyard

The tabernacle courtyard was at the centre of the camp and had the Levites camped immediately around it. The other tribes were set out as follows:-

- North - the tribes of Dan, Asher and Naphtali
- South - the tribes of Rueben, Simeon and Gad
- East - the tribes of Judah, Issachar and Zebulon
- West - the tribes of Ephraim, Manasseh and Benjamin

THE PRIESTS

Moses selected his brother Aaron as the first High Priest. The office was to be hereditary and preserved in perpetuity to Aaron's family, passing to the eldest son on the High Priest's death.

To help him, Aaron's sons, Nadab, Abihu, Eleazar and Ithamar, were appointed priests or helpers for the physical work of dealing with the offerings.

They were to be the priestly family, with their tribe assisting them in administration as required.

The skilled Hebrew men made the High Priest and the Priests their sacred garments to give them dignity and honour. The garments comprised a breastpiece, an ephod, a robe, a woven tunic, a turban and a sash. They were made of fine linen and decorated by an embroiderer with blue, purple, scarlet yarn, and gold.

The Garments of the High Priest

As the first High Priest, Aaron was in charge of all the other priests and organised them. The high priest was the only person allowed to enter the inner sanctuary on the Day of Atonement each year. He was provided with two sets of robes — white garments of linen for the Day of Atonement and Golden garments for the rest of the year.

All year round, the High Priest wore eight garments:

- The ephod,
- breastplate,
- robe,
- tunic,
- turban,
- belt,
- golden head plate, and

- undergarment.

Over the white undergarment, he put on the sky-blue robe, hemmed with decorative pomegranates and bells which rang as he moved around.

Then he put on the ephod, which looked like an apron fastened by a long belt.

There were two shoulder straps sewn onto the belt. These straps went behind, up and over the priest's shoulders. Two sardonyx stones were attached at the ends of these straps on the shoulders.

He also put on a breastplate set with twelve precious stones, one stone representing each of the twelve tribes of Israel.

His turban differed from those of the ordinary priests and had in front a golden plate inscribed "Holy for all" tied on by a blue cord.

The tunic and turban are both to be of fine woven linen. The sash is to be the work of an embroiderer.

The Ephod

The ephod was a tabard which covered the High Priest from the shoulders to the hips. It was made of finely twisted linen embroidered with gold, blue, purple and scarlet yarn. The front and back sections were attached by two shoulder pieces and a woven waistband of the same embroidered materials as the Ephod.

Each shoulder piece had an onyx stone mounted in a gold filigree setting and a braided chain of pure gold. The two onyx stones were engraved with the names of the tribes. These were in the order of their birth, with six on each stone.

The Robe of the Ephod

The robe of the ephod was made entirely of blue cloth. In the centre was an opening for the head, which had a woven edge to prevent tearing. The hem was embroidered, and alternately fabric pomegranates and gold bells were hanging from it. The sound of the bells could be heard as the High Priest walked.

The Breastpiece of Judgment

The breastpiece was made of the same fabric as the ephod, finely twisted linen, decorated by an embroiderer with gold and blue, purple and scarlet yarn. The fabric was folded twice to a finished size of 230mm square

It was then mounted with twelve stones with gold filigree set in four rows. The stones were engraved, like seals, with the name of each tribe as follows:-

- In the first row: there is a Ruby (Judah), a Topaz(Issachar) and a Beryl (Dan);
- Second row: a Turquoise (Reuben), a Sapphire (Simeon) and an Emerald (Zebulun);
- Third row: a Jacinth (Ephraim), an Agate (Manasseh) and an Amethyst (Benjamin);
- Fourth row: a Chrysolite (Gad), an Onyx (Asher) and a Jasper (Naphtali)

Four gold rings were fastened to the corners of the breastpiece.

- The upper two were tied to the rings of the Ephod by braided chains of pure gold.
- A blue cord tied the lower two rings to the waistband of the Ephon to stop it from swinging out.

The Urim and Thummim

One purpose of the breastpiece was to help make decisions:

> The Urim and Thummim were to be put into the breastpiece, between the two layers, so that it was over the heart of the High Priest.

These were two oracular stones; their names mean 'lights' and 'perfections' and represent the first and last letters of the Hebrew alphabet.

Their decision-making ability was based on drawing them as lots, meaning 'Yes' or 'No'. The skill was to ask the right question.

Other High Priest Items

A gold plate engraved with the words 'Holy to God' was fixed with a blue lace to the front of a sash. The High Priest wore this on his forehead. The other items were:

- A coat of checkerwork made in fine linen.
- A turban again of fine linen.
- A sash made by the embroiderer.
- Linen undergarment reaching from the waist to the thigh.

The Priests

The priests were from the tribe of Levi and were originally Aaron's sons. No priest could serve in the Tabernacle unless dressed in their robes of office to give them reverence and honour.

Their robes of office were tunics, sashes, turban, and undergarments. These were made from white linen and known as 'garments of white'.

Consecration of the First Priests

On the day of the Consecration (on the first day of the first month of the second year), Moses took to the Tabernacle:

- Aaron and his sons,
- the garments and
- anointing oil

They also placed a young bull, two rams, and a basket of unleavened bread. This bread comprised unleavened bread, cakes and wafers made from fine wheat flour. There were watched by the Hebrews congregation, with the elders standing within the courtyard.

Moses brought Aaron and his sons to the tabernacle and washed them with water from the bronze basin.

- He then took the garments and dressed Aaron in those of the High Priest. First, he put on the robe of the Ephod, then the Ephod was tied with the sash. Then he added the breastplate and put the Urim and Thummim over Aaron's heart.
- Next, he put the turban on his head and set the golden plate on the front like a holy crown.
- Moses then took the anointing oil and consecrated the Tabernacle and all its fittings.
- He anointed the altar, basin, and accessories by sprinkling them seven times.
- Moses then anointed Aaron on his head to consecrate him.

Then he brought Aaron's sons, dressed them in their coats, tied sashes, and put on their headbands.

He then anointed Aaron's sons. The priesthood was theirs by a lasting ordinance.

The Bull

Next, Moses took the bull and performed what would be called 'A sin offering':

- Aaron and his sons laid their hands on its head.
- Moses then slaughtered the bull
- He took the blood and put it around the horns of the altar with his finger
- He poured the rest of the blood at the base.

This purified the altar to sanctify and make atonement.

Moses took all the fat on the Bulls innards, the cover to the liver, and the two kidneys and burnt it on the altar.

Due to its size, the rest of the bull, its skin, flesh and dung were burnt outside the camp. This was in a clean place where the Altar's ashes were normally placed.

The First Ram

Moses next presented a ram and performed what would be called 'A burnt offering'.

- Aaron and his sons laid their hands on the head of the ram.
- Moses then slaughtered the ram and sprinkled the blood around the altar.
- Moses washed the innards and legs with water and then burned it all on the altar.

The Second Ram

Moses then took the other ram, called the 'Ram of Consecration'.

- Aaron and his sons laid their hands on the head of the ram.
- Moses then slaughtered the ram and took some of the blood.
- He put some of it on Aaron's right ear, the thumb of his right hand, and the big toe of his right foot.
- Then he brought Aaron's sons and put blood on them in the same place.
- The rest of the blood he sprinkled around the base of the altar.

The Bread

Moses then took:

- The fat and the fat tail,
- the cover of the liver,
- the two kidneys, and
- the right thigh.

Out of the basket of unleavened bread, he took one cake and wafer and put them on the fat and thigh.

He passed these to Aaron and his sons to wave in turn, as a 'Wave Offering'. Moses finally took them and burned them on the altar.

Moses then took the breast and waved it for a wave offering.

This was Moses' portion of the ram of consecration.

He then took some anointing oil and blood from the altar and sprinkled it on Aaron and his son's garments to sanctify them.

Seven Days

Moses then told Aaron and his sons to boil the flesh at the Tabernacle's entrance and ate it with the bread from the basket.

What they do not eat must be burnt with fire, as it is holy, and nobody else can eat it other than a priest.

It is to take seven days to ordain the priests.

Each day a bull is to be sacrificed as a sin offering to make atonement. So likewise, the altar was to be purified and anointed to consecrate it each day.

At the end of seven days, on the eighth day, Moses told Aaron to take a calf from the herd for a sin offering, a ram for a burnt offering and offer them on the altar.

He then told the Hebrews to take:

- a male goat for a sin offering,
- a calf and a lamb for a burnt offering, and
- a bull and a ram for a peace offering, and
- a meal offering mixed with oil.

Aaron and his sons proceeded with the rituals and carried them out correctly before Moses.

Two Lambs each day

There was an ongoing commitment to the Tabernacle, and each day, two one-year-old lambs were to be offered on the altar—one in the morning and the other at twilight. With the lambs, there was an offering of a tenth of an ephah of fine flour mixed with a quarter of a hin of oil from pressed olives and a quarter of a hin of wine as a drink offering.

For generations to come, this burnt offering was made regularly at the entrance to the Tabernacle.

Offerings at the Dedication of the Tabernacle

After the tabernacle and all the associated items were consecrated, the leaders of the Hebrews brought their offerings for its dedication. They presented them before the altar over the next twelve days. Following are their names and days when they brought offerings:

Table 39: Leaders making offerings

Day	Leader's Name	Son of	Tribe
1st	Nahshon	Amminadab	Judah
2nd	Nethanel	Zuar	Issachar
3rd	Eliab	Helon	Zebulun
4th	Elizur	Shedeur	Reuben
5th	Shelumiel	Zurishaddai	Simeon
6th	Eliasaph	Deuel	Gad
7th	Elishama	Ammihud	Ephraim.
8th	Gamaliel	Pedahzur	Manasseh
9th	Abidan	Gideoni	Benjamin
10th	Ahiezer	Ammishaddai	Dan
11th	Pagiel	Ocran	Asher
12th	Ahira	Enan	Naphtali

They all brought the same offerings comprising:-

- A silver plate and sprinkling bowl filled with fine flour mixed with oil as a grain offering. (total weight one hundred shekels)
- A gold dish filled with incense. (weight ten shekels), A young bull, a ram and a male lamb a year old, for a burnt offering;
- A male goat for a sin offering;
- To be sacrificed as a fellowship offering, two oxen, five rams, five male goats, and five male lambs a year old.

This made twelve silver plates, silver sprinkling bowls and gold dishes.

The leaders also jointly brought six covered carts and twelve oxen as gifts— an ox from each leader and a cart from every two.

These they presented before the tabernacle, and Moses gave them to the Levites to help move the Tent of Meeting under the direction of Ithamar, son of Aaron, the priest.

- The Gershonites received two carts and four oxen.

- The Merarites received four carts and eight oxen.
- The Kohathites did not receive any because they were to carry the holy things they were responsible for on their shoulders.

THE LEVITES

The headcount

While at Mount Sinai, after the tribes had been counted, Moses asked Aaron to take a census of the Levites. He was to count all the men aged from thirty to fifty who would work in and around the Tabernacle. The total counted was 1000, with the Kohathites numbered 300. The Gershonites numbered 500, and the Merarites numbered 200.

The Setting Apart of the Levites

Moses took his tribe, the Levites and explained to the Hebrews that he would give them to Aaron and his sons to do the work at the Tabernacle. He explained that in Egypt, they had claimed every firstborn male, whether man or animal, as his. So he had set them apart from those belonging to the Egyptians and now wished to swap them for the Levi tribe.

Moses said Levites men twenty-five years old or older should come to participate in the work at the Tent of Meeting. First, they would train for five years. Then, at fifty, they must retire from their regular service and work no longer, but they may assist their brothers in performing their duties.

He made the Levites purify themselves after he sprinkled 'water of cleansing' on them; they shaved their whole bodies and washed their clothes. They then took a young bull with its grain offering of fine flour mixed with oil; and a second young bull for a sin offering.

Moses then brought the Levites to the front of the Tabernacle and assembled the Hebrew community.

Moses told the Hebrews that he was bringing the Levites before them, and the Hebrews were to lay their hands on them. Aaron then presented the Levites as a wave offering from the Hebrews so that they may be ready to do their work. Finally, after the Levites had laid their hands on the heads of the bulls, one was used for a sin offering and the other for a burnt offering to make atonement for the Levites.

After that, the Levites came to do their work at the Tabernacle under the supervision of Aaron and his sons.

Rules for Priests

Moses spoke to the priests, Aaron's sons, and said to them: they must not make themselves unclean; they must not shave their heads or the edges of their beards or cut their bodies. They are to anoint new priests with oil. They can only marry a virgin.

Moses said to Aaron: 'For the generations to come, none of your descendants who has a defect or deformity may come near to offer the food. So Moses told this to Aaron, his sons and all the Israelites.

Moses told Aaron and his sons to treat with respect the sacred offerings the Hebrews consecrate to me so that they will not profane my holy name. The one who touches any such thing will be unclean till evening. He must not eat any of the sacred offerings unless he has bathed himself with water.

When the sun goes down, he will be clean, and after that, he may eat the sacred offerings, for they are his food.

No one outside a priest's family may eat the sacred offering, nor may the guest of a priest or his hired worker eat it. But if a priest buys a slave with money, or if a slave is born in his household, that slave may eat his food.

The priests must not desecrate the sacred offerings the Israelites present by allowing them to eat the sacred offerings and so bring upon them guilt requiring payment

Unacceptable Sacrifices

Moses spoke to Aaron, his sons, and the Israelites and said: Sacrifices must not have defects, allowing them to be acceptable. Only perfect and complete animals are to be offered. When you sacrifice a thank- offering, sacrifice it in such a way that it will be accepted on your behalf. It must be eaten that same day; leave none of it till morning.

Oil and Bread Set Before the Priests

Moses told the Israelites to bring clear oil of pressed olives for the light so that the Tabernacle lamps may be continually burning.

Also, bread is to be set out as a lasting covenant. This belongs to Aaron and his sons, who are to eat it in a holy place because it is the most holy part of their regular share of the offerings made by fire.

Redeeming What Is the Priests

Moses spoke to the Israelites and said the priest would deal with payments required from them to redeem items given to or owned by the priests.

These are the commands Moses gave on Mount Sinai to the Israelites.

Note: Mount Horeb or Mount Sinai?

Different sources for the text describe land features with other names. For example, locations and features like mountains, hills, rivers etc., were given various names over time.

For example, we find confusion with the place names of the Deserts and Mountains of Horeb and Sinai. These are the same location, but events appear to have taken place elsewhere.

Table XX: Mountain name in OT Book – number of mentions.

Book	Horeb	Sinai
Exodus	3	11
Leviticus	-	4
Numbers	-	1
Deuteronomy	8	1

Note: What was the difference between The Tent of Meeting, The Tabernacle, The Temple, or an Altar

God initially met the Hebrews publicly, perhaps one-to-one. But the Hebrew leaders wanted meetings to take place in private, where the priests could politically control them.

The Tent of Meeting

The name occurs in the Books of Exodus, Leviticus, and Numbers. It is the name of a place where God would meet with his people, Israel.

Before the tabernacle was constructed, God met with Moses in a temporary 'Tent of meeting', but references are a bit intermixed.

Exodus 33:7,9 says:

"Now Moses used to take a tent and pitch it outside the camp some distance away, calling it the 'Tent of meeting.' Anyone inquiring of the Lord would go to the tent of meeting outside the camp. . . . As Moses went into the tent, the pillar of cloud would come down and stay at the entrance, while the Lord spoke with Moses."

The fact that Moses set up the 'Tent of Meeting' outside of the camp follows the events of 'The Golden Calf' (Ex 33:3) at Sinai when the Hebrews stopped worshipping God.

The Tabernacle

The word means 'residence' or 'dwelling place' of God. It was a replacement within the Hebrew camp for the Tent of Meeting. God provided the details for its construction to Moses in Exodus 25-31 and 35-40. Once it was built, the 'Tent of Meeting' was no longer required.

The Tabernacle was a portable structure and enclosure which the Hebrews transported on their journey through the wilderness and conquest of the Promised Land. After some 440 years, Solomon's Temple in Jerusalem superseded it.

Table XX: The number of mentions in Various Books.

	The Tent of Meeting	The Tabernacle	The Temple	Altar
Genesis				11
Exodus	33	55		51
Leviticus	-	4		71
Numbers	54	36		23
Deuteronomy	1		1	6
Joshua	1			11
Judges			10	9
1 Samuel			5	4
2 Samuel			1	3
1 Kings			71	28
2 Kings			60	14
1 Chronicles		4	42	8
2 Chronicles		1	139	23
Ezra			56	3
Nehemiah			30	1
Isaiah			17	6
Jeremiah			45	
Ezekiel			45	16

EPILOGUE

The Next Book,

About the Bible : Volume 2

covers the period from:

Judges to Solomon

Included is an appendix to cover :

- The Laws
- Feasts and Festival Offerings
- The Priests
- The Temple
- Health

About the Author

Nicholas Dunning lives in Cambridgeshire and studied Architecture at the University of Bath. For many years he has worked on development projects in and around London.

He has a keen interest in Ancient Buildings and ecclesiastical architecture.

Over twenty years ago, he started work on this project, looking into the history of the Bible. This expanded to cover the development of Christianity in this country and beyond.

The 2020-2 Coronavirus lockdown has enabled him to work through this project and complete it as a series of reference volumes.

Such works are often difficult to publish due to the high costs of printing and copyright restrictions on the Bible text itself.

To make the work available to a wide range of readers, he has made use of Amazon's Kindle Direct Publishing. So now his books are readily available in both electronic and paperback formats.

The electronic *'Kindle'* version is immediately available to download and has the advantage of a fully searchable text for words, names, and subjects. In addition, this provides an in-depth live 'Index'.

This work will be of interest to a wide range of readers. In addition, many will see it as a useful reference source.

The following email address is available to provide comments and feedback:

aboutthebible@gmail.com

Back of Cover

The land of Israel has been at the crossroads of history for thousands of years. Its people have come and gone, over the years, for one reason or another.

But its real fame comes from being the prime location of the book called today 'The Bible' by Christians. This book is made up of two sections, referred today as the 'Old Testament' and the 'New Testament'.

The Old Testament draws on the Hebrew religious text and history. This section is used as the back story for what then follows.

The New Testament is the story of Jesus and the founding of the Christian church in the eastern Mediterranean.

In a series of volumes, this work attempts to put the bible into a historical context and make the text readable in a clear story format. It follows the development of Christianity from its origin into its final form as one of the primary religions in the world today.

It is an easy reference for those interested, but it is not intended to replace anyone's much-loved version of 'The Bible'.

This book covers the period from Creation to the Israelites arrival in the 'Promised Land'.

Nicholas Dunning is an architect living in Cambridgeshire, England. For many years he has worked on leading development projects in this country.

Printed in Great Britain
by Amazon

12794183R00149